# THE AFRICAN AMERICAN EXPERIENCE

## ISSUES AND ANALYSIS

*Edited by*
*Cottee Jerome White*
*Metropolitan State College*
*Denver—Denver, CO*

**KENDALL/HUNT PUBLISHING COMPANY**
2460 Kerper Boulevard P.O. Box 539 Dubuque, Iowa 52004-0539

Cover design by Michael Walker — Performance Images
Denver, Colorado

Printed in the United States of America
10  9  8  7  6  5  4  3  2  1

# CONTENTS

iii

# PREFACE

African American Studies programs in colleges and universities across the country were initially introduced due to community and student demands during the Civil Rights Movement of the 1960's. Although the nation was founded on pluralistic, democratic principles, those principles have unfortunately not always been observed with respect to persons of racial and ethnic backgrounds. American education has been both a means of subjugation and a means of liberation for African Americans and other ethnic minorities. Black Studies, not expected to survive past infancy, is now in its third decade of formal existence. African American Studies holds the potential to expand the dimensions of knowledge, and explore unchartered areas of research.

Studies about the heritage of Black people in literature, the arts, politics, and other phases of history are not new. Black scholars in Black colleges and historical and cultural independent organizations have been engaged in Black Studies for more than half a century. The climate of the 1960's demanded a new and more insistent urgency for scientific and objective studies of peoples of African descent.

There are still many unresolved issues, myths, and negative stereotypes existing in our society relative to African Americans. This collection of essays and studies have been undertaken to help point the way to a meaningful perception of the African American experience and offer some suggestions on how to probe more deeply and how to ask new questions. The essays and studies included in this book relate to the following topics:

1. Studying the African American Experience: Toward Objectivity;
2. The Afrocentric Approach: Meaning and Implications;
3. Race, Racism, Ethnicity and the African American Experience: Myths and Realities;
4. African American Culture: Historical Roots and Uniqueness;
5. The Struggle for Freedom and the Liberation of the African American.

These issues are central to an understanding of the African American experience — past, present and the future. I hope this collection of readings will stimulate discussion and provide information leading to a better understanding and appreciation of the African American experience.

This book is recommended as supplementary reading in conjunction with basic textbooks and standard works in African American Studies, ethnic studies, and sociology. A list of questions relating to each section of the book and appendices are included at the end of the book.

I wish to thank Dennis Green and Charles White, two students who have inspired and assisted me over the years. For the Ancestors, as recognized and praised by Dr. Margaret Walker Alexander in her poem, "For My People," I give thanks for my being.

Cottee Jerome White
Professor of Sociology and
African American Studies
Metropolitan State College – Denver

*Editor's Note:* Author's decisions about terminology—whether to use "African-American," "Afro-American," "Black America," and with or without hyphens, with capital or lower case—are complicated ones, and there are good arguments for each choice. All these choices are evident in the quotes and essays contained in this book. This author has chosen to use the concepts Black Studies and African American Studies (without the hyphen) interchangeably. Capitals (*B and W*) are used for Black and White when used as a designator for race and/or ethnic group.

# INTRODUCTION

The United States, with more than 30 million African Americans, has one of the largest Black populations in the world. Only 5 of the more than 40 independent African states have total populations that exceed the number of Blacks in the United States (Pinkney, 1993:34). Within the United States, Black Americans are the largest visible minority group. They constitute approximately 90 percent of the "nonwhite" population of the country (Pinkney, 1993:34). Despite their large numbers, due to institutional racism, the history and the culture of African Americans has been distorted or most often simply omitted from the curriculum of educational institutions. Black Studies developed as a response to this historical problem in American education. The Black Studies Movement of the 1960's demanded that in order for education to be representative of all aspects of the American experience, Black Studies should become an intricate part of the curriculum at all levels.

Today, approximately 25 percent of this society's school age children are ethnic minorities. It is estimated that by the year 2000, over 30 percent of our school age population will be children of color (Bennett, 1990:15). The public school population in many of our large urban areas is already predominantly Black. The changing demographics of our country have propelled many educators to consider a new approach to teaching and learning. This new approach would require public schools, colleges, and universities to expand their curriculum to reflect the diversity of the United States.

African American scholars maintain that Black Studies is a necessity in terms of the pluralistic society we have in the United States. In his discussion of the importance of an understanding of the African American experience to the goals of multicultural education, Banks (1987:193) concluded:

> The Black experience in the United States has strikingly revealed the gross discrepancies between American ideas and reality. Throughout their history in America, Blacks have been called

upon to make its dream a reality. Their cries have fallen on deaf ears. Afro-American history and culture must be studied to enable students to understand and to appreciate fully the great conflicts and dilemmas in American society and to develop a commitment to help make America's great ideals a reality.

Moreover, the experiences of African Americans cannot be studied in a vacuum. Various racial/ethnic and cultural groups must be included in African American Studies content in order to understand the oppression, the survival, and the prosperity of the African American community (Semmes, 1981:5). The holistic and multidisciplinary nature of African American Studies greatly contributes to the goals of multicultural education.

Teacher education programs in colleges and universities are being forced to rethink their curriculum as more school districts demand that their teachers incorporate issues relating to race, ethnicity, and gender. A curriculum that teaches only mainstream views and perspectives gives students a distorted view of the United States and the world (Banks, 1987: xiii). States and accreditation agencies are requiring teachers to have more training iin multi-culturalism. Teachers and administrators with expertise in African American Studies are being called upon for assistance in this effort.

Students planning a career in community service, government, health sciences, and business would benefit from being exposed to the field of African American Studies. It is less than responsible to avoid learning something about the background and experiences of persons one will serve, particularly when understanding cultural background is essential to providing adequate service. A study of the African American experience will enhance students to think critically about race, class, and culture as it relates to all aspects of the human experience.

African American scholars have made important advances in challenging the assumptions held by those in traditional disciplines concerning Africa and peoples of African descent. As we approach the 21st century, an ongoing review of the accomplishments of Black Studies is necessary. In its twenty-five years of formal existence, Black Studies has not completely transformed the educational system in the United States as its early proponents had envisioned. But during its short period of formalized existence, African American Studies has had a noticeable impact on higher education in the United States. The contemporary Black Studies Movement gave rise to demands for inclusion by other groups, Hispanics, American Indians, Asian Americans, and women. African American Studies has been in the forefront for developing and strengthening the intellectual, social, and political thought necessary for human liberation.

*Cottee Jerome White*

## LITERATURE CITED

Banks, James A. 1987. *Teaching Strategies for Ethnic Studies*: Boston: Allyn and Bacon.

Bennett, Christine I. 1990. *Comprehensive Multicultural Education — Theory and Practice*. Needham Heights, MA: Allyn and Bacon.

Pinkney, Alphonso. 1993. *Black Americans*. Englewood Cliffs, NJ: Prentice-Hall, Inc.

Semmes, Clovis E. 1981. "Foundations of an Afrocentric Social Science — Implications for Curriculum Building, Theory and Research in Black Studies." *Journal of Black Studies*. Vol. 12, Number 1/Spring.

## RECOMMENDED READING

Alkalimat, Abdul. 1985. *Introduction to Afro-American Studies: A Peoples College Primer*. Chicago: Twenty-first Century Books and Publications.

Anderson, Talmadge (editor). 1990. *Black Studies—Theory, Method, and Cultural Perspectives*. Washington State University Press.

Azevedo, Mario (editor). 1993. *Africana Studies— A Survey of Africa and the African Diaspora*. Durham, N.C.: Carolina Academic Press.

Berry, Mary Francis and Blassingame, John W. 1982. *Long Memory: The Black Experience in America*. New York: Oxford University Press.

Blackwell, James. *The Black Community*. 1991. New York: Harper Collins Publishers.

Boamah-Wiafe, Daniel. 1993. *The Black Experience in Contemporary America*. Omaha: Wisdom Publications.

Franklin, John Hope. 1988. *From Slavery to Freedom — A History of Negro Americans*. New York: Alfred A. Knopf.

Hayes, Floyd W. III. (editor). 1992. *A Turbulent Voyage—Readings in African American Studies*.

Karanga, Maulana. 19XX. *Introduction to Black Studies*. Los Angeles: Kawaida Publications.

Schaefer, Richard T. 1993. *Racial and Ethnic Groups*. Glenview, Ill.: Scott, Foresman.

# 1

# STUDYING THE
# AFRICAN AMERICAN EXPERIENCE:
# TOWARD OBJECTIVITY

"Education is our passport to the
future, for tomorrow belongs to the
people who prepare for it today."
*Malcolm X*

# THE INTELLECTUAL AND INSTITUTIONAL DEVELOPMENT OF AFRICANA STUDIES

*Robert L. Harris, Jr.*

Africana studies is the multidisciplinary analysis of the lives and thought of people of African ancestry on the African continent and throughout the world. It embraces Africa, Afro-America, and the Caribbean, but does not confine itself to those three geographical areas. Africana studies examines people of African ancestry wherever they may be found for example, in Central and South America, Asia, and the Pacific Islands. Its primary means of organization are racial and cultural. Many of the themes of Africana studies are derived from the historical position of African peoples in relation to Western societies and in the dynamics of slavery, oppression, colonization, imperialism, emancipation, self-determination, liberation, and socioeconomic and political development.

There have been four stages in the intellectual and institutional development of Africana studies as an area of scholarly inquiry. The first stage began in the 1890s and lasted until the Second World War. During this first stage, numerous organizations emerged to document, record, and analyze the history, culture, and status of African peoples. For example, the Bethel Literary and Historical Association of Washington, D.C., formed in 1881, sponsored lectures on numerous topics, such as the Egyptians, the Zulus, and various aspects of African culture, in addition to contemporary issues affecting African Americans. Other organizations functioned in a similar manner for example, Philadelphia's American Negro Historical Society, established in 1897; Washington, D.C.s American Negro Academy, also started in 1897; and New York's Negro Society for Historical Research, organized in 1911.

These early black literary and historical associations sought to preserve and to publicize the legacy of African peoples. They were superseded in 1915, when Carter G. Woodson formed the

Reprinted with permission from Three Essays—Black Studies in the United States by Robert L. Harris, Jr., Copyright © 1990 by the Ford Foundation. Reprinted with permission from the Ford Foundation, New York, N.Y.

Association for the Study of Afro-American (formerly Negro) Life and History (ASALH), which still survives today. Woodson laid the groundwork for systematic study of African peoples through the associations annual meetings; the *Journal of Negro History*, launched in 1916; the national observance of Negro History Week (now Black History Month), started in 1926; publication of the *Negro History Bulletin*, begun in 1933; and the formation of Associated Publishers to print books on the black experience in America and throughout the world. ASALH has been the premier organization in promoting historical consciousness and in generating greater understanding of African heritage in the United States.

In 1897 W.E.B. DuBois initiated an ambitious program at Atlanta University to examine various categories of African-American life in ten-year cycles. He proposed that such studies be continued for at least 100 years to provide knowledge and understanding of the black family, church, social organizations, education, and economic development in the United States. From 1898 to 1914, the Atlanta University studies produced sixteen monographs, which consisted of more than 2,100 pages of research. DuBois, Woodson, Lorenzo J. Greene, Charles H. Wesley, E. Franklin Frazier, Ralph J. Bunche, Charles S. Johnson, Abram Harris, Sterling Brown, and other pioneering black scholars produced an impressive body of scholarship to correct the errors, omissions, and distortions of black life and history that prevailed among white academics and the American public.

The second stage for Africana studies began with the study of black America by Gunnar Myrdal. This stage was in some respects a setback. Myrdal, who began his project for the Carnegie Corporation in 1939, confined his analysis to the American social, political, and economic order. There was growing concern about the role and place of the black population during the Second World War, as a majority of African Americans became urban. Black migration northward, which had begun in large numbers during the 1890s, had accelerated during World War I, and had slowed during the Depression of the 1930s, mushroomed during World War II, making the black presence in America more a national than a regional or primarily southern concern. Believing that black people in the United States were fundamentally Americans who had no significant African cultural background or identity, Myrdal accepted the formulation of the University of Chicago School of Sociology that ethnic and racial contact led not only to conflict but also to inevitable assimilation and absorption into the dominant society. His two-volume study, *An American Dilemma: The Negro Problem and Modern Democracy*, published in 1944, had an important influence on scholarship, especially the work of white academics during this second stage.

White scholars, by and large, had ignored black people. The Columbia University historian John W. Burgess had boldly stated: "[A] black skin means membership in a race of men which has never itself succeeded in subjecting passion to reason; has never, therefore, created any civilization of any kind." After World War II, as the black population in the United States became predominantly urban and as scholarship in general shed notions of inherent racial inferiority and superiority with the Nazi debacle, white scholars devoted increasing attention to African Americans' status in the United States. They sought environmental rather than biogenetic explanations for African Americans' inferior status.

In *Mark of Oppression* (1951), Abram Kardiner and Lionel Ovesey hypothesized that African Americans emerged from slavery without a culture, with "no intra-psychic defenses--no pride, no group solidarity, no tradition." They argued: "The marks of his previous status were still upon him--socially, psychologically, and emotionally, and from these he has never since freed himself." Stanley Elkins in his book *Slavery* (1959) concluded that African Americans were not genetically inferior but were made inferior by the process of enslavement, which they internalized and passed on to succeeding generations. In *Beyond the Melting Pot: The Negroes, Puerto Ricans, Jews, Italians, and Irish of New York City* (1963), Nathan Glazer and Daniel P. Moynihan attributed African-American status to the absence of middle-class values and norms among the black population in general. Two years later, in *The Negro Family: The Case for National Action*, Moynihan wrote: "Three centuries of injustice have brought

about deep-seated structural distortions in the life of the Negro American." He concluded that "the present tangle of pathology is capable of perpetuating itself without assistance from the white world."

Whereas Burgess had implied that Africans had never created anything of worth and therefore African Americans were descended from an inferior people, post-World War II white scholars, in the main, identified African-American status not with an inglorious African past but with deficiencies occasioned by slavery, segregation, and discrimination. It is important to note that these scholars believed that the end of racial oppression would not immediately produce racial equality, not because of lack of social opportunity but because of the accumulated pathological behavior of black people. In other words, black people were not divinely created inferior but were made inferior over time. The sum of racial oppression and its alleged internalization by black people dramatically affected their lives across generations.

Another significant post-World War II development was the creation of African studies programs that had no real link to black people in the New World. Although Melville Herskovits, a white anthropologist and proponent of African studies, tried to join the study of Africa with the lives of black people in the New World, African studies became wedded to a modernization theory that measured African societies by Western standards. African history, culture, and politics were explored more within the context of the colonial powers than with any attention to African cultural continuities in the Western hemisphere. This compartmentalization of knowledge regarding black people departed significantly from the scholarship of individuals such as DuBois and Woodson during the first stage in the development of Africana studies.

The civil rights revolution, the black power drive, and the black consciousness movement initiated a third stage of Africana studies. During this era, larger numbers of black students entered predominantly white colleges and universities. Most of these students were the first generation of their families to attend college. They encountered faculties that were almost entirely white and a curriculum that was primarily Eurocentric in perspective. The "melting pot" thesis prevailed as the paradigm of American society in which all groups, regardless of background, assimilated to an ideal that was primarily white, Anglo-Saxon, and Protestant. Ironically, at a time when African nations were achieving independence from colonial rule, Africa seemed unrelated to black people in the United States. If Africa was discussed in classes, it was generally as an adjunct to European imperialism. In large measure, black people were seen as pawns rather than as actors, as victims more than as victors.

Together with many black scholars from the first stage of Africana studies, black college students challenged the prevailing orthodoxies on predominantly white campuses. They demanded the employment of black professors and the establishment of Africana studies departments and programs. They pressed for the inclusion of African studies in the newly formed Africana studies programs. The inclusion of African studies was important for several reasons. First, African Americans have historically linked their destiny with the future of Africa. Second, the image of Africa has had significant consequences for the status of African Americans. Third, African ancestry has informed the cultural heritage of African Americans as much as their presence in the United States. Fourth, the history, politics, and culture of Africa could stand as a counterweight to the dominance of Western culture in American education.

The Eurocentric focus of the college curriculum basically excluded people of African ancestry or studied them through a European filter. Eurocentrist scholars ignored the growth of civilization in Africa, especially in Egypt, or coopted Egyptian civilization as part of a European rather than an African continuum. They also ignored the African heritage of African Americans, characterizing them as having begun their existence in North America as *tabulae rasae*--blank slates to be imprinted with Euro-American culture.

Although some colleges and universities were willing to establish Africana studies programs, they were less willing to organize Africana studies departments. Faculty within the traditional departments were reluctant to give up their prerogative of determining what constituted a course in history, literature, or government; who would take such courses; and how the professors teaching them would be evaluated for employment, promotion, and tenure. Advocates of Africana studies departments questioned how members of traditional departments that had not offered courses on the black experience or hired black faculty could sit in judgment on the nature and quality of work being done in this newly emerging field of study.

The third stage of Africana studies, from about the mid-1960s to the mid-1980s, was a period of legitimization and institutionalization. Few scholars were prepared to teach Africana studies courses. The shift in perspective from Eurocentrism to Afrocentrism required the recovery, organization, and accessibility of research materials that made black people, their lives, and their thoughts the center of analysis and interpretation. Many white scholars in particular had assumed that there was not sufficient documentation on which to base sound judgments about the personal and collective experiences of black people in the United States. However, with the new interest in black life and culture, federal, state, and local archivists combed their collections for materials on the African-American experience and published several useful guides. Major projects began assembling and publishing the papers of black leaders, writers, and organizations. It is now clear that there are abundant materials (print, visual, and sound) to reconstruct and to interpret the African-American past.

The prodigious research of black and white scholars has dramatically changed the manner in which we now view African Americans. Most scholars today acknowledge the persistence of African culture in the United States. They no longer accept the idea that African-Americans passively acquiesced to oppression, recognizing that, on the contrary, they actively resisted oppression in a variety of ways. In large measure, scholars have come to accept the United States as a pluralistic society with multiple viable cultures, rather than as a "melting pot." We think more of acculturation, with give-and-take, than of assimilation--particularly in the form of total absorption into the dominant culture, which itself is now being redefined.

Africana studies has achieved legitimacy and has become institutionalized within higher education. It has now moved into a fourth stage of theoretical refinement and more sophisticated analysis and interpretation. The fundamental research tools have been developed, although there will certainly be a need to update and to supplement them as new materials become available. In general, the field is in fairly good condition, but there are some problems, or perhaps opportunities to improve it.

Because the formats for multidisciplinary programs vary from campus to campus, there will probably not be a single method of organization for Africana studies. The ideal format is the department structure, which allows for selection of faculty and development of curriculum. Programs with faculty in traditional departments can also be successful, provided that they have some control of faculty lines. The program, however, becomes a more complex arrangement, especially in decisions for hiring, promotion, and tenure. Joint appointments carry similar problems, especially for junior faculty. They are less burdensome for senior faculty, whose tenure has already been established. Cross-listing of courses is one means by which departments and programs can take greater advantage of faculty resources on their campuses. However, before such cross-listing can be effective, there must first be a strong core faculty within the department or program. Otherwise, the Africana studies curriculum becomes too dependent on the priorities of other departments.

One goal for the fourth stage of Africana studies should be to broaden and deepen the field of inquiry. This prospect becomes somewhat difficult for those departments and programs with limited numbers of faculty. Small faculties are stretched thin when they attempt to offer a major and to cover Africa, Afro-America, and the Caribbean. Offering a comprehensive program in Africana studies has meant that some departments and programs play primarily service roles in providing introductory courses that are used to fulfill one or more distribution requirements for graduation. These efforts have little opportunity to supply depth in the field of study. Faculty become very much occupied with servicing large introductory courses and have little time for research and writing in an area of specialization. There is a tendency for faculty to become generalists familiar with a broad range of knowledge rather than specialists who advance the frontiers of specific areas of knowledge.

As Africana studies moves into its fourth stage, as well as its third decade on predominantly white campuses, there is a need to re-examine the curriculum on many campuses. Some departments and programs offer a hodgepodge of courses that have evolved over time in response to student interest and faculty availability. Many departments and programs, particularly those with small faculties, need to determine what they can do best with their resources. Some have specific strengths upon which to build; others need to reconsider where they want to concentrate their resources. Unless they have the faculty and the administrative support, many departments and programs cannot offer successful comprehensive Africana studies courses. In a 1986 report on the "Status of Afro-American Studies in the State University of New York," Dr. Kenneth Hall showed that the preponderance of students are attracted by courses on Afro-American history, the civil rights movement, film, music, and contemporary Africa. Courses on history and culture (literature, music, film, drama, and dance) seem to appeal most to a cross section of students (black and white), with politics close behind.

In many respects, Africana studies faculty need to return to the basic question: Africana studies for what? There was much discussion and debate on this question during the early days of organizing, when the focus was on the quest for legitimacy and institutionalization. On many campuses, Africana studies was to provide the black presence, to supply role models for students, to have an active advising and counseling function, to organize film series, lectures, and symposia, and to influence traditional departments in the composition of their faculty and curriculum. This was a tall order that exhausted many Africana studies faculty. Having expended their energy on getting the new field off the ground, many faculty had not devoted sufficient time to research and publication and thus were caught short when evaluated for promotion and tenure.

Today, there is some debate about whether Africana studies faculty should play their former roles of counselors and mentors or give more time to research. Some of this tension would be eased if administrators supported campus-life specialists who would organize cultural activities for black students in particular and for all students in general. Faculty development is an important element within the university, and it is especially important for Africana studies faculty, many of whom need to reorient themselves toward greater scholarship.

Public colleges that are clustered in metropolitan areas have a unique opportunity to foster scholarship in Africana studies departments by establishing master's degree programs and research institutes. Such projects might encourage Africana studies departments and programs to develop strengths in specific areas. These strengths could be drawn upon for graduate programs and research institutes to promote greater scholarship by identifying areas of investigation and by bringing together scholars with similar interests. Research institutes might also be a means to influence more students to pursue advanced degrees and expand the number of minority scholars.

Answers to the question of "Africana studies for what?" will have a significant effect on the shape and content of the curriculum. To address these issues, the National Council for Black Studies has already embarked on a program of summer institutes for college teachers. Such responses will also influence the role of Africana studies on different campuses. Africana studies will continue to vary from college to college. Ultimately, however, there is a need for greater clarification and understanding through more dialogue about its specific function on various campuses.

# BLACK SCHOLARS AND THE SOCIAL SCIENCES

*Carlene Young*

Black social scientists in the United States of America have been consistently faced with the dilemma of attempting to study various aspects of man's existence while they exist in social environments which either deny, seriously question, or attribute genetically inferior capabilities, to their own humanity.

How have they dealt with these contradictions? Have they contravened or acquiesced? Have black scholars been able to maintain their integrity and inviolate status? Have they been able to use the tools of scholarship? What contributions have they made to knowledge, to their chosen disciplines and most importantly to their own people and society at large. Have they been successes or failures? This essay is an attempt to deal with these questions and place the role of black social scientists in perspective. This will enable us to both assess and better understand their contributions and the significance of their work.

The birth of the social sciences parallels in many respects the birth of this country, insofar as the plight and condition of black people are concerned.

There is the idealism, the noble concepts of freedom, justice, equality, and liberty which are "democratic for the master race but tyrannical for the subordinate groups."[1]

The glaring contradictions that exist between the freedom rhetoric which sustained the undercore of revolutionary fervor essential to the American Revolution and at the same time countenanced enslavement of fellow human beings, who although black were nonetheless entitled to be free, has persisted in various forms until today.

Thomas Jefferson's attempt in the Declaration of Independence to lay blame for this apparent contradiction was short lived. His statement that Kind George III had "waged cruel war against human nature itself, violating the most sacred

rights of life and liberty in the persons of a distant people, who never offended him, captivating and carrying them into slavery in another hemisphere, or to incur miserable death in their transportation thither," was deleted as a result of sentiment which did not wish to sully this illustrious document with any mention of the festering reality which would serve to make this nation one of the wealthiest in the world but would also undermine its moral fibre.[2] "The document which emerged as the Constitution would have nothing to say about eliminating the institution of slavery, accepted the notion of the Negro as property, and recognized no discrepancy between a democratic form of government and racial slavery."[3] The mask of democracy and freedom was donned.

The Badge of Color became the official identifying symbol of inferiority and subordination. As the exploitative economic system grew and flourished so did the tenets of racism. The entire society proceeded to enter a conspiracy of accommodation to ensure the subjugation of the black populace.[4] Van den Berghe makes an astute assessment of the contradiction that exists between ideals of liberty and equality as spread by the American and French Revolutions while at the same time also paradoxically contributed to the development of racism.

> Faced with the blatant contradiction between the treatment of slaves and colonial peoples and the official rhetoric of freedom and equality, Europeans and white North Americans began to dichotomize humanity between men and submen (or the "civilized" and the "savages"). The scope of applicability of the egalitarian ideals was restricted to "the people," that is, the whites . . .[4]

This was the era when the United States was beginning to establish itself as one of the greatest imperialist powers of the world.

The conquest of colored peoples in Hawaii, Cuba, Philippines, Puerto Rico, Mexico and the "anti-Oriental agitation" in the Western states provided rationalizations which justifies the ideologies of Social Darwinism or the notion of survival of the fittest and Manifest Destiny.

Juan Comas' report to the United Nations Economic and Social Council (UNESCO) in *Race and Science* discusses "Racial Myths" and makes a significant observation, when he states:

> ... the truth is that with coloured societies becoming potential competitors in the labour market and claiming the social advantages regarded as exclusively the heritage of the whites, the latter were obviously in need of some disguise for the utter economic materialism which led them to deny the inferior peoples any share in the privileges they themselves enjoyed. For that reason they welcomed with satisfaction, distortion and adaptation of it in conformity with their own particular interests, transformed it into the so-called "Social Darwinism" on which they base their right to their social and economic privilege.[5]

Charles Darwin's *The Origin of Species* (1859), which was the basis of Social Darwinism, refuted "the hypothesis of a multiplicity of human species." However, his theory provided the framework for incorporating ideas of race superiority and inferiority.

> The idea of natural selection was translated to a struggle between individual members of a society, between members of classes of a society, between different nations and between different races. This conflict, far from being an evil thing, was nature's indispensable method for producing superior men, superior nations, and superior races.[6]

The development of American universities and scholarship was coincident with the spread of Social Darwinism, Teutonic Origins Theory and the Eugenics movement. In his work, *Race: The History of An Idea in America* (which may be one of the most significant treatises on the subject), Gossett traces the development of the prevailing ideologies of white supremacy. The nineteenth century was a most fertile period for the nature and spread of these ideas. Gossett reports that "One does not have to read very far in the writings of nineteenth century social scientists to discover the immense influence of race theories among them." "In studying human societies," he goes on to say, "they generally assumed that they were also studying innate racial character. Races were thought to represent different stages of the evolutionary scale with the white race--or sometimes a subdivision of the white race--at the top."

Herbert Spencer, one of the founding fathers of sociology, sought to apply Darwin's ideas to the analysis of human society. Spencer's concept of social evolution led to coining of the terms "survival of the fittest" and "struggle for existence." William G. Sumner, another trailblazer in sociology, and a founder of American sociology was a discipline of Spencer. Later social scientists have for the most part severely criticized and discarded these theories.

The Teutonic Origins Theory was essentially concerned with attributing to the Teutonic race the source of world civilizations. These "superior" people were to be found principally in Germany, England and the United States. "For about a quarter of a century the Teutonic Origins Theory was the dominant school of thought among American historians."[7] One of the most avid proselytizers of the Teutonic theory was the political scientist at Columbia University, John W. Burgess, together with Henry Baxter Adams, historian of Johns Hopkins. Burgess was at Columbia for 36 years and sent many of his students to Germany. "By 1905, Burgess himself could speak of the virtual control of American universities by men educated at German universities."[8] Theodore Roosevelt was one of his most famous students.

The supposed peculiar talent of the Teutonic race--their political genius--was the ability to form stable governments even in countries where they were a minority. "Historians and political scientists as well as anthropologists contributed to the racist milieu by discovering that every quality which they considered to be good in civilization somehow or other emanated from ancient Teutons, Celts, Anglo-Saxons, or Normans."[9]

Other proponents of these ideas, or equally pernicious concepts stemming from a belief in the inherent inferiority of black people, are found in each of the disciplines. The tremendous influence of scholars like the following reverberates in our midst today.

Louis Agassiz, a brilliant anthropologist, believed the black child to be as bright as the white child until puberty, then animal nature took over and white child's intellectual development continued. G. Stanley Hall, first Ph.D. in psychology in the United States, founder of the psychology laboratory at Johns Hopkins (1883) and the *American Journal of Psychology* (1887) and later president of Clark University (1899-1919), "associated the peculiar emotional intensity of Negroes with unbridled sexuality, leading him to discuss the question of rape, lynching, and social control."[10]

William McDougall's instinct psychology attributed greatest achievements to those with "Nordic" blood.

Albert Bushnell Hart, distinguished Harvard historian, wrote "the theory that the Negro mind ceases to develop after adolescence perhaps has something in it." He served on the board of trustees of Howard University for twenty-three years.

David Starr Jordan, president of Stanford University, and sociologist Franklin H. Giddings published similar views particularly with respect to analysis of poverty and crime.

Howard W. Odum, president of American Sociological Association, 1930, had published a research study, *Social and Mental Traits of the Negro: A Study in Race Traits, Tendencies and Prospects* (1910). This research was sponsored by Columbia University. Odum reports that:

> The Negro has little home conscience or love of home. . . He has no pride of ancestry, and he is not influenced by the lines of great men. The Negro has few ideals and perhaps no lasting adherence to an aspiration toward real worth. . . . He is shiftless, untidy, and indolent. . . . The young educated Negroes are not a force for good in the community but for evil.[11]

Odum later admitted the error of his views.

As in all matters there were exceptions. There were and are scholars who challenged the proponents of white superiority-black inferiority. Johann Blumenbach, co-founder of anthropology, Benjamin Rush, Franz Boas are but a few.

Their voices were muted in the chorus of those who found support in racist ideology.

The tenor of the times and social milieu in which these scholars found themselves was the antithesis of erudition.

The legal, social, political and economic circumstances of the late nineteenth century culminated in what has been described by the eminent historian, Rayford Logan, as "The Nadir" and "The Golden Age of Racism" by Van den Berghe.

This was the period which countenanced disfranchisement statutes and practices, lynchings as a means of social control, physical violence, intimidation, race riots, and strict enforcement of Jim Crow laws. From 1867 to 1877, organizations

formed for the express purpose of implementing violence on "uppity blacks" who did not know their place flourished and multiplied. Ku Klux Klan, White Leagues, Knights of White Camelia, Pale Faces, White Brotherhood and Mississippi Rifle Clubs were some of the organizations dedicated to white supremacy and the restoration of absolute power over the fate of black "citizens." In the decade from 1889 to 1899 there were 1,875 reported lynchings.

Schwartz and Disch remind us that the leadership of the Universities between 1877 and 1920 likewise reflected the racist norms of the society as a whole and contributed to the generally "permissive" atmosphere in which violence was perpetrated.

This is the scene in which black social scientists came to ply their skills and expertise. They came primarily to the field of race and intergroup relations. Someone *had* to deal with race detractors since "the racists had the immense advantage of the strong backing of scientists and social scientist."[12] They did not shy away from their task, but much of the brilliance and potential was never fully realized because of the narrow constraints within which black scholars were forced to function.

Jim Crow laws denied them admission to libraries, attendance at meetings of the national organizations of their respective disciplines as well as honorary societies like Phi Beta Kappa.

Opportunities for research were almost nonexistent due to the fact that white institutions would not hire them and black institutions would not hire them and black institutions committed the majority of their resources to teaching.

One of these scholars provides us with some insight into the matter:

> If he doubted himself, it would be understandable, for he had been brainwashed, completely and almost irrevocably, by assertions of Caucasian superiority endorsement of Social Darwinism, with its justifications for the degradation of the Negro, and political and legal maneuverings that lowered the Negro still further on the social and intellectual scale. *But the aspiring Negro scholar did not doubt himself, and he turned on his detractors with all the resources he could summon in the effort to refute those who claimed he was inferior.*[13] (Emphasis added by author.)

It is commonly believed that institutions of higher learning are repositories of knowledge, peopled with seekers of truth and wisdom as well as centers for the training of leaders and decision makers in society. However, investigation of the real functioning of these institutions reveals that in more instances than not, the value, ideologies and social norms of the society are as extant here as in the most representative community.

Racism with all its concomitant variables of prejudice, discrimination, segregation, exploitation and subjugation, does not wait outside the doors of these learned towers--but enters with all the vigor and authority which comes with the statues and influence of its members.

The seductiveness of white superiority and racism which pervade every institution in this society has captured many a brilliant scholar.

The tenor and tone of some of the most prestigious universities in this country are suffused with sometimes subtle but frequently overt manifestations of racist ideology.

It is sheer fallacy to believe that education and scholarship are immune to the infectious nature of ideologies of white supremacy. Harvard University is a case in point. Although Harvard has produced some of the most distinguished scholars of the black world, its subsequent treatment of these graduated is sad commentary on the pervasive nature of institutional racism. These scholars have carved a place for themselves not merely in the annals of black scholarship, but scholarship in general.

W.E.B. DuBois is without a doubt an alumnus of whom any institution would be proud, and one of Harvard's finest. There are other Harvard alumni of equal stature: historians Carter G. Woodson, John Hope Franklin, Benjamin Brawley, Rayford Logan; Alain Locke, first Black American Rhodes Scholar, and critic and art historian; economists Robert Weaver, William Dean; chemist Percy Julian; poets Sterling Brown, Countee Cullen, political scientist Ralph Bunche. Outstanding graduates have also been trained at other institutions including Yale, Columbia, University of Chicago.

Among some of them are distinguished scholars such as sociologists St. Clair Drake, E. Franklin Frazier, Charles S. Johnson, Allison Davis, Horace Cayton and Ira Reid, psychologists Herman Canady, Kenneth Clark; economist Abram L. Harris; historian Benjamin Quarles; political scientist Ralph Bunche; and Arthur Schomburg, noted bibliophile and collector of Negro historical materials.

The South can be credited with having pro-duced proportionately more educated and successful blacks in various fields than any other area. Oftentimes the only employment a black scholar could obtain was in the black colleges of the South, international reputations notwithstanding. "Segregation had produced the situation where superior men were consigned to schools inferior in facilities and encouragement of research . . ."[14]

The condition and plight of black people has for the most part been attended to under the rubric of race relations. Race relations has been a major area of concentration for social scientists, both white and black. The premise underlying much of the focus in this area stemmed all too frequently from a social pathology or deviation frame of reference.

The "prevailing scholarship" has exerted profound influence on the subject matter chosen for investigation, the methodology, assumptions and interpretations of data.

> . . .Black social scientists have for the most part expended the ir energies "correcting" and "modifying" traditional offerings rather than proceeding from fresh hypotheses not dependent on accepted premises. In consequence, the socio-historical image of the black American has always either a distortion or the modification of distortion.[15]

Although the social sciences make a point of emphasizing the scientific method as an essential component of its truth-seeking endeavors, the objective, value-free researcher has been a phantom--of which one hears much but is rarely manifest in reality. Kinloch reminds us that:

> The field of race relations in the United States has closely followed social change in the general society: beginning as a rationalization of slavery, it moved to a justification of segregation, then an applied attempt to implement the "American Creed" in the acknowledgement of widespread prejudice and discrimination. For this, it is obvious that the field has been far from objective and, in many respects, exemplifies the utilization of "knowledge" by a colonial elite for its own purpose.[16]

Black scholars, as a result of membership in the "out-group" were most often forced into the position of having to set the record straight. They frequently had to forsake their chosen professional interests in order to respond to the attacks on the race by the scholarly literature of their white colleagues.

The tragedy of this posture lies in the fact that men, who otherwise for color, would have had brilliant, rewarding careers in their chosen fields--whether the sciences, medicine, or social science--were relegated to institutions and positions that either could not or would not utilize their talents.

Despite these handicaps the research productivity of the Negro historians, sociologists, and economists in the 1930's is surprising, especially when the small number of Negro Ph.D.'s at that time is considered. In 1936, for example, there were only nine in history, fifteen in sociology, and five in economics.

Carter G. Woodson, educated at the University of Chicago and Harvard (Ph.D., 1912), is another in the long line of academicians whose contributions have never been given the recognition they deserved. Woodson, a rigorous scholar and activist in his resistance to anti-Negro scholarship, founded the Association for the Study of Negro Life and History (1915), and the *Journal of Negro History* in 1916. This journal became one of the most respected of American historical journals and also provided a vehicle for publication of the research of black scholars.

Charles H. Thompson, founder of one of the most influential periodicals of the time, *Journal of Negro Education* (1932), provides an example of the quality of scholarship in existence and its impact on society.

The *Journal of Negro Education* has been described as "the most potent continuing critique of the public policy of segregation." In addition to condemnation of segregated schools and focus on legal policies, "Thompson also published a steady stream of research by Howard H. Long, Martin D. Jenkins and others on the question of the intelligence of Negroes and on intelligence testing which exposed the distortions of white psychologists and educators."[18] There are countless others whose stories echo these, with better or worse circumstance, but always with the element of racism serving as the determinant factor.

Oliver C. Cox, one of the first black sociologists to utilize Marxian ideas as an analytical tool, challenged the "caste" hypothesis popularized in sociological analysis of race relations. Cox maintained that race relations in the United States was dynamic, not static. The caste hypothesis could not explain the violence necessary to enforce segregation, nor the inevitability of violent racial conflict which he predicted in 1948. The crucial variable--power--is explored by Cox. Few others up to that time had the insight or the courage to explore the subjugation of blacks in terms of power.

Negroes and whites in the United States stand toward each other in the relationship of subordination and superordination, a relationship implying suspended conflict. Conversely, castes stand toward each other in the relationship of superiority and inferiority, a relationship implying *natural*, socially accepted, peaceful status ordering of the society. In the first case, we have a power relationship in which definite aims and ends of each group are opposed; the second is a situation of *mutual emulousness* among little status-bearing groups.[19]

Recognized as a classic in the field of community studies by contemporary sociologists and one of the most frequently cited reference works of all those dealing with race relations, *Black Metropolis* by St. Clair Drake and Horace Cayton, is as valid a piece of work today as it was when first published. It is included in a list of seven works of which the noted sociologist, Oliver Cromwell Cox, states "no study of race relations could be considered adequate without a knowledge of the contributions made by such works as . . . Gunnar Myrdal, *An American Dilemma*; St. Clair Drake and Horace R. Cayton, *Black Metropolis*; and W.E.B. DuBois, *The Souls of Black Folk*."

Black scholars have influenced the direction and development of black community life; they have staved off the onslaught of racist scholarship; and they have produced works of scholarship which have withstood the tests of time, surviving on their merit and not merely as representative of "Negro" scholarship. As with all black people, they come from different backgrounds experiences and perspectives, but one universal force in their lives was the fact of being black in a society that has never accepted black as equal to white and has always acted out the contradiction inherent in this definition of inequality.

The opprobrium of racism has never been sufficient to counteract the profits and benefits that accrue from the exploitative process.

One of the outstanding scholars of our generation, John Hope Franklin, reflects on this anomaly:

The world of the Negro scholar is indescribably lonely, and he must, somehow, pursue truth down that lonely path while, at the same time, making certain that his conclusions are sanctioned by universal standards developed and maintained by those who frequently do not even recognize him. Imagine the plight of the Negro historian trying to do research in archives in the South operated by people who cannot conceive that a Negro has the capacity to use the materials there.[20]

Obstacles such as these have not deterred the many who have been productive and at the same contributed most significantly to the field of knowledge.

It is with a great deal of respect for their dedication, perseverance and fortitude that these works should be approached. This is not to say that their works should be accepted without critique or analysis--for that would deny the role of scholarship and the goals to which many of then dedicated their professional lives.

The following titles are representative of the type of scholarship referred to in the essay. There are no lists that are exhaustive and this one certainly makes no attempt to pretend otherwise. It is representative but limited, yet in the best judgement of the author provides a sampling of consummate social science scholarship.

The essence of the social sciences is man. Each discipline attempts to study man with respect to its own area of focus. The social science fields are most commonly thought to be: History, Political Science, Anthropology, Psychology, Economics and Sociology.

The parameters of this essay and the following bibliographies have been limited to these fields. There has been no attempt to incorporate any of the outstanding or significant works found in other forms such as the essay autobiography, fiction or poetry.

Each title listed herein represents a form of systematic or documentary analysis based on a particular theoretical frame of reference and significant scholarship. The backgrounds in terms of formal training, experiences and viewpoints are diverse. However, the unifying thread amongst these works is the evidence of scholarship commitment to better understanding and alleviation of the conditions of racism and of oppression among black peoples of the world.

The bibliographies are divided into (1) Earlier Literature, which includes works published through the 1950's; and (2) Recent Contributions, dating from 1960 to the present.

## EARLIER LITERATURE BIBLIOGRAPHY

Blyden, Edward Wilmot, *Christianity, Islam and the Negro Race*, First published in 1887, Reprinted 1967, Edinburgh University Press; Distributed in U.S.A. by Aldine Publishing Co., Chicago. Traces the influence of Islam or Mohammedanism and Christianity on the development of Africa with particular attention paid to the concept of Negro personality.

Bond, Horace Mann, *History of Education in Alabama 1835-1935: A Study of Cotton and Steel*, Washington, 1939. Marxian analysis is used to point out the plight of black people in Alabama as directly related to the productivity of the cotton and steel industry.

Brawley, Benjamin, *A Social History of the American Negro*, First published 1921 by the Macmillan Company, Reprinted 1970, The Macmillan Company. One of the first works to study the actual life of Negro people in the United States beginning with their African Origins. The scholarship evident in this work dealt effectively with many of the distortions of the period which had found acceptance in academia.

Bunche, Ralph, *World View of Race*, Washington, 1936. Treatise on political and economic interests served by race theories as they influence world affairs. Incorporates a Marxian analysis of relationship between race, colonialism and imperialism.

Cayton, Horace and Mitchell, George, *Black Workers and the New Unions*, Chapel Hill. University of North Carolina Press, 1939. This work contributed much to an understanding of blacks and the development of labor unions. Racism, segregation and the conflict between union, nonunion members and the effect on black workers is depicted.

Cox, Oliver Cromwell, *Caste, Class, and Race*, First published in 1948 by Doubleday: Monthly Review Press, edition 1959. Cox, one of the first black sociologists to utilize Marxian ideas as an analytical tool, challenged the "caste" hypothesis popularized in sociological analysis of race relations and explored power as a crucial variable. The caste hypothesis could not explain the violence necessary to enforce segregation, nor the inevitability of violent racial conflict which he predicted in 1948.

Davis, Allison, Gardner, Burleigh, and Gardner, Mary, *Deep South: A Social Anthropological Study of Caste and Class*, Chicago, Illinois: University of Chicago Press, 1942. One of a series of studies of black communities in the South (Mississippi) with their status differentiations. The authors found social classes present in this rural community but little differentiation among the classes.

Drake, St. Clair and Cayton, Horace, *Black Metropolis*, Vol 1 & 2, First published 1945, New York: Harcourt, Brace & Co. Paperback edition 1962, Harper & Row. Revised and enlarged edition 1970. Classic study of urban life describes black community in Chicago. Life styles, institutions and values of blacks who have migrated to large urban centers of the North are presented with insightful analysis. Raw pride, group solidarity and self-help are significant themes. The observations and conclusions are as pertinent today as when first written.

DuBois, W.E.B., *Black Reconstruction In America: An Essay Toward A History of the Part Which Black Folk Played in the Attempt to Reconstruct Democracy in America, 1860-1880*, New York: Harcourt, Brace & Co. 1935. Important study which presents data to counter balance the biases and distortions of white historians on the Reconstruction. Includes chapter "The Propaganda of History" which explains the situation under which black scholars suffered, and an extremely helpful bibliography.

DuBois, W.E.B., *The Negro*, First published 1915, Henry Holt & Co. Retitled and reprinted in 1939 as *Black Folk: Then and Now*, New York: Henry Holt & Co. First effort by black scholar to directly attack concepts of Social Darwinism and its effect on African peoples of the world.

DuBois, W.E.B., *The Philadelphia Negro: A Social Study*, First published in 1899; Schocken paperback edition, 1967. First important sociological study of Negro Community in United States--established model for urban studies. Precedent setting with its emphasis on class and social environment as determinants of personality and behavior rather than heredity.

Franklin, John Hope, *From Slavery to Freedom: A History of Negro Americans*, First published in 1947. Paperback edition, 1969, Vintage Books, New York: Alfred A. Knopf, 1975, 4th Edition. Comprehensive history of black Americans tracing their African Heritage, development in the United States and contributions to American society.

Frazier, E. Franklin, *Black Bourgeoisie: The Rise of a New Middle Class in the United States*, First published in 1955 as *Bourgeoisie Noir*, Paris: Librairie Plon. Glencoe, Ill.: Free Press, 1957. Collier Books Edition, 1962. Case study of the emergent middle-class defined primarily as wage earners and salaried professionals. Emphasis is on values and patterns of behavior and the make-believe world created by black bourgeoisie to compensate for its feeling of inferiority in a white world dominated by business enterprise.

Frazier, E. Franklin, *The Negro Family in the United States*, First published in 1939 by University of Chicago. Revised and abridged 1948 by Dryden Press. Paperback edition, 1966, University of Chicago Press. First black elected President of the American Sociological Association, Frazier presents an incisive account of problems faced by slave families and their subsequent development as mobility and social conditions exerted their influence on them in urban settings.

Harris, Abram L., *Negro As Capitalist*, Philadelphia: American Academy of Political and Social Science, 1936. Definitive study of black banking from the founding of the first all black bank, "True Reformer Bank" in 1888, to 1932. This work is significant because banks represented an important symbol of bourgeoisie spirit. Other business enterprises are also discussed.

James, C.L.R., *The Black Jacobins*, First published in 1938. Paperback edition, 1963; Random House. Recounts Haiti's struggle for independence and the brilliance of one of its greatest leaders, Toussaint L'Overture.

Johnson, Charles, *Growing Up in the Black Belt: Negro Youth in the Rural South*, Washington, D.C.: American Council on Education, 1941. One of a series of research works prepared for the American Youth Commission on Negro Youth problems in the rural Deep South. Presents attitudes of youth toward dominant caste controls.

Lewis, Hylan, *Blackways of Kent*, Chapel Hill, North Carolina: The University of North Carolina Press, 1955. Continuation of tradition of community studies assessing the caste and status differentiations of blacks in North Carolina. The pattern had been set by Drake & Cayton's *Black Metropolis* and Davis' *Deep South*.

Locke, Alain, Ed., *The New Negro: An Interpretation*, First published in 1925 by Albert and Charles Boni, New York: Reprinted 1969, Atheneum. First black Rhodes Scholar and intellectual father of Harlem Renaissance analyzes this period in a series of essays.

Logan, Rayford, *The Negro in American Life and Thought: The Nadir 1877-1901*, First published in 1925 by Dial Press, Collier paperback edition, retitled *The Betrayal of the Negro: From Rutherford B. Hayes to Woodrow Wilson*, 1965. An outstanding documentation of the concentrated and systematic efforts of the government, politics, economic social, literary forces to reinstitute white supremacy and ensure the subordinate status of black citizens.

McKay, Claude, *Harlem: Negro Metropolis*, First published in 1940, New York: E.P. Dutton & Co., Harvest paperback edition, 1968. One of the major writers of the Harlem Renaissance, provides a vivid pulsating study of the Aframerican capital of the world. The Harlem of Marcus Garvey, Father Divine, small businesses, Labor and Numbers is explored in the period after the Harlem Renaissance and up to World War I.

Padmore, George, *Pan-Africanism or Communism? The Coming Struggle for Africa*, London: Dennis Dobson, Ltd., 1957, New York: Doubleday & Co. Paperback edition, 1972, Anchor Books. Ideologist for Pan-Africanism and Participant-Historian who developed major theoretical framework for analysis and understanding of Pan-African movements.

Rogers, J.A., *Sex and Race*, 3 Vols., New York: H.M. Rogers Publishers, 1942. Survey from antiquity to the present of published sources supplemented by research in museums and art galleries to document the extent of black-white miscegenation; covers ancient Egypt, Greece and Rome.

Williams, Eric, *Capitalism and Slavery*, First published in 1944 by University of North Carolina Press. Paperback edition, 1966; Capricorn Books. Economic study of slavery and slave trade as the underpinning of British capitalism and the Industrial Revolution. The triangular trade of England, France and Colonial America provided the immense capital necessary to finance British industry.

Woodson, Carter G., *Mis-Education of the Negro*; first published in 1933 by Associated Publishers, Inc.; under the direction of the Association for the Study of Negro Life and History, Inc. Reissued, 1969, Associated Publishers. Critical assessment of educational system with its distortion of Afro-American history and stereotypic depiction of black people.

Wright, Richard, *Black Power: A Record of Reactions in a Land of Pathos*, New York, 1954. First use of the term "Black Power." Recounts Wright's reactions to the African situation.

Wright, Richard, *12 Million Black Voices*, 1949. Documentary recounting of the movement of blacks from South to North.

## RECENT CONTRIBUTIONS BIBLIOGRAPHY

Allen, Robert L., *Black Awakening in Capitalist America*, Doubleday, 1969. Important social analysis of black liberation movements, black nationalism and their relationship to capitalism.

Bennett, Lerone, *Before the Mayflower: A History of the Negro in America 1619-1962*, Chicago, Illinois: Johnson Publishing Co., 1962. Paperback edition, 1966, Penguin. Social history of blacks in American society from pre-slavery to Civil Rights sit-ins, demonstrations and school desegregation of the 1960's. Written for the general reader, it is no less valuable.

Billingsley, Andrew, *Black Families in White America*, Prentice-Hall, 1968. Provides social systems analysis of black families which emphasizes the interrelatedness of the family as an institution in society responding to "the other institutions and subsystems." A significant contribution is the typology of black families which delineates their structure into three general categories: (1) primary; (2) extended; and (3) augmented; and twelve subtypes within these categories.

Blackwell, James, *Black Community: Diversity and Unity*, New York: Dodd, Mead and Co., 1975. The formation, structure and maintenance of black communities as a direct response to racism oppression. Three of the most frequently used theoretical frameworks for study of black community: (1) Pluralism; (2) Internal Colonialism; and (3) Systems analysis.

Bontemps, Arna, *Great Slave Narratives*, Beacon Press, 1969. Slave narratives used as documents of historical, social and political analysis.

Carmichael, Stokley and Hamilton, Charles, *Black Power: The Politics of Liberation in America*, New York: Random House, Inc., 1967. The concept of Black Power is presented as a means of economic, political and social control. Black Americans urged to define their own goals, lead their own organizations and reject racist institutions and values of this society.

Cruse, Harold, *The Crisis of the Negro Intellectual*, New York: William Morrow & Co., 1967. History of black intellectuals with a stinging criticism of their anti-theoretical basis and inheritance of "leading failures of the black bourgeoisie of previous generations." A resounding critique of the role the black intellectual has played--or not played--in the black masses struggle for civil rights.

Clark, Kenneth, *Dark Ghetto: Dilemmas of Social Power*, New York: Harper & Row, 1965. Paperback edition, 1967, Harper Torchbook. Depiction of ghetto life, especially Harlem, with emphasis on "interpretation of the meaning of the facts of the ghetto, the truths behind the delinquency, narcotics addiction, infant mortality, homicide and suicide statistics." The powerlessness, hopelessness, and despair of residents is explored together with their dependency on the oftentimes hostile white communities that surround them.

Diop, Cheikh Anta, *The African Origin of Civilization, Myth or Reality*, 1974. An impressive scholarly re-appraisal of Egyptian History which presents convincing argument that it is reality and not myth.

Essien-Udom, E.U. *Black Nationalism: A Search for Identity in America*, Chicago, Illinois: University of Chicago Press, 1962. Dell paperback edition, 1964. The early history of Black Nationalism is explored with in-depth analysis of the Nation of Islam.

Fanon, Frantz, *Black Skin, White Mask*; First published in 1952 as *Peau Noire, Masques Blancs*, Paris, France by Editions de Seuil, New York: Grove Press, 1967. A searing analysis of the process by which the black man develops his identity as a member of a colonized people. Sexual relationships in superordinate and subordinate group together with the role of language is explored. "To speak a language is to take on a world, a culture."

Fanon, Frantz, *Wretched of the Earth*; New York: Grove Press, 1963. Brilliant analysis of the revolutionary process particularly as it applies to a colonized people. Essential to his premise is the role of violence "it is the intuition of the colonized masses that their liberation, must, and can only be achieved by force" . . . "decolonization is always a violent phenomenon." Fanon's assessment of class structure in neo-colonial Africa provides sound basis for understanding contemporary governments and the military in politics.

Grier, William H. & Cobbs, Price M., *Black Rage*; New York: Basic Books, Inc., 1968. Paperback edition, 1969, Bantam Books. Two black psychiatrists explore frustrations, anger and damage to black psyches and subsequent development which is a result of being black in a society that still maintains them in subordinate inferior position in society.

Hernton, Calvin C., *Sex and Racism*; New York: Doubleday & Co., 1965. Paperback edition, 1966, Evergreen Black Cat. The race problem in the United States as intricately tied to sex dating from slavery to the present is explored by this author. The stereotypes of blacks center on sexual aspects rather than economic or power issues. The manner in which blacks and whites relate to and perceive each other sexually and "as a result of living in a world of segregation and racial bigotry" is assessed.

Hill, Robert B., *The Strengths of Black Families*; New York; Emerson Hall Publishers, Inc., 1971. Robert Hill, Director, Research Department, National Urban League, surveys literature of black families which identifies their "existing strengths, resources and potential." U.S. Census data is provided for supportive information.

Quarles, Benjamin, *The Negro in Revolutionary War*, North Carolina: University of North Carolina Press, 1961. Pioneering comprehensive study of the role of black Americans on both sides of the Revolutionary War.

Rodney, Walter, *How Europe Underdeveloped Africa*; First published in 1972. Dar es Salaam: Tanzania Publishing House and London: Bogle-L'Ouverture Publications, Washington, D.C.: Howard University Press, 1974. Explicit and forthright analysis of the direct relationship between the exploitation of African resources and labor (underdevelopment) and capitalist productivity (development) in Western societies.

Staples, Robert, *Introduction to Black Sociology*, New York: McGraw-Hill, 1976. One of the first works by a black sociologist which attempts to define Afro-American or Black Sociology "as a discipline which: (1) "has emerged out of the need to define countertheories about the nature of black life in this country," and must be used (2) "as an introduction of black liberation." The task is defined as developing a sociology that can provide a balanced prospective of blacks and in theory that are peculiar to the needs of an oppressive social system.

Williams, Chancellor, *Destruction of a Black Civilization: Great Issues of a Race from 4500 B.C. to 2000 A.D.*, Chicago, Illinois: The Third World Press. The history of Africa with emphasis on the invasions and their subsequent negative effects on the people and societal development. Black Nationalist perspective.

## FOOTNOTES

1. Pierre L. Van den Berghe, *Race and Racism*, New York: John Wiley & Sons, Inc., 1967.
2. Bradford Chambers, *Chronicles of Black Protest*, New York: The New American Library, 1969, p. 48.
3. Barry Schwartz & Robert Disch, *White Racism*, New York: Dell Publishing Co., 1970, p. 23.
4. Van den Berghe, *op. cit.*, p. 17.
5. Juan Comas, "Racial Myths," in *Race and Science*, UNESCO, New York: Columbia University Press, 1969.
6. Thomas F. Gossett, *Race: The History of an Idea in America*, New York: Schocken Books 1969, p. 1945.
7. Gossett, p. 101.
8. *Ibid*, p. 114.
9. Schwartz & Disch, *op. cit.*, p. 17.
10. Michael Winston, "Through the Back Door: Academic

Racism and the Negro Scholar in Historical Perspective," *Daedalus*, Summer 1971, p. 685.

11. Howard Odum, *American Sociology: The Story of Sociology in the United States Through 1950*, New York: Longmans, Green, 1951, p. 154.

12. Gossett, *op. cit.*, p. 253.

13. John Hope Franklin, "The Dilemma of the American Negro Scholar," in Herbert Hill (ed.) *Soon, One Morning*, New York: Alfred A. Knopf, 1969, p. 65.

14. Winston, *op. cit.*, p. 708.

15. C. Eric Lincoln, "Introduction," in Benjamin Brawley, *Social History of the American Negro*, New York: Macmillan, 1970.

16. Graham Kinloch, *The Dynamics of Race Relations*, New York: McGraw-Hill, 1974, p. 36.

17. Winston, *op. cit.*, p. 70.

18. *Ibid*, p. 698.

19. Oliver C. Cox, *Caste, Class and Race*, New York: Doubleday, 1948, p. 431.

20. Franklin, *op. cit.*, p. 72.

# BLACK HISTORY'S DIVERSIFIED CLIENTELE

*Benjamin A. Quarles*

Along with many other denials since he arrived on these shores, the Black American has until recently been denied a past. The consequent damage to his psyche can hardly be imagined. In a poem entitled "Negro History," appearing in the volume *From the Ashes: Voices of Watts* (Budd Schulberg, editor), young Jimmie Sherman depicts the past as his grandfather viewed it:

> A ship
> A chain
> A distant land
> A whip
> A pain
> A white man's hand
> A sack
> A field
> of cotton balls--
> The only things
> Grandpa recalls.

Such an outlook on the past has a stultifying effect, making for apathy and despair. Hence, black leaders since the birth of the Republic have been advocates of Negro history, obviously envisioning a far broader coverage of it than Jimmie Sherman's grandpa had come to know. Black scholars, led by Carter G. Woodson in 1915, began to remove the layers of ignorance and distortion that had encrusted the Afro-American past. One of these scholars, W.E.B. Du Bois, in the closing line of his autobiography, written during his last months, bespoke anew his lifelong devotion to history: "Teach us, Forever Dead, there is no Dream but Deed, there is no Deed but Memory." A quarter of a century earlier Du Bois fired back a sharp rejoinder to a magazine editor who had rejected a Du Bois essay because it had touched upon the past. "Don't you understand," Du Bois wrote, "that the past is present; that without what was, nothing is."

During the past decade the cry for Black history

Reprinted with permission from *Africa and the Afro-American Experience* edited by Lorraine A. Williams. Copyright © 1971, 1972, 1973, 1977, 1981 (paper edition) by Howard University Department of History.

has been stronger than ever before. Numbered among the proponents of such history are the newer Black militants. "We Blacks," writes Imamu Amiri Baraka (LeRoi Jones), must "learn our collective past in order to design a collective destiny." Of his period of confinement at the Norfolk (Massachusetts) Prison Colony, Malcolm X wrote: "I began first telling my Black brother inmates about the glorious history of the Black man-- things they had never dreamed." On another occasion he referred to history as "a people's memory" without which "Man is demoted to the lower animals." In his assessment of the past, Malcolm X did not ignore the less glorious aspects of the Black pilgrimage in America. Speaking to a ghetto audience in Detroit in 1953 he evoked a deep response with the words: "We didn't land on Plymouth Rock, my brothers and sisters--Plymouth Rock landed on us!"

Eldridge Cleaver, who, like Malcolm X, became a serious student of history while serving time in prison, spoke its praises. In his essay "To All Black Women, From All Black Men," in *Soul on Ice*, he writes:

> Be convinced, Sable Sister, that the past is no forbidden vista upon which we dare not look, out of a phantom fear of being, as the wife of Lot, turned into pillars of salt. Rather the past is an omniscient mirror: we gaze and see reflected there ourselves and each other--what we used to be and what we are today, how we got this way, and what we are becoming. To decline to look into the Mirror of Then, my heart, is to refuse to view the face of Now.

One of the sable sisters who has needed no convincing about history's role is poet Sarah Webster Fabio, who writes:

> Now at all costs, we must heal our history. Or else our future rots in the disease of our past.

Although Black history is now coming into its

own as never before, not all of its proponents are in pursuit of the same goal. Indeed, today Black history is being called upon to serve an increasing variety of publics, four of whom we may scrutinize briefly. These are the Black rank and file, the Black revolutionary nationalists, the Black academicians, and the white world, both scholarly and lay. Not mutually exclusive, these groups often overlap. But this fourfold typology enables us to illustrate the major contemporary uses of Black history. We may take these in turn, first describing their aims and then noting their general content and style.

For the Black rank and file, the man in the street, the laity, Black history's main objective is to create a sense of racial pride and personal worth. To the rank and file the new Black history is good therapy, its end result an improved self-image. In a world that has traditionally equated blackness with inferiority, Black history serves as a balm to make the wounded whole. In a world that has traditionally equated blackness with low aim, Black history serves as a stimulus to success. To a Black person seeking to resolve an identity crisis, Black history is ego-soothing; it places one in the thick of things, thereby diminishing his sense of alienation, of rootlessness. Black history is a search for the values and the strengths imbedded in the Black subculture. Black history strikes at the Black American's legacy of self-rejection, the burden of shame that he had been taught was his to bear going back to the curse of Cain. "I always wanted to be somebody," runs the title of the autobiography of a Black tennis champion. Black history tells the Black reader that he is somebody, however vicariously.

In its content, Black history for the masses reflects somewhat "the great man" theory of history. White or Black, the typical American, himself individualistic, conceives of his country's past as the achievements of a group of outstanding characters, pushing on against herculean odds. History is a tableau of heroes set in bold relief. To the generality of Blacks their men of mark constitute their history, the bulk of their attention falling upon individual achievers--an underground railroad conductor like Harriet Tubman, a dedicated bishop like Daniel E. Payne, an educator like Mary McLeod Bethune, a sports celebrity like prize fighter Peter Jackson or jockey Isaac Murphy, and a singer like Elizabeth Taylor Greenfield (the "Black Swan") or Bessie Smith. The list is endless, ranging from an early African king to a present-day ghetto leader.

Upbeat and achievement-oriented, Black history for the rank and file stresses victories--the peak that was scaled, the foe that was vanquished, the deep river that was crossed. Moreover, to the masses, youth makes a special appeal, the younger Frederick Douglass arousing more interest than the Sage of Anacostia. Local Black historical figures likewise meet with a readier response than out-of-staters, however more nationally important the latter may be. Moreover, history designed for the laity will of necessity devote as much attention to popular culture and the lively arts as to the more traditional staples, politics and economics, particularly since the Black stamp on the former is more readily discernible.

The emphasis on the lively arts and popular culture lends itself to the mass media. Hence, Black history for laymen has found a natural ally in television, commercial as well as educational, but obviously of far greater proportions in the latter. Radio, too, especially in the folkways recordings, lends itself to Black cultural history. Other mass media such as newspapers and magazines are increasingly carrying Black history articles, biographical sketches, and pictorial materials. Sensing the growing interest in Black history, commercial firms have brought out coloring books, alphabet books, Black history games, and Black history in comic-book format.

History as hero worship is hardly the kind of history espoused by the second Black group under survey--the Black revolutionary nationalists. This group focuses upon exploiters and oppressors, a case study in man's inhumanity to man. This group views history as grievance collecting, a looking back in anger. Black nationalist history is essentially the story of a powerful white majority imposing its will upon a defenseless Black minority. Black nationalists hold that American society needs to be reconstructed and that Black history is, or should be, a means of ideological indoctrination in the revolutionary cause of Black liberation.

Black nationalist history is not without its traces of paranoid thinking, one which holds that the forces of evil are banded in an eternal conspiracy to maintain their oppressive sway. Of very ancient origin, this devil theory of history is deeply rooted in the human psyche and hence should occasion no surprise when met in any of its multiple guises.

Like so much else in American life, Black nationalism has, as it has always had, a variety of forms--cultural, religious, and economic, among others. Revolutionary nationalism moves a step beyond the others in its goals and does not rule out violence in achieving them. Revolutionary Black nationalists, having carefully examined the almost unbelievable pervasiveness of color prejudice in our society have, in essence, given up on America. Estranged from the land of their birth, they ponder its dismantlement.

As to content, revolutionary Black history is not as interested in historical spadework as in providing new interpretations of that which is already known. Black nationalist history emphasizes racial contrast, physical and cultural. It propounds a Black aesthetic and implies a Black mystique. It bespeaks the essential kinship of Black people on whatever continent they be located or in whatever walk of life. Its central theme is oppression, slavery in one guise or another. Rebelliousness against the oppressor likewise looms large in nationalist lore.

A compound of Black rage and white guilt, revolutionary Black history makes much of the analogy of colonialism, holding that Black Americans live in a state of vassalage to white Americans. Black America is a semi-colony of white America.

Going further, the revolutionary school of thought stresses separatism, insisting that Black Americans have always constituted a nation. To those who hold these views, Black history has one overriding purpose; namely, to promote nation-building.

In tone, Black revolutionary history is judgmental, with overtones of recrimination, moral condemnation, and prophetic warning. Apocalyptic and polemical in temper, it scorns objectivity, which it equates with a defense of the status quo. Revolutionary Black history may, on occasion, read like social commentary, sometimes taking on a man-the-barricades urgency.

Selective in content, black revolutionary history ignores as irrelevant those aspects of the past which do not relate to its philosophy. As will be noted in just a moment, however, this tendency to pick and choose is nothing new in the historical profession.

The third group under survey are the Black academicians--the intellectually sophisticated, the college and university trained, the well-read. Like the revolutionary nationalists, they operate on a more studious level. They would concur with the revolutionary nationalists in holding that history is a weapon in the warfare. But to the academically oriented mind the basic foe is ignorance, be it willful or otherwise. It hardly need be added that ignorance is a somewhat impersonal foe and hence less easily pinpointed, less starkly isolated.

To the Black academician, history is a discipline, an attempt to recapture and mirror the past as accurately as possible. Admittedly this is a tall order, considering the nature of the evidence and the unreliability of so many of the witnesses. Black academicians hardly need to be reminded that history, as we know it, is not neutral, not value-free. Who can tell the Black academician anything new about the insensitivity of past generations of white scholars, of their neglect or distortion of the role of Black peoples? But the Black academician would question the viewpoint that prejudiced history must be met with prejudiced history; he would doubt that the best way to strike at the mythmakers of history is to imitate them. In *The Fire Next Time*, James Baldwin has observed that "an invented past can never be used; it cracks and crumbles under the pressures of life like clay in a season of drought." As we have noted, however, white Americans have made some use of an invented past. But Black Americans must realize that a powerful majority may for a time be able to afford the luxury of fantasy. Such indulgence on the part of a minority is a species of living beyond its means, a minority having to husband carefully its limited resources.

Like the laymen and the nationalist, the Black academician finds in Black history a deepening sense of racial worth and of peoplehood. He, too, reads Black history with pride. The Black academician views America as a civilization upon which his ancestors have left their stamp. Hence, he does not regard America as a white civilization exclusively; to him it also has its Black, red, and yellow components. The Black academician holds that his forbears helped to build America, and this being the case no one should sensibly expect him to pack his belongings and leave for other shores.

In addition to personal and racial gratification, the Black academician reads Black history because he feels that it will contribute to his knowledge and understanding of mankind, of his fellow travelers in time and space.

For academicians, the content of Black history would be more selective than for the laymen, in an attempt to avoid the obvious or the well known. Black history for the academician would deal less with persons and more with processes, less with general Black history than with selected topics in Black history. It would include comparative studies and pose methodological problems. On the grounds that academicians do not shy away from the unpleasant, Black history for them would not ignore the less glorious aspects of the Black past--the African tribesmen who engaged in the slave trade, the slave drivers on the Southern plantations, the Black informers who divulged the slave conspiracies or those who revealed the hiding place of a runaway slave. History has its share of those Blacks who turned out to be all too human.

The academician would grant that, more often than not, the truth makes one sick. But he believes the New Testament adage about truth also making one free. The academician holds that truth, including the search for it, has a liberating effect. To be truly free is to be free first and foremost in the great franchise of the mind. To a group like Black Americans, who have been subjected to so much falsehood by others, it would seem that the quest for truth should be held in high favor, having a relevance never failing.

Black history written for the academic fraternity will in the main take on a reflective, judicial tone, taking its cue from the careful winnowing and sifting that preceded it. The style will be sober, the rhetoric restrained. Passionate and deeply emotional language is highly necessary and desirable in human affairs, but such expression is more the province of the poet, the orator, and the charismatic leader than of the professional historian. An orator may give full vent to his innermost feelings, and to the innermost feelings of his audience, but a social scientist works in a discipline which has imperatives of its own, imperatives which may point to conclusions that run counter to his private wishes.

The codes of his discipline bring the Black academician face to face with one of the major problems confronting every social scientist; namely, whether his citizen role should overshadow his professional role, whether he should give priority to social action or to scientific inquiry. Should an academician strive for competence in his discipline or should he seek primarily to become personally involved and relevant? To the Black academician this dilemma takes on an unusual urgency inasmuch as he is fully aware of the long-standing discriminations against Black people in the American social order. Addressing himself to this question of citizenship role versus profes-

sional role, sociologist Ernest Q. Campbell comes to the conclusion that "there is no intrinsic reason why the roles of scientific inquirer and staunch advocate are incompatible" ("Negroes, Education, and the Southern State," *Social Forces*, March 1969). But to play these two roles simultaneously would seem to require unusual abilities and energies. In their absence each Black academician must come to some hard choices as to his own major commitment.

To the final audience under survey, the white community--academic and lay--Black history has an important message. Black history should not be confined to Blacks alone--this would be like confining the Gospel to those already converted, to use a familiar figure. Black history, like other phases of Black studies, is no longer a matter of limited concern. Whites need to know Black history. As Theodore Draper points out in *The Rediscovery of Black Nationalism* (New York, 1970), "In the interest of the entire society, white students need Black Studies as much or even more than black students." At a meeting of the Organization of American Historians in 1969, C. Vann Woodward voiced much the same sentiment in his presidential address, "Clio with Soul." Woodward spoke of Black history as being "too important to be left entirely to Negro historians."

To begin with, whites should realize that the major reason for the long neglect of Black history falls upon the historical guild itself. As Carl Becker has pointed out, "The historian selects from a number of particular facts certain facts which he considers most important to be known." Historians, continues Becker, "unconsciously read the objective facts of the past in the light of their own purposes, or the preoccupations of their own age." To point out that written history has a subjective element is certainly nothing new--Becker's observations were made in 1910. But to mention this matter at the outset makes for the open-mindedness so essential to a proper perspective on the Black American. Whites who read history should know by now that white historians have until recently dealt with the American past in such a way as to ignore the Black presence or to minimize its importance in the making of America.

The aim of Black history for white readers is twofold; first to eliminate the myth that our country's past was rosy and romantic, a new Eden "with liberty and justice for all," and second, to illustrate the centrality of the Black American in our national experience. White historians have until recently tended to play down the somber aspects of Black-white relationships in America--the deeply ingrained sense of white superiority dating back to Jamestown and Plymouth, the brutality of slavery, the mockery of post-Reconstruction, and the twentieth-century offshoots of these persistent pathologies. The American past has a tragic component which cannot be brushed away. White Americans must need take a second thought as they sing the familiar lines, "Thine alabaster cities gleam,/Undimmed by human tears."

Black history would enable whites to more realistically appraise some of our country's boasted achievements and some of its acclaimed public figures. For example, whites generally view the age of Andrew Jackson as one in which the right to vote was extended to the common man. But whites need to know that it was during this period that states like North Carolina and Pennsylvania were explicitly prohibiting Blacks from exercising this privilege. White readers of American history have thought highly of Woodrow Wilson for his espousal of the "New Freedom" and for his doctrine of "making the world safe for democracy." But white readers need to know that during Wilson's presidency, and with his acquiescence, Black federal workers in the District of Columbia were systematically segregated and were given inferior working conditions and restroom facilities such as had not existed up to this time in the federal government.

Black history would be remiss if it did not call attention to these sobering aspects of the American past. But Black history does not consist solely of white denial and discrimination. Hence Black history for whites would indicate the myriad ways in which this country's history and culture would have been different without the presence of the Black man. Many of these ways--economic, political, constitutional, and military--are more quickly spotted than others. In some fields--art, literature, music, the dance, and popular culture in general--the Black contribution centers in the common core, making its stamp more difficult to isolate. But whether obvious or subtle, the Black man's gifts to America have been freely received if slowly acknowledged. To this extent all Americans are part Black in their cultural patrimony. Blacks in general would concur in the sentiment expressed by a stanza from James Weldon Johnson ("Fifty Years, 1863-1913," in his *Fifty Years and Other Poems*, Boston, 1921):

> This land is ours by right of birth,
> This land is ours by right of toil,
> We helped to turn its virgin earth,
> Our sweat is in its fruitful soil.

The acceptance of Black history by whites has been greatly facilitated by the current emphasis on social history. "It is a good moment to be a social historian" writes E.J. Hobsbawn (*Daedalus*, Winter 1971), history professor at the University of London. This branch of history pays particular attention to the anonymous common man and to the manners and customs of everyday life. And even more importantly for a Black orientation, this branch of history emphasizes social movements and the phenomena of social protest.

For the white reader of Black history the content would, at least initially, suggest the centrality of the Negro American and his identification with this country's great, professed goals. Therefore such history would comprise a general presentation of the American past with the Black component interwoven throughout, appearing at its proper chronological juncture and not separately, somewhat like a disjointed subtheme for the curious, Clio's underworld.

In style and technique Black history for whites would differentiate between the white layman and the white intellectual. For the white layman the approach would be much the same as for his Black counterpart, that is, an emphasis on biographical sketches and on the lively arts and popular culture, including sports. Again, as for the Black layman, books would be greatly supplemented by the mass media. Indeed, of course, the mass media outlets used to reach Black people will inevitably reach many whites.

For the white academician the approach to Black history might be broader than the biographical and less fearful of the recipient's short attention span. Black studies for white intellectuals would back assertion with documentation, presenting proof and citing authorities. A footnote is not an end unto itself. But those of an academic bent have been trained to look for the hard evidence; to them a statement must be intellectually tenable, its sources as trustworthy as possible. For the open-minded scholar--the seeker after truth--the will to believe is not an acceptable substitute for the data that corroborates.

We have dealt with Black history for four different audiences. But in written history the use of different approaches and viewpoints need come as no surprise. No one category of events, no single interpretation, can furnish the cloth for that seamless garment we call history. There is not single compass by which to unravel the course of historical causation. Written history, in form and content, is many-sided, however much this may disconcert the doctrinaire types.

This short excursion into Black history has taken note of varying viewpoints as to its function. Although varied, these approaches are often complementary rather than contradictory. More than anything else they demonstrate that there are alternate ways of looking at the past. The viewpoints of the revolutionary nationalist and the academic historian are not necessarily antagonistic. The academician, for example, may disavow an activist role and say that he is dealing with ideas for their own sake. But ideas are weapons and, as a rule, action is germinated by ideas.

In the formation of the new Black history the academician--the traditionalist--will continue to be of major importance. But if Black history is to come of age, revolutionary Black nationalists will also have much to contribute. The nationalist historians will force a reexamination of the historic patterns of color prejudice in America, not only in its grosser, more obvious manifestations, but in its manifold subtle forms, its protective coloration one might say. The nationalists will bring into purview the Blacks of the so-called Third World, comparing and contrasting them with their counterparts in America. The tone of moral outrage that characterizes the nationalist school has its value, too, a healthy anger often acting as a social catalyst.

And finally the revolutionary Black nationalist has made it clear that to properly assess the Black past we need newer, nontraditional techniques. A multidisciplinary approach is called for, one not relying so largely on written records. Historical inquiry is already profiting from the methodology of the behavioral sciences--sociology, anthropology, and psychology. Interdisciplinary history opens vistas across and beyond the traditional chronological and geographic boundaries. These widening approaches to appraising the past have led to such newer periodicals as the *Journal of Interdisciplinary History*, its first issue appearing in the autumn of 1970 and its avowed purpose to "stimulate historians to examine their own subjects in a new light, whether they be derived from psychology, physics, or paleontology."

This is the age of ideological cross-fertilization. It is to be noted, for example, that today in the study of early man on this planet no fewer than twelve different special skills are necessary--six field skills and six laboratory skills. In properly assessing the Black role in American history a comparable if less numerous list of skills is needed. Without the use of these newer tools the past will remain an incompleted past. In fine, historians of the Black past must take into consideration "the changing character of historical evidence, the development of new techniques and concepts in related disciplines and the growing body of research by non-historians into historical problems," to borrow a phrase from David S. Landes and Charles Tilly ("History as Social Science," in Social Science Research Council *Items*, March 1971).

The newer Black history, looking afresh down the corridors of time, has a revolutionary potential of its own. For Blacks it is a new way to see themselves. For whites it furnishes a new version of American history, one that especially challenges our national sense of smugness and self-righteousness and our avowal of fair play. Beyond this the new Black history summons the entire historical guild--writers, teachers, and learners-- to higher levels of expectation and performance. History, as all of its disciples know is both continuity and change. Change stems from our readiness to challenge the current order, using the best tools of our trade. A new Black history would revitalize education, quickening whatever it touches.

In 1925 in the foreword to his pathbreaking volume *The New Negro*, Alain Locke, one of the many illustrious Howard University scholar-humanists, said many things that have a contemporary ring: "Negro life is not only establishing new contacts and founding new centers, it is finding a new soul. There is fresh spiritual and cultural focusing . . . There is a renewed race-spirit that consciously and proudly sets itself apart." Locke, of course, was speaking primarily of creative expression in the arts, but his words aptly characterize the current Black thrust in history. In its work of restoring history's lost boundaries, the Black history of today is establishing new contacts and finding a new soul.

# BENIGN NEGLECT?
# ANTHROPOLOGY AND THE STUDY OF
# BLACKS IN THE UNITED STATES

*E.L. Cerroni-Long*

The distinction between "pure" and "applied" anthropology has always been rather difficult to define. In fact, according to Partridge and Eddy (1978: 4-5), such distinction "is largely a fiction of popular culture" even if, they go on to say, "there is an important differentiation to be made between 'abstract' and 'applied' anthropology." In the authors' view, what distinguishes "applied" anthropologists is that they "study living cultures and contemporary people . . . conduct research oriented toward the problems of those they study . . . seek application of their findings, data, and analyses beyond anthropology" (Partridge and Eddy, 1978: 5). Going by this definition, however, it is certainly not necessary to wait for the foundation of the American Society for Applied Anthropology at Harvard in 1942, to find examples of excellent anthropological research that can be defined as "applied." In fact, one could perhaps stretch the argument and suggest that not only must some of the best anthropological works, both before and after 1941, be defined as works of applied anthropology, but the discipline itself was born out of the necessity to resolve practical problems.

In Goody's (1973: 19) words, anthropology "emerged as an attempt at understanding the colonial (or primitive) present and the European (or civilized) past." As a matter of fact, the evolutionism that characterized early anthropology implied the *equation* between the past of "civilized" people and the present of the "primitives," and through the study of the savages anthropologists endeavored to investigate the "origin, or rather the rudimentary phases, the infancy and childhood of human society" (Frazer quoted by Voget, 1975:143). In the process, the new elites created by the Industrial Revolution were provided with a theory of progress that not only gave scientific support to their intellectual supremacy but also justified the escalating exploitation of the primitive people that Western expansion was making necessary (Burridge, 1973). But, both in Britain and in the United States, the social impact of anthropology was not confined only to the ideology it supported, its most direct influence was exerted through those anthropological studies that either had immediate social application or were at least stimulated by concrete problems of policymaking and administration (e.g., see Hunt, 1863, Nott and Gliddon, 1854).

This was especially true in the United States, where the interest of anthropologists was, from the beginning, overwhelmingly directed to the study of American Indians, whose administration was evidently a concrete and urgent concern of the American government. In Britain, after the flurry of "applied" interest that characterized anthropology in the 1860s (see Reining, 1962), scholars directed their efforts at getting anthropology established as an academic discipline and the involvement in practical matters decreased markedly. The "academicization" of anthropology took place in due course also in the United States, but in this country the interest in actively applying anthropological analyses and findings remained very much alive.

In fact, the history of American anthropology shows recurrent "explosions" of the "applied orientation" usually bringing along remarkable flourishing in all areas of the discipline (see Goldschmidt and Sanday, 1979).

In view of all this, one question needs to be asked: Why did not anthropologists apply their specific training and expertise to the study of minority relations, the one problem that seems so fundamental in American society, with more frequency than was done? In particular, why did not anthropologists contribute more conspicuously to the study of blacks, especially since they could be seen both as a problematic aspect of American society and as an exotic culture, at least just as exotic as the American Indians, the study of whom was taken up by hundreds of American anthropologists? To analyze why American anthropologists have not studied the black minority should tell us something both about the nature of American anthropology and about the relationship between anthropology and society in the American setting. Also if this relationship is studied in its dynamic components one can attempt to predict the potential for change American anthropology retains. However, before attempting to explain why American anthropologists have not studied blacks one must try to define the extent of this accusation. It is not true in fact that no studies at all were carried out on this subject. To see what was done, how it was accepted and used within the intellectual community and by American society at large, and why the studies that were done remained isolated should be of help in assessing the relationship between anthropology and the study of blacks in America.

## HISTORICAL OVERVIEW

Before offering a rapid outline of the history of anthropological involvement with the study of blacks in the United States one clarification is in order. When I say *anthropological studies of blacks* I mean studies in which blacks are analyzed as a culture or, perhaps, as an American subculture. Thus the various references to Negroes as a race often found in the works of early anthropologists, certainly do not qualify for our purposes.

Quite interestingly, even Boas, who dedicated much of his career to bringing forth a scholarly refutation of deterministic theories based on race, apparently did not recognize the existence of a distinctive Afro-American culture. His anthropometric studies of black and white Americans led him to reaffirm his belief in the unreliability of "racial identity as a means of predicting cultural capacity" but also "to infer that blacks, as a group, simply 'overlapped' white American culture, if only imperfectly" (Szwed, 1972: 157). In my view, however, this fact does not prove Willis's contention that Boasian scientific antiracism was essentially stimulated by the desire to combat anti-Semitism and thus was essentially a weapon in the struggle with the white Protestant establishment over the domination of anthropology in the United States (Willis, 1972: 138-139). Rather, it could be argued that it was just the antiracism, humanitarianism, and political liberalism typical of Boas and of many of his students that led them

to propound the notion that blacks should not be considered as a distinct sector of American society since their "racial" heritage had all but been lost during the traumatic period of slavery (e.g., see Benedict, 1959a: 86-87; Benedict, 1959b: 26).

Besides, two other factors should not be overlooked. First of all, it must be remembered that Boas had emigrated from Germany to escape anti-Semitism and that a good number of Boasians were European Jews. Thus one can speculate that they had a personal emotional investment in supporting a theory of black acculturation that fitted neatly into the general ideology of amalgamation, which indeed was a typical "minority utopia" (Newman, 1973: 63-67). In effect, behind Boas's racial theories there does seem to be a desire to defend the basic "goodness" of amalgamation as it was occurring in the American setting (e.g., see Boas, 1909). Second, and most important, to consider American blacks as a separate cultural group was made difficult for the Boasians by their very definition of culture as an integrated whole rooted in a well-defined physical setting. Furthermore, the paramount Boasian interest in "conservation ethnography" led to a total dedication to cultures in which "purity" had not been contaminated by prolonged contact with Western civilization (Mintz, 1970: 14).

All these considerations must not make us forget, however, that Boas felt true sympathy for the cause of the blacks. In his lifetime he became actively involved with W.E.B. DuBois and with other political leaders fighting for civil rights, and while his own position on the matter of black culture may be considered ambiguous, he must be credited with stimulating his students' interest in the direction of black studies. Obviously, the student that did most in this field was Melville Herskovits, but Boas was also the go-between for the prolific marriage between anthropology and the study of black folklore that produced, among others, the works of Elsie Clew Parsons, Zora Neale Hurston, and Martha Beckwith (Whitten and Szwed, 1970: 32-34). In this period, studies of black folklore were also carried out by Arthur Huff Fauset, a student of Frank Specks's and one of the very few black anthropologists of this period, who also produced a dissertation, entitled *Black Gods of the Metropolis* (Fauset, 1944), which is one of the earliest examples of urban ethnography (Szwed, 1979: 101).

At the beginning of the 1930s, another "second generation" anthropologist, Hortense

Powdermaker, following a suggestion by Edward Sapir, completed a period of fieldwork in a Mississippi community she fictitiously named Cottonsville from which she derived an ethnographic study (Powdermaker, 1939) particularly interesting as an analysis of interracial relations. In effect, however, Powdermaker's work belongs to a tradition of studies of black communities that were carried out throughout the 1930s and the 1940s by scholars who directly or indirectly came under the influence of either Robert E. Park or of W. Lloyd Warner. Many of these scholars were sociologists and the few anthropologists among them were informed, mainly through Warner, by a British social anthropological perspective.[1] Considered together, "these studies provided a massive documentation of inequality and the disadvantaged position of the Negro in American life" (Hicks and Handler, 1978: 313), but from a theoretical point of view they simply offered supporting evidence for the sociological theory of black "cultural deprivation" that remained the orthodox view among liberal scholars well into the 1960s.

Because of its longevity and popularity and because it is on this theory that rested many of the government's meliorative policies triggered by the unrest of the last two decades, the sociological position certainly deserves separate attention. For the moment, however, I would like to conclude my overview of the specifically anthropological contributions to the study of blacks with a brief analysis of the work of Melville J. Herskovits. His position was, in fact, so original and controversial and his conclusions have been gathering such growing popularity in recent years that one is tempted to put this scholar in a category of his own.

Herskovits's initial position on the subject of the blacks' heritage was very similar to that of Boas and of other Boasians. In his *The Negro's Americanism* (1968), published in 1925 at the height of the Harlem Renaissance, he argued that blacks represent a case of complete acculturation. This attitude had probably been stimulated by early anthropometric studies that may have led him to the same confusion of race and culture that Boas himself may have incurred (Szwed, 1972: 157, 175, note 3). However, various fieldwork experiences in Surinam, Haiti, Trinidad, Brazil, and West Africa gradually led him to reconsider radically his position and to reach original conclusions that he expounded in his *The Myth of the Negro Past* (1941).

In this work, in open polemic with what was the "consensus of virtually all of the white and black intellectuals and laymen of his time" (Szwed, 1972: 164), he argued that the culture of black Americans reveals a remarkable persistence of African traits. In so doing, Herskovits had precise "political" purposes besides his scholarly ones. His major aim was to provide the blacks with a surely grounded sense of cultural heritage and a feeling of pride in their past, but he was also hoping that the emphasis on the richness of black culture would lead the whites to change their attitudes toward the potentialities of the Negro "and thus contribute to a lessening of interracial tensions" (Herskovits, 1941: 32).

Perhaps, as Szwed argues, these were unrealistic hopes for the times, and they were confronted instead by the very real danger that "Herskovits' conclusions might be used by racists and the ethnocentrically inclined to build a case against integration and social equality" (Szwed, 1972: 164). Thus it could be thought that the ostracism with which *The Myth of the Negro Past* was received by the intellectual community was caused by a fear for this kind of consequence. Certainly most of the supporters of the theory of "Negro cultural deprivation" rejected Herskovits's position on both theoretical and ideological bases, but it is important to remember that his theories were also attacked by many anthropologists on purely technical grounds. The fact is that in approaching the study of Afro-American cultures, Herskovits had entered a territory that had been traditionally dominated by British social anthropologists. Moreover, he had studied these cultures by emphasizing the importance of the symbolic or broadly cultural elements in them, relying on psychological principles for interpretation and, above all, almost disregarding the analysis of social structure. This attitude was, of course, "heretical" in the eyes of social anthropologists in the British mold and as a consequence "theoretical opposition over the significance of Afro-American date was inevitable" (Whitten and Szwed, 1970: 29).

In the furor over Herskovits's treatment of cultural facts, the facts themselves were ultimately discarded (Szwed, 1972: 164) and *The Myth of the Negro Past* remained isolated both from the mainstream of anthropological research and from that of studies concerning blacks. As mentioned above, these studies were practically monopolized by sociologists and the theory they developed not only became the orthodox social science view on the issue but was to have long-range repercussions at the level of policymaking.

## SOCIAL THEORY AND THE BLACK REACTION

Ironically, it was anthropology itself that stimulated a certain attitude toward the study of American blacks, the implications of which were taken over and developed by sociologists to the point in which any conflicting theory, such as Herskovits's, was ostracized or ignored. Not only that, but in the study of blacks, social scientists made frequent use of anthropological concepts, while anthropological methods of research were generally avoided. The concept that was used, and misused, most was certainly the very idea of "culture." In this respect, one must remember that the focusing of sociological interest on the black "problem" took place at the end of World War I and developed through the 1930s. It was at that time that northward migration and black unrest, resulting from the disappointment in the great hopes aroused by Wilsonian promises of "real democracy," transformed what had been a Southern problem since the "compromise of 1877" into a national problem (Hicks and Handler, 1978: 315). By the time the sociologists began to develop their theories about the black "problem," scientific racism was already on the wane and they accepted and made use of the anthropological concept of culture. However, this concept was mainly used to demonstrate the fact that blacks lacked a culture of their own (e.g., see Frazier, 1934: 194).

This was, to be sure, just a development of the theory of "cultural loss" that Boas and the Boasians had put forth to support the notion of successful black acculturation. Also, this theory was clearly stimulated by sympathy for the plight of the blacks and by a sincere desire to ameliorate their living conditions. After all, the center for sociological investigation in this period was Chicago, where indeed the conditions of recently urbanized blacks were quite wretched, and the two scholars who most contributed to the formulation of this theory were Robert Ezra Park and E. Franklin Frazier, the latter of whom was black, both of whom were confirmed liberals. However, the problem with the theory the Chicago sociologists developed was that it was not built on ethnographic data. In effect, it seems to have been put forth a priori as a suitable rationalization for the fact that blacks had become a national problem in the United States, and subsequently it was supported and reinforced by data derived from statistical surveys that punctually demonstrated what they had been carried out to demonstrate: Blacks were plagued by social and personal disorganization that could be explained only as a consequence of their "cultural deprivation" (e.g., see Embree, 1931: 10-11; Frazier, 1939: 21; Reuter, 1938: 106). Thus a self-fulfilling theory was founded and a "pejorative tradition" (Valentine, 1968) initiated.

In trying to understand the overwhelming popularity and the sweeping influence of the "sociological theory," the most important factor to take into consideration is, in my view, its historical acceptability. In other words, historical factors made such a theory acceptable at both the ideological and social levels. First of all, it fitted neatly into the tradition of "moderate liberal reformism" that became the orthodoxy for the American intelligentsia in the period between and around the two wars. Second, by showing concern for the plight of the Afro-Americans the white elites could hope to please the black electorate, increasingly important in northern urban areas, to unify the country for "the exigencies of international conflict first again the Axis, and later against 'world Communism,'" and to achieve the social peace so important for a bureaucratized industrial society (Frederickson, 1971: 331). Third, and most important, in offering a "cultural" explanation for "the plight of the Negroes" sociologists not only provided a rationalization for the maintenance of the status quo[2] but paved the way for the ultimate interpretation of the social inequality suffered by blacks as being a consequence of their own "cultural inadequacy" (Hicks and Handler, 1978: 315-317).

In all fairness it must be pointed out that the studies sociologists and sociologically inclined anthropologists produced during this period in documentation of the inequality suffered by blacks in American society did have some positive influence at the policymaking level. An anthropologist, Robert Redfield, "served as an expert witness in *Sweatt v. Painter*, as it was argued before the United States Supreme Court" (Van Willigen, 1977: 40) and later some of these studies were used as supporting evidence for the Court's opinion in the 1954 *Brown v. Board of Education* (see Kluger, 1976). One wonders, however, whether or not it was the impact of these studies that influenced the antisegregationist rulings of the 1950s or rather the mounting pressure of black unrest. After all, "the American dilemma" was, as presented in the works of these scholars, an essentially moral problem. It is quite symptomatic in this respect that, when the increasing social unrest of the 1960s pushed the federal government to ask social scientists for suggestions on policies apt to ameliorate the relationship between the white elites and the blacks, the advice offered concerned the desirability of a general attitude of "benign neglect" toward black unrest and the creation of programs directed at changing black ethos (Hicks and Handler, 1978: 315).[3]

It is a measure of the sociologists' sincere belief in the correctness of their theories that they were taken completely by surprise by the fact that after the blacks acquired enough social strength to be able to make precise demands, these implied the total rejection of the "sociological theory." Where the social scientists had theorized about their "cultural deprivation," blacks emphasized their African heritage; where the sociologists had implied or openly stated that the highest Negro aspiration was for complete assimilation, black leaders demanded separatism, autonomy, and, in fact, a reinforcement of segregation.

It has been suggested that this apparently incoherent reaction was caused directly by the realization, on the part of the blacks, that no matter how many studies were done to demonstrate the inequality prevalent in American society there would persist a basic unwillingness on the part of the government and of the white elites to support the implementation of concrete measures that could eliminate that inequality (Tumin, 1972). Alternatively, it has been said that perhaps blacks "began to tire of the stigmatization and forced change" they had to accept in order to achieve integration in the white world (Szwed, 1972: 169). It could also be argued, however, that historical changes in American society and in the world at large[4] slowly allowed blacks to gather enough self-confidence and authority to be able to challenge a "scientific theory," and the policy based on that theory that not only did not correspond to a reality in the way they perceived it but could even be seen, at least from a certain point of view, as supporting the vested interests of the white elites. Thus the new "Dream" blacks now seem to pursue has nothing to do with becoming "more American than the Americans," which is seen as what the whites have always wanted the blacks to become; rather it is built on the desire to reaffirm the group's ancestral "difference" and to obtain equality on

the basis of the recognition of this difference, not on the basis of the white man's values and criteria of fitness and competence.

Confronted by the black reaction to the "sociological theory," the questions Americans should ask themselves are obvious. Are blacks just mainstream Americans or, for that matter, can they ever be or do what they want to be? Is their culture just the culture of poverty or do they display such poverty of culture that all they need is "cultural retraining" in order to aspire to and enjoy the bliss of middle-class American life? Is the sociological interpretation of black personality, family, and community structure in terms of "pathology" (e.g., see Clark, 1965; Harrington, 1968; Lasch, 1969; Moynihan, 1965; Rainwater, 1968) based on anything but self-serving accumulation of data or ethnocentric interpretation and speculation? Answers to these questions can be found and it is the anthropologists that are best equipped to offer them. It seems obvious that if there is sincere willingness to understand and accede to Negro demands, an effort should be made to fill with objective data the details of a picture that for too long many have been filled out with fantasy (Szwed, 1972: 170-171).

Judging from recent trends it seems evident that an increasing number of anthropologists are now indeed directing their training to the study not only of blacks but of other aspects of American society that have become unexpectedly problematic. As a result, anthropology is simply fulfilling anew its role as a "pragmatic" discipline. However, since a discipline evolves according to the nature of the problems it is applied to, there are intimations that for anthropologists to be able to deal effectively with the new subjects they are called on to analyze they will have to expand and renew considerably their theoretical tenets and their methodology.

## RETROSPECT AND PROSPECT

It has been said that to foresee the future one must know the past well. In this view, it can be useful to try to analyze in depth the various reasons possibly behind the fact that anthropologists have kept their distance from the study of American blacks until very recent years.

First of all, it should be clear from what has been said so far that once the study of blacks was taken over by the sociologists and the "pejorative tradition" was established there was little space for isolated anthropological contributions that did not fit into that specific tradition; the case of Herskovits proves this fact amply. Second, it has also been pointed out that, at least to a large extent, the sociologists were in fact influenced by the Boasian position on the matter of black acculturation. However, the specific direction that anthropological studies took in America since very early times is a phenomenon that cannot be explained simply by the specific notions Boas and the Boasians may have entertained on the matter of black heritage.

In trying to analyze the overwhelming attention given by American anthropologists to the study of American Indians vis-a-vis the blacks, William Willis has recently offered a list of factors that certainly merit attention. Among them there is the romantic allure that Indians held for most Americans, as indigenous inhabitants of the New World and as a part--even if on the enemy side-of the heroic pioneer period (Willis, 1970: 35). Also important is to consider the political liability the study of blacks could have created in the period in which there was still a specific Southern problem and any study of them would have "struck at the very heart of the Jim Crow system of White Supremacy" (Willis, 1970: 37). Finally, as remarked by Ann Fisher (1969), the figure and status of the Negro was likely to arouse in a prospective student feelings of guilt or at least of emotional discomfort (Willis, 1970: 35) certainly not conducive to that bond of interest, affection, and respect that was thought to be a sine qua non between researcher and informant in the early period of anthropological development.

In my view, however, what made American anthropologists overwhelmingly choose American Indians and neglect Afro-Americans as the subjects of their studies, before and after Boas, is a more general factor: the very special relationship that anthropology--and not just the American brand--has traditionally had with the concept of "primitivism." It was the developmentalism of the Enlightenment that "invented," so to speak, the figure of the "savage" as the necessary deuteragonist to the "civilized" in the morality play to which the intellectuals of the time equated history. But nineteenth-century evolutionism then proceeded to codify the "primitive" as a qualitatively different kind of human being and a basic dichotomy was created that the subsequent shift of anthropology to social environmentalism did little to dispel. Boas and the Boasians simply substituted culture for race or the other biological limitations emphasized by the evolutionists to explain human diversity, but they retained the evolutionist notion that the primitives should be the paramount object of investigation for anthropologists since they are so different from "us" that to study them can allow precious insights into our hidden self and can help us understand human nature as such. Boas himself stated very generally that "conditions of life fundamentally different from our own can help us to obtain a freer view of our own lives and of our own life problems" (Boas, 1940: iv), but that "fundamentally different" really meant "primitive" is well exemplified by the fieldwork sites Boas himself suggested for many of his students and by the fact that for years anthropologists have all but neglected the study of complex societies, however "different" they may have been from Western ones. Of course there was also the factor of availability and certainly American anthropologists found American Indians amenable to becoming objects of study just as much as the British found perfect laboratories in the primitive societies incorporated by their far-flung empire. However, the very disinterest displayed by American anthropologists-- or, for that matter, by anthropologists of any nationality--for the study of American blacks reveals more deep-seated biases: This group simply did not fit the image Westerners had in their minds for the "natural" subject of anthropological investigation.

Finally, it must be remembered that the very methodology that Boas and the Boasians propounded as the anthropological methodology in their attempt at giving the discipline intellectual autonomy and scientific respectability in a certain way determined the objects of their study. The traditional rationale behind fieldwork, as distinct from the sociological techniques, has always been that anthropologists studied societies that were thought to be so pristine, isolated, and homogeneous--characteristics typically associated with "primitiveness"--that the part of them the researchers could actually study through their techniques could be safely used to stand for the whole (see Kaplan and Manners, 1972: 191-194). Thus, in a way, the Benedictian image of cultures as integrated wholes can be seen as at least partly deriving from the fact that the exigencies of the traditional anthropological method dictated that just such apparently integrated societies be chosen as objects of study in the first place. In this sense,

American blacks, coming from various tribes and from different parts of Africa and living in scattered areas of the United States could certainly not qualify for investigation, even if they had not been considered as completely acculturated.

Evidently the problem of methodology is a particularly difficult one for anthropology to solve in this period of internal renewal. As John Szwed (1979: 106) wrote:

> what is at issue if the distinction between private and public levels of culture. Anthropologists have traditionally specialized in studies of private dimensions of cultural organization--the personality, the family, the neighborhood, the small village, etc.--and have sought to define a people from these perspectives. But in even moderately complex societies this is extremely difficult if not impossible to carry out, not only because private domains are finally, by definition, impenetrable by outsiders, but also because there is no necessary relationship between what a people define as their private behaviors and those which they use in public domains.

However, anthropologists are increasingly dealing precisely with the relationship between the private and public domains, not only because they are now more often dealing with complex societies but also because they have come to realize that the static, integrated model of culture they have been using so far is ultimately unsatisfactory even in the approach to simple societies. For decades cultures have been studied as if they were static not only in time but also in their structural functioning. Because of this assumption, anthropologists have traditionally focused their attention on the groups of which the societies were thought to be made as if they were the permanent mechanisms of a structure in constant equilibrium. Thus not only were informal social groupings disregarded or not even noticed (see Boissevain, 1974: chap. 1) but the *dynamic process* by which informal organizations affect the maintenance and transformation of the more conspicuous aspects of the social structure was completely overlooked.

But the very problems anthropologists are called on to analyze require that this dynamic aspect of culture be taken into consideration. Quite interestingly this shift at the theoretical and, necessarily, methodological levels is being mirrored and sustained--or perhaps has been prepared--by historical developments and by the new ideology

that has come from them. Whatever the very complex reasons behind the worldwide phenomena of ethnic revival (see Glazer, 1975), fight for minority rights, and increasing erosion of centralized authority (see Bell, 1975: 142-152) the fact is that these historical factors have sensitized large masses of people to the problems of acquisition, distribution, and management of power. Specifically, in America the traumatic effects of the 1960s and of the early 1970s have forced society at large to question traditional notions on matters of the location, the legitimacy, and the use and abuse of power. As a consequence, anthropologists have become extremely sensitive about the role their discipline may be thought to have played in situations of "institutionalized inequality" and have gone through a protracted period of recriminations, mea culpa, and "rethinking." The outcome of this process seems, however, extremely positive at the theoretical level: Now not only anthropology but the social sciences in general are giving increasing attention to aspects of social life that have to do specifically with the nature and exercise of power.

The study of American blacks seems to be an almost ideal case to test the validity of this novel approach. On the basis of the admittedly still scarce data offered by those scholars that in recent years have approached the study of this subject in a new way[5] we are tentatively building an image of black culture as practically emerging out of the conflict created by an institutionalized unbalance of power. In Blauner's terse summarization, the culture of the Afro-Americans finds its sources in a heterogeneous African heritage, the experience of slavery, and the antebellum Southern plantation life, the trauma of Emancipation, northern migration, civil fights, life in the ghettoes, poverty, and, above all, the continuous endurance of racism (Blauner, 1970: 352-359).[6] The study of such a culture should then provide answers to a variety of important general questions. What is the relationship between people's perceptions of their ethnic roots and forced acculturation? In what sense is the character of a minority group shaped by the kind of first contact its members have with the host country? In a situation of forced acculturation, what elements of its ethnic heritage does a minority retain and what does it lose and why?[7] Does poverty actually create a specific "culture" or is the experience of poverty reinterpreted and lived "ethnically" by different minorities (see Valentine, 1968)? Besides, in what sense do American blacks partake of a macroculture of Negritude (see Drachler, 1975)? What contribution does the study of blacks give to the understanding of African and of mainstream American cultures in a world in which nations are becoming increasingly "plural" and in which class struggle is enmeshing more and more with minority conflict often based on ethnicity (Glazer, 1975: 13)? The insights we could derive from the study of blacks should be actively sought.

Whether such insights are actually gained will depend, in my view, on two factors. First of all, the methodology we bring to this field of study must be sharpened and adapted to the new subject of investigation. In general, sociolinguistic and microbehavioral analyses seem to have great potentialities for the study of ethnicity "especially as these behaviors are the nexus at which questions of identity, culture, and stereotyping all meet" (Szwed, 1979: 106). Also, a multidisciplinary approach seems in order[8] and a significant contribution can be expected from those native anthropologists that should now be increasingly attracted by a discipline in the process of emerging from its middle-class mold, lily-white composition, and ivory-towerish remoteness (see Willis 1970: 38-39). Second, anthropologists must become conscious of the effect "telling it like it is" (Valentine and Valentine, 1970: 415) is bound to have on the research population, the research commissioner(s), the public at large, and the intellectual community when their studies are carried out in their own society and specifically directed to problematic aspects of it.

However, the very fact that anthropologists are finally becoming interested in the study of power and its working indicates that they have also acquired sensitivity for the role they play in the power relationships of researcher/informant, scholar/public, grant-givers/research population.

It must also be clearly realized that the formulation of policy is a political process and that good data do not automatically generate good public policy (Partridge, 1978: 371). Thus anthropologists must overcome their dislike for direct involvement with power (see Goldschmidt, 1977: 297) and dispel the suspicion of escapism their traditional interests and activities have so far created (see Willis, 1972: 141-142). Effective use of the data in educating the public and the policymakers on the substance of the problem at issue should be complemented by actual presence at the level of policy formulation. In Nadel's (as quoted in Hogbin, 1957:263) words:

> The "defeatist" argument that anthropological advice cannot change policy seems to me just that; policies are not sacrosanct and have been known to give way before just (and courageous) criticism. That the criticism should be just is the responsibility of the anthropologist. So is the honesty of his approach, in the sense that he must at every step make explicit the premises and reasoning that guide him. . . . And if . . . this means that the anthropologist must enter the arena with politicians, business men, moralists, or that popular her "the practical man", he has nothing to be ashamed or frightened of; his armory is strong and his weapons respectable.

The study of American blacks is just one of the many cases in which the "new" anthropologists can put to fruit their training, expertise, and commitment. In so doing they will simply best serve the most fundamental scope of their discipline, which Tylor himself recognized as a reformer's science (1871:410).

## NOTES

1. Among them one must remember Allison Davis, himself a black, who, together with Warner and Burleigh and Mary Gardner did a study of a Mississippi town later published in *Deep South* (Davis et al., 1941). Also important was the contribution of St. Clair Drake, especially for his study of Chicago blacks, conducted with Horace R. Cayton and published in *Black Metropolis* (Drake and Cayton, 1945).
2. Robert E. Park himself was a moderate and supporter of Booker T. Washington's "accommodationism" (see Park, 1950). "Park's model of race relations postulated the status quo as a natural stage in a developmental cycle: race prejudice would eventually disappear (Hicks and Handler, 1978:315).
3. The programs that sprouted from the War on Poverty--for example, VISTA, Job Corps, Head Start--were "aimed at changing attitudes, beliefs, and values, rather than on redistributing wealth and power" (Hicks and Handler, 1978:322). Blacks, not being credited with an ethnic culture of their own, were more and more thought to be acting "deviantly" because they belonged to a large subculture of poverty that dictated their attitudes and behavior (see Gladwin, 1967).
4. A complete outline of these historical changes exceeds the limits of this article but they certainly included the new social strength acquired by blacks as a result of a decade of Supreme Court decisions condemning segregation and of the achievements of organizations such as the NAACP (National Association for the Advancement of Colored People) and Dr. Martin Luther King's "Movement" (Drake, 1971:282). Also, as a result of the Voting Rights Act of 1965, blacks began to believe that "in-group solidarity, not integration, was necessary for the maximization of political strength" (Drake, 1971:282). Finally, it must also be remembered that the struggle for independence many black nations successfully carried out in Africa against white colonialism during the 1950s created a powerful symbolic

catalyzer for the blacks' rediscovery and acceptance of their own African heritage. In my view, the African revitalization movement among American Negroes was not a case of "ethnogenesis" (see Singer, 1962), understood in the strict sense of artificial adoption of an almost fictional ethnic identity. Blacks had always been conscious of their African roots but they had been led to believe, not least by the sociologists, that the only way to acquire equality in American society was by being "a thousand percent American."

5. These scholars include anthropologists, sociologists, and psychologists who have balanced their knowledge of the "pejorative tradition" with what blacks themselves have been saying about their heritage in recent years. Furthermore, and most important, these scholars have been prepared to build their speculations on black culture not ready-made theory but on first-hand ethnographic material. Among the early works produced through this approach see, for example, Hannerz (1969), Keil (1966), Liebow (1967), McAdoo (1978), Nobles (1975), Stack (1974), and Valentine and Valentine (1970).

6. In Blauner's view, this specific situation is a result of the fact that blacks were internally colonized (Blauner, 1969). If this view is accepted (for the argument against it (see Glazer 1971) it would then be extremely interesting to compare the culture of American blacks with the ones that have emerged from an out and out process of colonization, such as that or urbanized black South Africans.

7. In this regard a reconsideration of Herskovits's much maligned concept of "cultural focus" would perhaps be in order.

8. Quite interestingly, Herskovits did approach the study of American blacks by drawing from extremely rich and heterogeneous material from fields as varied as folklore, ethnomusicology, dance, art, literature, ethnohistory, and also from fields that now would be defined as kinesics and proxemics but for which, when he worked on them, anthropologists had not yet developed clear theoretical frameworks (Whitten and Szwed, 1970:28).

# REFERENCES

Bill, D (1975) *Ethnicity and social change*, pp. 141-174 in N. Glazer and D. P. Moynihan (eds.) Ethnicity, Cambridge, MA. Harvard Univ. Press.

Benedict, R. (1959a/1934) *Patterns of Culture,* New York: Mentor.

Benedict, R. (1959b/1940) *Race: Science and Politics*, New York: Compass.

Blauner, R. (1969) Internal colonialism and ghetto revolt. *Social Problems* 16. 4-393-05.

Blauner, R. (1970) "Black culture, myth or reality?" pp. 347-366 in N. E. Whitten, Jr. and J. F. Szwed (eds.) *Afro-American Anthropology: Contemporary Perspectives*, New York: Free Press.

Boas, F. (1909) "Race problems in American." *Science* 29 (May): 839-849.

Boas, F. (1940) *Race, Language and Culture,* New York: MacMillan.

Boissevain, J. (1974) *Friends of Friends: Networks, Manipulators and Coalitions*. Oxford: Basil Blackwell.

Burridge, K.O.L. (1973) *Encountering Aborigines*. New York: Pergamon.

Clark, K. B. (1965) *Dark Ghetto*. New York: Harper & Row.

Davis, A., B. B. Gardner, and M. R. Gardner (1941) *Deep South.*

Chicago: Univ. of Chicago Press.

Drachler, J. (ed.) (19675) *Black Homeland/Black Diaspora*. Port Washington, NY: Kennikat.

Drake, St. C. (1971) "Prospects for the future," pp. 280-302 in N. I. Huggins, M. Kilson, and D. M. Fox (eds.) *Key Issues in the Afro-American Experience*. New York: Harcourt Brace Jovanovich.

Drake, St. C. and H. P. Cayton (1945) *Black Metropolis*. New York: Harcourt, Brace.

Embree, E. R. (1931) *Brown America*. New York: Viking Press.

Fauset, A. H. (1944) *Black Gods of the Metropolis*. Philadelphia: Philadelphia Anthropological Society.

Fisher, A. (1969) "The effect upon anthropological studies of U.S. Negroes of the professional personality and subculture of anthropologists," Presented at the annual meeting of the Southern Anthropological Association, New Orleans, March 13-15.

Frazier, E. F. (1934) "Traditions and patterns of Negro family life in the United States," pp. 191-207 in E. B. Reuter (ed.) *Race and Culture Contacts*. New York: McGraw-Hill.

Frazier, E. F. (1939 *The Negro Family in the United States*. Chicago: Univ. of Chicago Press.

Frederickson, G. M. (1971) *The Black Image in the White Mind*. New York: Harper & Row.

Gladwin, T. (1967) *Poverty U.S.A.* Boston: Little, Brown.

Glazer, N. (1971) "Blacks and ethnic groups: the difference and the political difference it makes." pp. 193-211 in N. I. Huggins, M. Kilson, and D. M. Fox (eds.) *Key Issues in the Afro-American Experience*. New York: Harcourt Brace Jovanovich.

Glazer, N. (1975) "The universalization of ethnicity" *Encounter* 44, 2: 8-17.

Goldschmidt, W. (1977) "Anthropology and the coming crisis: an autoethnographic appraisal." *Amer. Anthropologist* 79, 2:293-308.

Goldschmidt, W. and P. R. Sanday (1979) "Postscript: the present uses of anthropology: an overview." pp. 253-267 in W. Goldschmidt (ed.) *The Uses of Anthropology* (Special Publication No. 11). Washington, DC: American Anthropological Association.

Goody, J. (1973) "L'antropologia sociale nella tradizione britannica e nelle sue prospettive attuali," pp. 19-36 in B. Bernardi (ed.) *Etnologia e Antropologia Culturale*. Milano: F. Angeli.

Hannerz, U. (1969) *Soulside: Inquiries into Ghetto Culture and Community*. New York: Columbia Univ. Press.

Harrington, M. (1968) *Toward a Democratic Left*. New York: Vintage.

Herskovits, M. J. (1941) *The Myth of the Negro Past*. New York: Harper & Brothers.

Herskovits, M. J. (1968/1925) "The Negro's Americanism," in A. Locke (ed.) *The New Negro*. New York: Atheneum.

Hicks, G. and M. J. Handler (1978) "Ethnicity, Public Policy and Anthropologists," pp. 292-325 in E. M. Eddy and W. L. Partridge (eds.) *Applied Anthropology in America*. New York: Columbia Univ. Press.

Hogbin, H. I. (1957) "Anthropology as public service and

Malinowski's contribution to it," pp. 245-266 in R. Firth (ed.) *Man & Culture*. London: Routledge & Kegan Paul.

Hunt, J. (1863) "On the study of anthropology," *Anthro. Rev.* 1: 1-20.

Kaplan, D. and R. A. Manners (1972) *Culture Theory*. Englewood Cliffs, NJ: Prentice-Hall.

Keil, C. (1966) *Urban Blues*. Chicago: Univ. of Chicago Press.

Kluger, R. (1976) *Simple Justice: The History of Brown v. Board of Education and Black America's Struggle for Equality*. New York: Knopf.

Lasch, C. (1969) *The Agony of the American Left*. New York: Vintage.

Liebow, E. (1967) *Tally's Corner: A Study of Negro Streetcorner Men*. Boston: Little, Brown.

McAdoo, H. P. (1978) "Factors related to stability in upwardly mobile black families." *J. of Marriage and the Family* 40. 761-776.

Mintz, S. W. (1970) "Foreword," pp. 1-16 in N. E. Whitten, Jr. and J. F. Szwed (eds.) *Afro-American Anthropology: Contemporary Perspectives*. New York: Free Press.

Moynihan, D. P. (1965) *The Negro Family: The Case for National Action*. Washington, DC: Government Printing Office.

Newman, W. M. (1973) *American Pluralism*. New York: Harper & Row.

Nobles, W. W. ((1975) *A Formulative and Empirical Study of Black Families*. Washington, DC: Department of Health, Education and Welfare, Office of Child Development.

Nott, J. D. and G. R Gliddon (1854) *Types of Mankind; or Ethnological Researches Based upon the Ancient Monuments, Paintings, Sculptures and Crania of Races, and upon their Natural Geographical, Philological and Biblical History*. Philadelphia: Lippincott.

Park, R. E. (1950) *Race and Culture*. New York: Free Press.

Partridge, W. L. (1978) "Uses and nonuses of anthropological data on drug abuse," pp. 350-372 in E. M. Eddy and W. L. Partridge (eds.) *Applied Anthropology in America*. New York: Columbia Univ. Press.

Partridge, W. L. and E. M. Eddy (1978) "The development of applied anthropology in America." pp. 3-45 in L. M. Eddy and W. L. Partridge (eds.) *Applied Anthropology in America*. New York: Columbia Univ. Press.

Powdermaker, H. (1939) *After Freedom: A Cultural Study of the Deep South*. New York: Viking.

Rainwater, L. (1968) "The American working class and lower class: an American success and failure." pp. 29-46 in S. Tax et al. (eds.) *Anthropological Backgrounds of Adult Education*. Boston: Center for the Study of Liberal Education for Adults.

Reining, C. C. (1962) "A lost period of applied anthropology." *Amer. Anthropologist* 64. 593-600.

Reuter, F. B. (1938) *The American Race Problem*. New York: Crowell.

Singer, L. (1962) "Ethnogenesis and Negro-American today." *Social Research* 29: 419-432.

Stack, C. (1974) *All Our Kin: Strategies for Survival in the Black Community*. New York: Harper & Row.

Szwed, J. F. (1972) "An American anthropological dilemma: the politics of Afro-American culture." pp. 153-181 in D. Hymes (ed.) *Reinventing Anthropology*. New York: Vintage.

Szwed, J. F. (1979) "The ethnography of ethnic groups in the United States, 1920-1950," pp. 100-109 in W. Goldschmidt (ed.) *The 32 Uses of Anthropology* (Special Publication No. 11). Washington, DC: American Anthropological Association.

Tumin, M. M. (1972/1968) "Some social consequences of research on racial relations," pp. 444-455 in B. E. Segal (ed.) *Racial and Ethnic Relations*. New York: Crowell.

Tylor, E. B. (1871) *Primitive Culture*. London: John Murray.

Valentine, C. (1968) *Culture and Poverty: Critique and Counter Proposals*. Chicago: Univ. of Chicago Press.

Valentine, C. and B. L. Valentine (1970) "Making the scene, digging the action, and telling it like it is: anthropologists at work in a dark ghetto." pp. 403-418 in N. E. Whitten, Jr. and J. F> Szwed (eds.) *Afro-American Anthropology: Contemporary Perspectives*. New York: Free Press.

Van Willigen, J. (1977) *A Bibliographic Chronology of the Development of Applied Anthropology*. Lexington, KY: Univ. of Kentucky Press.

Voget, F. W. (1975) *A History of Ethnology*. New York: Holt, Rinehart and Winston.

Whitten, N. E. Jr. and J. F. Szwed (1970) "Introduction," pp. 23-60 in N. E. W. Whitten JR., and J. F. Szwed (eds.) *Afro-American Anthropology: Contemporary Perspectives*. New York: Free Press.

Willis W. S. Jr. (1970) "Anthropology and Negroes on the souther colonial frontier," pp. 33-50 in J. C. Curtis and L. L. Gould (eds.) *The Black Experience in America*. Austin, TX: Univ. of Texas Press.

Willis, W. S> (1972) "Skeletons in the anthropological closet," pp. 121-152 in D. Hymes (ed.) *Reinventing Anthropology*. New York: Vintage.

# BEGINNING IN AN-OTHER PLACE: OPPUGNANCY AND THE FORMATION OF BLACK SOCIOLOGY

*Rhett S. Jones*

In 1973 Joyce Ladner edited a volume titled *The Death of White Sociology*, the contributors to which not only advanced a number of reasons why the end of White Sociology was near, but predicted a new Black Sociology would replace it.[1] Many of these contributors--the present writer among them--assumed that White Sociology as then practiced distorted black life and that a more sensitive discipline would have to replace it if the experiences of African Americans were to be fully understood. This was not the simple-minded argument that only black scholars could study black people--an argument which seemed to have existed more in the minds of naive black undergraduates than among mature black intellectuals--but rather a sensible position which argued knowledge of a people could not advance without some understanding of how the people saw themselves. White scholars can understand African Americans, but to do so, they must give up some of their most cherished assumptions, the principle one being that African Americans and Euro-Americans can be studied by means of the same technique.

In order to fully grasp the significance of this difference and construct a Black Sociology, it is necessary to understand African American history, for it is in the past where the differences between black and white folks have their origin. It is surprising that few historians have interested themselves in the study of American race relations in the seventeenth and eighteenth centuries.[2] Most focus on the post-Civil War era. Unfortunately, at the time Lander was organizing her anthology, the two books which were to transform understanding of American racial slavery were not yet in print. Neither John Blassingame's *The Slave Community* nor George Rawick's *Between Sundown and Sunup*, each chronicling the emergence of a separate black culture within the constraints of slavery, had been published.[3] Nor had

the many articles, monographs, and books on Afro-American history which characterized the late 1970s and early 1980s yet made their appearance. In the absence of a Black History, no Black Sociology could be constructed, and in the early 1970s Afro-American History had simply not developed to the point where it could provide a justification for a separate discipline, much less provide sufficient data for sociologists to draw on in construction theories of black life.

As a result, while sociologists interested in black life published a number of useful studies in the 1970s, but a genuine Black Sociology did not emerge. Most sociological works on the black community were organized along the lines of conventional sociology texts.[4] Even more destructive to an understanding of African American life was the effort made to incorporate Afro-American Studies into the new field of Ethnic Studies, a field originally developed to facilitate study of Euro-Americans whose ancestors originated from places in Europe other than England. With the exceptio of the French, Germans, Dutch, and Scots, the ancestors of most of these "ethnics" (as they came to be called) did not arrive in North American in large numbers until well after the United Stated had won its independence from England. For example, large numbers of Irish immigrants did not arrive until the nineteenth century, while Poles, Greeks, Italians, and Slavs did not come in sizeable numbers until the twentieth century. While these people have long rich histories in their native lands, their American experience as compared to that of African Americans is brief and truncated. By the time of the Revolutionary War the majority of the ancestors of living African Americans were themselves the grandchildren of black folk born in the New World.[5] The black experience in North America is therefore an old one and cannot be reduced to the Ethnic Studies constructs. Although Ethnic Studies is a more recent discipline than White Sociology, neither has demonstrated any capacity for providing

Reprinted with permission from *The Griot*, Fall 1992, Vol. 10, Spring 1992.

understanding of the black experience and both share a tradition of indifference to the unique historical experience of black people.

## HISTORY, INDIVIDUALISM, AND SELF-AWARENESS

Black intellectuals must recognize this uniqueness and construct a Sociology which will be sensitive to African American culture. Charles Long's term "oppugnancy" acknowledges a black awareness which must be at the heart of any useful exploration of black America. He writes:

> What is portrayed here is a religious consciousness that has experienced the 'hardness' of life, whether the form of that reality is the slave system, God, or simply life itself. It is from such a consciousness that the power to resist and yet maintain one's humanity has emerged. Though the worship and religious life of blacks have often been referred to as forms of escapism, one must always remember that there has been an integral relationship between the hardness of life and the ecstasy of religious worship.[6]

While Long writes here of religion, the oppugnant tradition is much broader in that it signals recognition by blacks that their life has long been different from and "harder" than its white counterpart. Black people know their experience is different from whites but it is the failure of White Sociology to take into consideration black awareness of this knowledge that accounts for the failure of a useful sociology of black folk to emerge. Black knowledge of self is what most sociologists do not accept as valid datum.

In addition to its failure to seriously incorporate the black perspective of self into its work, White Sociology has also failed to effectively grapple with black life because of its preoccupation with *organizations* not *individuals*. But, as will be demonstrated below, African American organizational life, when compared to its Euro-American counterpart, is underdeveloped. There are three reasons for this sociological preoccupation with institutions rather than people. First, the two men who are generally regarded as the founding fathers of Sociology, Emile Durkheim (1855-1917) and Max Weber (1864-1920), were not only preoccupied with organizations but determined to demonstrate that Sociology was and ought to be a separate and distinct science.[7] While psychologists were concerned with the individual, sociologists ought to be concerned, at least in the opinion

of Durkheim, with the "social fact", a separate and distinct form of data from the ideas of individuals. With regard to Weber, his organizational insights into the working of bureaucracies have been among the most lasting of his contributions.[8] Second, American sociologist have also been at some pains to distinguish their work from that of their psychological colleagues. Talcott Parsons and Robert Merton, who saw American Sociology into its maturity [and many would argue into the height of its influence], also wrote more about institutions and organizations than about individuals.[9] Third, the Euro-American middle class is itself centered about organizations, and as many white American sociologists come from middle class backgrounds ,it has been natural for them to cast their research into conceptual frameworks derived from groups, whether formal or informal, not individuals. Those white sociologists whose class origins are not middle class are almost without exception working class ethnic in background. Euro-American ethnic communities have been organized about such institutions as churches, schools, fraternal associations, and small businesses, so that it has been natural for such sociologists to concern themselves more with institutions than individuals.[10]

The exceptions to this preoccupation with organizations is found in the work of those who term themselves humanistic sociologists.[11] There are also scholars who write in the tradition of humanistic psychology and anthropology and each of these groups has its own journal. Black journals also publish papers by scholars writing in humanistic traditions.[12] By humanism its practitioners generally mean a commitment to understanding of people and their interpretation of their own reality.

As Long points out, black people understand their ancestors were involuntary migrants whose very presence as slaves called into question the alleged Euro-American commitment to equality, democracy, and liberty for all. The Black experience differs from the white one in that by their decision to migrate to the New World, Europeans gained additional freedom for themselves. Even while the thirteen colonies were ruled by England, its inhabitants enjoyed greater freedom than was true of Englishmen who remained at home. Most of those who chose to migrate to North America were not members of the nobility, nor even of the gentry, but rather persons from the lower orders of English life. In english North

America they gained far more control over their lives than had been the case back home.[13] Even those ethnics who migrated to the United States from Southern and Eastern Europe as late as the twentieth century had far more say in government on this side of the Atlantic that was the case in their homelands. Jews, for example, who came in large numbers in the twentieth century, while they had long exercised some economic influence in Europe were able in the United States to also participate fully and openly in the political process.

The experience of black folk was just the reverse. In West Africa--the region of Africa from which most slaves were transported to North America--there was a tradition of participation of governance by ordinary citizens. Rulers were elected, and while elector qualifications varied in almost all states, rulers were subject to recall.[14] In sharp contrast to the monarchial national states of Europe where power was exercised from the top down, West Africa power was exercised from the bottom up. By virtue of their enslavement and transportation to North America, West Africans lost whatever say they had in government.

Moreover, in order to maintain control over the slaves, the colonists agreed on a strategy of cruelty.[15] No one put it better than Kenneth Stampp who in his classic work titled one of the chapters, "To Make Them Stand in Fear"[16] Slaveholders beat, tortured, maimed, raped, and even killed their slaves as part of a deliberate, brutal campaign aimed at reducing black men and women to docility. And while they did not succeed, centuries of cruelty inevitably had an impact on African American life. The slave community was operated not by the slaves for the benefit of those who lived within it, but rather by the slavemaster for his benefit. As a result, during the centuries of enslavement black people developed no traditions of disciplining one another for the good of the Black community.

For example, most slave revolts in North America failed not because they were poorly planned but because they were betrayed.[17] Even though the slaves might know who had betrayed a rebellion, they had no way of publicly disciplining him. Of course, it would be possible to strike in a covert manner, to assault the guilty bondsman or even to kill him, but the slaveholders did not permit the enslaved to publicly hold a trial for the purpose of condemning one who sold out his people. Nor were the slaves permitted to publicly reward one

of their own who contributed to the community. It was possible for slaves to secretly express their appreciation for one who had served the community and the bondsman proved remarkably clever at finding ways to demonstrate their appreciation without the slavemaster's knowledge. They complimented one another by means of folklore, songs, and even religious ceremonies, but all such communications had to be circumspect, without the public proclamations which not only encourage the recipient, but inspire the audience as well. While Euro-Americans boldly celebrated themselves and taught thereby numerous lessons to their young, African Americans were forced to hide their lessons behind tales of hares, spiders, and other creatures. While these tales--along with black Christianity--carried black folk through terrible times even thought their meanings could not be publicly stated, African Americans could not politically rally around them. Nor could they use the tales to inspire their children to collectively come together for the good of black folk.

Since much of what has been written thus far is about slaves, it is necessary to introject a brief note about free blacks. For a period in the seventeenth century free blacks briefly enjoyed the "equal opportunity" white Americans later denied them.[18] Winthrop Jordan may be correct in arguing that the rudiments of racial consciousness made racism inevitable or the separate yet related arguments of Kovel, Morgan, and Fredrickson, which claim that racism was deliberately created on this side of the Atlantic, may be closer to the truth.[19] All scholars agree, however, that by the last quarter of the seventeenth century the migrants were committed to excluding blacks from participation in economic and political life. Free blacks gradually became a tiny minority of the black population. As the new American nation moved through the nineteenth century, free blacks, even in the North, were stripped of civil rights. While free blacks were not unimportant in the evolution of black American life, African American culture was formed in the crucible of slavery and it is to the slave experience one must look in attempting to construct a Black Sociology. The slave experience made blacks very different from whites. And only when one recognizes the extent of this difference does a sociology capable of grappling with black life on its own terms become possible.

Not only was African American culture shaped by slavery, but Afro-Americans have long been aware of the central role played by the peculiar institutions in moulding themselves. Oppugnancy, as Long indicates, is rooted in this self-knowledge and it therefore follows that any meaningful Black Sociology must be based on oppugnant awareness.

## WHITE ORGANIZATIONS— BLACK INDIVIDUALS

According to Long, the slaves "had to experience the truth of their negativity and at the same time transform and create *an-other* reality."[20] White Sociology has never come to grips with *an-other* reality constructed by black people and so has continued to study African Americans and Euro-Americans by means of the same techniques. Yet the two races differ in that whites gained freedom by migrating from Europe, while blacks lost freedom by being transported as slaves from Africa. They also differ in that whites are concerned with organizations, while blacks are concerned with people. A genuine Black Sociology must therefor take into consideration black preoccupation with persons.

This preoccupation with persons stems directly from the failure of African Americans to build effective organizations during the slave era. Black people developed no tradition of coming together in a public, collective sense to rely on one another. Instead each slave learned to rely on himself, or at best on a small group of friends or a few family members. These folk were not organized in any systematic manner, nor were they publicly able to proclaim their goals as did white Americans. Even the most important institution, the church, operated for the most part as underground associations. By subtitling his highly acclaimed works on slave religion "The Invisible Institution," Albert Raboteau suggests that no matter how important the church may have been, it did not dare emerge from underground and operate as a visible institution from which slaves could publicly proclaim their cause.[21] Instead, the church remained a loose association of individuals committed to one another but not to an impersonal institution. Thus, this preoccupation with persons characterized and shaped African American culture during slavery.

The slave narratives make it clear that while fugitive slaves generally assumed that other slaves encountered in their attempts to escape would be supportive, they approached each bondsman with caution. The runaway sought to read the character of other blacks and learn something of what they thought of slavery before revealing themselves. Some of these narratives, edited by Gilbert Osofsky in a work titled *Puttin on Ole Massa*, also make it clear that slaves had this same watchful reflectivity in their day-to-day dealings with whites.[22] In order to "put on" the slaveholder, his slaves had to sharpen their character assessment skills. In the course of surviving and improving their lives, blacks developed skills in reading one another and in reading whites.

In the course of surviving and improving their lives, whites developed skills in using and, when possible, dominating formal organizations. The extent to which Euro-Americans have centered their lives around institutions has been obscured by their celebration of themselves as rugged individualists. They present themselves as a people characterized by an independent individualism, able and willing to accomplish a great deal on their own without the aid of large, powerful institutions. But this self-reliance has been exaggerated. With the exception of the initial settlers, most whites, particularly when compared to blacks, were and are supported by a rich array of organizations. Schools, colleges, the military, churches, banks, and a wide range of other institutions provided support for whites from the beginning of the colonial period. Later these formal organizations were joined by Fraternal orders, unions, film studios, certification boards, think-tanks and other associations too numerous to mention. These institutions either completely excluded blacks or, at best, admitted a token few. Whites are therefore assured of a level of organizational supported denied blacks. While Euro-Americans were coddled by these institutional aids, African Americans had to survive without them. Blacks, not whites, have been America's rugged individualists.

Of course, there are black organizations, but there are five reasons why they are underdeveloped and hence less capable of providing support as compared to their white counterparts. First, the black population is much smaller, so black organizations have not had the population base which could make them large and influential. Some Afro-American institutions are sizeable but the largest black insurance companies, universities, and cosmetic firms do not begin to approach in size the largest white ones. Second, the black population is much poorer so it simply does not have the resources to support a museum, a scholarship program, or a summer camp on the same scale as do whites. Third, many black organizations are influenced, if not controlled, by whites and therefore do not always operate in the best interest of blacks. For example, the private black colleges usually have and have long had whites on their board of trustees. Many did not have a black president until decades after they had been established. Organizations such as the National Association for the Advancement of Colored People and the Urban League have long prided themselves in having board members who are not black. For the most part, non-black members of organizations devoted to blacks serve them to the best of their ability, but their presence sometimes introduces the question of who knows what is best for the community. For example, while there were blacks on both sides of the Industrial Education versus College Education debate which raged a century ago, whites who argued for the training of black women as domestic servants were as much concerned with the needs of the white community--some admitted as much--as with the black. Numerous activists in the "movement" claimed that the presence of whites in leadership positions in black organizations undercut black self-confidence, while reinforcing the idea that Euro-Americans know what is best for African Americans.[23]

A fourth reason why black organizations are weak and underdeveloped is that black people simply do not have the cultural experience of managing one another, much less managing formal organizations, for the good of blacks. Until recently African Americans were excluded from both formal training management and from informal learning within white organizations which might have led them to executive positions. Far more important than this is that blacks have little experience in the effective management of one another. The slaveholders allowed African Americans only limited control over other African Americans. Research on black overseers (or drivers) reveals that while they were often supportive of the slave community, their power had its origins in white authority.[24] Blacks in fact had little respect for those who had gained limited authority in an organization built to serve white people, speaking of such individuals contemptuously as the "HNIC." The Head-Nigger-In-Charge was equivalent to an Uncle Tom and in return for the power granted over other blacks, served his master without reservation. The last, and perhaps most important reason why black organizations

are weak is that black people do not believe in them. The mortality rate of black organizations is notoriously high. Their high rate of failure makes millions of African Americans unwilling to invest money, time, or other resources in black organizations. But their failure to support black institutions in turn makes for a self-fulfilling prophecy for in the absence of such support black organizations weaken and go under. Blacks then look at this failure and are even less willing to help the next black organization which appeals for support.

The white ethnic experience has been quite different as they supported their organizations in a way in which blacks did not. First, being isolated from the larger white American community by culture, language and religion, they had no alternative but to help one another and to utilized the wide variety of available strategies. Some chose to completely escape from their ethnic past by learning to speak English, anglicizing their names, moving out of the "old" neighborhood, and converting to another religion. At the other end of the spectrum were those who refused even to learn English, much less change their names, leave the neighborhood, or convert. There were a host of persons in between. The overlapping communities helped one another. The more integrated used the leverage they had gained to help their countrymen, while those who remained behind acted as a bloc and providing thereby the necessary political muscle to support those who had left the community.[25]

As part of their oppugnancy and grappling with *an-other* reality, African Americans compare themselves to ethnics, citing their willingness to help one another and unfavorably comparing the failure of blacks to support each other. In their self-condemning anger blacks overlook an important distinction between the support blacks and whites in the United States provide one another.[26] White folk support and have a long history of being supported by organizations. Black folk support and have a long history of being supported by individuals. The Euro-American orientation is organizational, the African American orientation is individual.

In an organizational society, the African American preoccupation with the personal puts black folk at a disadvantage. The history of black people leads most of them to focus on reading the character of others, not on learning the organizational rules of the game. The black church, which is frequently cited as the strongest African American institution, turns out on closer examination to be based on individuals not on organization. There are only handful of black churches in the United States today in which a call to their pulpit legitimizes a minister as a person significant in the life of African American Christendom. In all the other churches, the pastor makes the church, not the other way around. Black people are attracted to and follow a preacher and when he leaves and moves to another church, especially if it is in the same area, his congregation, fame, and influence will follow.

## A PERSONAL PEOPLE

Because of the African American interest in the person and lack of interest in the organizational, it has been easy to present black communities as disorganized in the sociological literature. In one sense black communities are more disorganized, lacking as they do the wide range of institutional structures which characterize Euro-America. And in another sense black communities are disorganized in that they are not controlled by the people who live within them. For example, blacks were unable to prevent whites from placing houses of prostitution, gambling dens, after-hours bars and a host of other illegal and quasi-legal establishments in their neighborhoods.[27] Nor were they able to prevent drugs in general or heroin in particular from invading black residential areas. Recently, despite the election of black officials in unprecedented numbers, African Americans have not been able to prevent the spread of "crack," an increase in teen-age pregnancies, a growth in gangs, and an increase in attack on the black aged. Black people are no more in control of their communities in the 1990s than slaves were in control of their communities in the 1780s.

Yet the same social scientists who regarded the black community as disorganized and out of control also acknowledge that black youngsters score high in tests of self-esteem and self-confidence.[28] In fact many black inner-city children score higher on such tests than do white youngsters. Upon reflection, however, this should not seem surprising. These young people are being raised in an environment which requires self-reliance, one which teaches each day that there are few black formal organizations on which they can rely.

At the same time black youngsters also learn their community is not as disorganized as it appears at first glance; there are informal structures organized around individuals by which black people support one another. Like the "Invisible Institution" of the slave era, these support systems do not always operate above ground and therefore are not publicly acknowledged. They are often missed by social scientists in search of more formal institutions, and even when they are uncovered, misunderstood. For example, the distinguished black sociologist E. Franklin Frazier as part of this scathing report on the black middle-class, pointed out that its members did not really command powerful economic and political resources. The political organizations and the business enterprises which they represented, Frazier argued, were a tiny part of the nation's political and economic infrastructure.[29] The organizations of the black bourgeoisie seemed to Frazier to be not only politically but economically unimportant in the American scheme of things. Instead of functioning as did comparable white organizations, they operated instead to serve the psychological needs of the black middle-class. In effect, Frazier claimed, such organizations operated solely to give these African Americans a sense of achievement and to help them deny they had failed to accomplish much of anything in the larger white world. A man of his time, Frazier regarded this as a form of escape thereby failing to see that while these allegedly powerful black organizations existed for the most part in the minds of their owners and in black press, they were positive, not negative, institutions. They were by means by which black folk supported one another.

At lower socio-economic levels, even these imitations of white organizations are not available to blacks, yet they still manage to support one another. This is how Katrina Hazzard-Gordon describes the institution of the rent-party, a common phenomenon of northern cities in which blacks cooperate with one another not just to enable a given family to pay the rent, but to make it possible for a group of people to meet their bills. Successful rent parties were not hurriedly thrown together affairs, but instead needed a complex, though informal, infrastructure if they were to work.[30] Elliot Liebow describes a similar black support system. First, he details the problems of the unemployed black male who without a job either losses or believes he loses the respect of his family. He then looks elsewhere for support and as Liebow writes "Increasingly he turns to the streetcorner where a shadow system of values constructed out of public fictions serves to accommodate just such men as he, permitting them to be men once again provided they do not look too closely at one another's credentials."[31] Similarly, the street gangs of Chicago described by R.Lincoln Keiser and John R. Fry have created elaborate structures which enable them to help each other.[32]

These African American structures have in common that they are personal and built around people and not impersonal and base don organizational guidelines. They demonstrate that black people can work well together even without formal supports, provided they are able to work with persons they know. Even Afro-American humor is personal. The ritual trading of insults characteristic of black life not just in the United States but elsewhere int he Americas is not only personal in the sense that two people trade insults on a face-to-face basis, but that a personal relationship must exist between *them before* the game even begins.[33] In describing *tantalism*--the Guyanese equivalent of signifying--Edwards emphasizes that "only friends 'play tantalise.' The expression 'me and you don't play tantalise' is tantamount to a social rejection of the addressee."[34] Black people readily extend personal support whether they are simply passing the time or trying to help those they know maintain a positive image of self.

They do not, however, respond so well when personal needs are presented by impersonal, formal organizations. The plight of black children in need of adoption is a case in point. They are classified by adoption agencies as hard to place. The majority of prospective adoptive parents are white and their preference is for a healthy white infant. Although black infants available for adoption may be both physically and psychologically healthy, they are not adopted by white parents, many of whom will make efforts to adopt Asian children from overseas. The depth of American racism is seldom more clearly demonstrated as thousands of black children are placed in foster homes and community center each year while they wait in vain for white adoptive parents who never appear. But, neither do black adoptive parents. This at first seems strange for during the slave era black adults readily and easily assumed responsibility for children whose parents were sold away. After emancipation black families routinely stepped in and assumed responsibility for homeless black youngsters.[35] Black families today are not so quick to step forward to adopt such children because appeal son the behalf of un-known black children are made by impersonal Euro-American agencies. The same African Americans who generously support one another in raising money for the rent and in saving personal face remain seemingly indifferent to the plight of these children. It is not that they cannot relate to the children, only that the Afro-American tradition makes it difficult for them to relate to the institutions which speak for the children.

Finally, race conflict in North American is personal. For more than a generation scholars in a field that has come to be known as comparative American race relations have been debating a thesis set forth by the distinguished scholar of Latin America, Frank Tannenbaum. In his little book Tannenbaum argued that race relations were less harsh and confrontational in the nations of Latin America than in the United States.[36] According to Tannenbaum, Blacks received better treatment in Latin America because slavery was a natural and normal part of social life in Iberia at the time the New World was settled. The Spaniards and Portuguese simply imported to the Americas an institution with which they were comfortable. The English, on the other hand, had to justify slavery in their colonies and eventually settled on the rationalization that Africans were inferior to Europeans. The other part of what has come to be called Tannenbaum Thesis is that while the Roman Catholic church recognized the humanity of black folk and intervened on their behalf in Latin America, the many Protestant denominations in North America were divided over whether or not blacks were human and often supported slaveholders in the cruel treatment of blacks. In the years since Tannenbaum published his book, a sizeable literature has grown up, much of it devoted to demonstrating his many errors.[37] Black historians such as Franklin Knight and the late Leslie B. Rout, Jr. have been in the forefront of Tannenbaum critics.[38]

The personal dimension has been overlooked in the many comparative studies of race in the New World, The slave system of the Caribbean and South America on the one hand, and those of North America on the other, differ in the average size of the plantations on which bondsmen lived. In such places as Haiti, Brazil, Jamaica, and St. Croix it was not uncommon for slave to labor on plantations populated by hundreds of slaves who might labor for weeks and not see a white man. But in North America a plantation of 50 slaves was rare. Most slaves served on small holdings with less than five other bondsmen and saw whites on a daily basis. In the many debates on comparative slavery and the Tannenbaum thesis, the perspective of the bondsmen themselves has seldom been taken into consideration. Caribbean and Latin American slaves were separated from their owners both by the size of the plantation and by the fact that there were comparatively few whites. While these bondsmen clearly understood their lives were dominated by whites, they were distant unknown creatures. On the smaller North American holdings however, relations between blacks and whites were up-close, intimate, and personal. While a slaveholder in Barbados might not even know the names of all his slaves, one in Maryland knew them well. While a slavemaster in Brazil might well screen his treatment of slaves through the many corporate structures Ibero-Americans were so adept at creating, one in Georgia assumed full personal responsibility for treatment of the slaves. Slavery in North America was personal and so, as a consequence, was race hate. While slaves in the Caribbean and South America may have hated a system, those in North American usually hated a person. This personal dimension of race hatred in the United States has been largely neglected in debates over the Tannenbaum thesis.

## CONCLUSION

Similarly those who have sought to construct a Black Sociology have neglected the personal dimension that is the essence of oppugnancy. In seeking to explain oppugnancy, the "hardness of black life." Long turns to a well known black folk saying:

> What you mean I gotta do that?
> Ain't but two things I got to do--Be black and die.[39]

Unlike the Caribbean and South America where what historian Carl Degler terms the "mulatto escape hatch"[40] existed for persons of African descent to make their way from blackness and up into one the intermediate mixed castes, those in the United States had no choice but to be black. Blackness in North America is as inevitable as death. African Americans cannot escape The Mark of Oppression according to two psychiatrists.[41] Abram Kardiner and Lionel Ovessey wrote without benefit of Long's term oppugnancy just as did Ladner and her colleagues nearly a quarter of a century later.

Each group of social scientists approached the black experience through the prism of white scholarship despite the fact that one worked firmly within the Euro-American scholarly tradition while the other sought to break free from it. Those who contributed to the Ladner volume--including the present writer--understood that White Sociology as then constructed could contribute little to the understanding of the black experience. Indeed, many felt White Sociology both distorted and demeaned the long black struggle for justice in North America. Yet, at the same time it was not clear how Black Sociology needed to be organized to better reflect black life and culture. Oppugnancy provides a basis on which to build a genuine Black Sociology in that it first acknowledges that long history of black Americans; second, demonstrates black folk have an awareness of this history; and third, (perhaps of greatest importance) reflects the personal orientation of African Americans as distinct from the organizational orientation of whites.

## NOTES

1. Joyce A. Ladner (ed.), *The Death of White Sociology*. New York: Random House, 1973.

2. Notable exceptions are Peter H. Wood, *Black Majority; Negroes in Colonial South Carolina form 1670 through the Stono Rebellion*. New York: Norton, 1975; Edgar J. McManus, *Black Bondage in the North*. Syracuse (NY): Syracuse University Press, 1973; and A. Leon Higginbotham, Jr., *In the Matter of Color-Race and the American Legal Process: The Colonial Period*. New York: Oxford University Press, 1980. Useful overviews of literature are Peter H. Wood, "'I Did the Best I Could for My Day:' The Study of Early Black History during the Second Reconstruction," *William and Mary Quarterly*, Third Series 35 (April, 1987), pp. 185-225; also Rhett S. Jones, "Race Relations in the Colonial Americas: An Overview." *Humboldt Journal of Social Relations* 1 (Spring/Summer, 1974), pp. 73-82.

3. John W. Blassingame, *The Slave Community: Plantation Life in the Antebellum South*. New York: Oxford University Press, 1972; and George P. Rawick, *From Sundown to Sunup: The Making of the Black Community*. Westport (CT): Greenwood Press, 1972.

4. Typical are Daniel C. Thompson, *Sociology of the Black Experience*. Westport (CT): Greenwood Press, 1974; and James E. Blackwell, *The Black Community: Diversity and Unity*. New York: Dodd, Mead, 1975.

5. The problems of the earliest Afro-Americans are discussed in the context of the evolving racial climate of the thirteen colonies by Gary B. Nash, *Red, White, and Black: The Peoples of Early America*. Englewood Cliffs (NJ): Prentice-Hall, 2nd edition, 1982; see especially chapters 7, 8, and 12.

6. Charles H. Long, *Significations: Signs, Symbols, and Images in the Interpretation of Religion*. Philadelphia: Fortress Press, 1986, p. 178.

7. On Emile Durkheim see his *Suicide: A Study in Sociology*, translated by John A. Spaulding and George Simpson. New York: The Free Press, 1951, first published 1987; for Weber see Reinhard Bendix, *Max Weber: An Intellectual Portrait*, Garden City (NY): Anchor Books, 1962.

8. See Hans H. Gerth and C. Wright Mills (eds.), *From Max Weber: Essays in Sociology*. New York: Oxford University, 1958, especially Chapter VIII and IX.

9. Good examples are Robert K. Merton, *Social Theory and Social Structure*, New York: The Free Press, Revised and Enlarged Edition, 1957; and Talcott Parsons, *Essays in Sociological Theory*. New York: The Free Press, Revised Edition, 1964.

10. See, for example, the discussions of various ethnic groups in Part II of James R. Halseth and Bruce A. Glasrud (eds.), *The Northwest Mosaic: Minority Conflicts in Pacific Northwest History*. Boulder (CO): Pruett, 1977.

11. White Humanistic Sociology is one of the most significant alternatives to mainstream Sociology it is perhaps worth noting that of two widely read critiques of the discipline, neither mentions the term in the table of contents. See Maurice Stein and Arthur Vidich (eds.), *Sociology on Trial*. Englewood Cliffs (NJ): Prentice-Hall, 1963; and J. David Colfax and Jack L. Roach (eds.),*Radical Sociology*. New York: Basic Books, 1971.

12. See, for example, Rhett S. Jones, "Finding the Black Self: A Humanistic Strategy." *Journal of Black Psychology* 7 (August, 1980), pp. 17-26.

13. Nash, *Red, White and Black*, pp. 214-215 argues, however, that by the time eighteenth century Americans began to celebrate their open, egalitarian society, actual opportunities for mobility were already decreasing. Edmund S. Morgan, *American Slavery--American Freedom: The Ordeal of Colonial Virginia*. New York: Norton, 1975 believes that the closing off of opportunities created problems in Virginia as early as the seventeenth century; see especially Chapters 11, 12, 15, and 16.

14. Compare on this issue W. E. Abraham, *The Mind of Africa*. Chicago: University of Chicago Press, 1962, Chapter 2: John S. Mbiti, *African Religions and Philosophy*. Garden City (NY): Anchor Books, 1970, Chapters 15, 17; and Jacques Maquet, *Africanity: The Cultural Unity of Black Africa*. New York: Oxford University Press, 1972, pp. 56-66 and 76-88.

15. Rhett S. Jones, "Structural Isolation, Race and Cruelty in the New World." *Third World Review* 4 (Fall, 1978), pp. 34-43.

16. Kenneth M. Stampp, *The Peculiar Institution: Slavery in the AnteBellum South*. New York: Vintage Books, 1956, Chapter IV.

17. A recent, detailed account of one of the eighteenth century West Indian revolts is found in David Barry Gaspar, *Bondmen and Rebels: A Study of Master-Slave Relations in Antigua*. Baltimore: Johns Hopkins, 1985, Part I.

18. So argue T. H. Breen and Stephen Innes, *"Myne Owne Ground:" Race and Freedom on Virginia's Eastern Shore, 1640-1676*. New York: Oxford University Press, 1982; first published 1980.

19. Joel Kovel, *White Racism: A Psychohistory*. New York: Vintage,1970; Morgan, *American Slavery* George M. Fredrickson, *White Supremacy: A Comparative Study in American and South African History*. New York: Oxford University Press, 1982, first published 1981.

20. Long, *Significations*, p. 177.

21. Albert J. Faboteau, *Slave Religion: The "Invisible Institution" in the Antebellum South*. New York: Oxford University Press, 1980, first published 1978.

22. Gilbert Osofsky (ed.) *Puttin' on Ole Massa*. New York: Harper and Row, 1969.

23. See, for example, Stokely Carmichael and Charles V. Hamilton, *Black Power: The Politics of Liberation in America*. New York: Vintage Books, 1967, especially Chapter III.

24. See Randall M. Miller (ed.), *"Dear Master:" Letters of a Slave Family*. Ithaca (NY): Cornell University Press, 1978; also William L. Van DeBurg, *The Slave Drivers*. Westport (CT): Greenwood Press, 1979.

25. A somewhat different interpretation is provided by Oscar Handlin, *Race and Nationality in American Life*. Garden City (NY): Anchor Books, 1957.

26. Worse still, this anger can lead to betrayal. See Aaron David Gresson III, *The Dialectics of Betrayal: Sacrifice, Violation and the Oppressed*. Norwood (NJ): Ablex, 1962, especially Chapters 2 and 3.

27. On this practice see Allan H. Spear, *Black Chicago: The Making of a Negro Ghetto, 1890-1920*. Chicago: University of Chicago Press, 1967, pp. 25-26; also Gilbert Osofsky, *Harlem: The Making of a Ghetto--Negro New York, 1890-1930*. New York: Harper Torchbooks, 1968, first published 1965, pp. 146-147.

28. An excellent overview of this literature, through the 1970s is Judith R. Porter and Robert E. Washington. "Black Identity and Self-Esteem: A review of Studies of Black Self-Concept, 1968-1978." *Annual Review of Sociology* 5 (August, 1979). For ideas on how to develop positive black-concept see James A. Banks and Jean D. Grambs (ed.), *Black Self-Concept: Implications for Education and Social Science*. New York: McGraw-Hill, 1972.

29. E. Franklin Frazier, *Black Bourgeoisie: The Rise of a New Middle Class in the United States*. New York: Collier Books, 1967, first published 1957, especially Chapters VII, IX, and X.

30. Katrina Hazzard-Gordon, *Atiba's a Comin': The Rise of Social Dance Formation in Afro-American Culture*. Unpublished Ph.D. Dissertation, Cornell University, 1983.

31. Elliot Liebow, *Tally's Corner: A Study of Negro Streetcorner Men*. Boston: Little, Brown, 1967, p. 213.

32. R. Lincoln Keiser, *The Vice Lords: Warriors of the Streets*. New York: Holt, Rinehart and Winston, 1969; and John R. Fry, *Fire and Black-Stone*. Philadelphia: J.B. Lippincott, 1969.

33. This point is made in discussions of signifying by Roger D. Abrahams, *Deep Down in the Jungle: Negro Narrative Folklore from the Streets of Philadelphia*. Chicago: Aldine, 1970, pp. 45-58; and by Alan Dundes (ed.), *Mother Wit from the Laughing Barrel: Readings in the Interpretation of Afro-American Folklore*. Englewood Cliffs (NJ): Prentice-Hall, 1973, pp. 277-328.

34. Walter F. Edwards, "Speech Acts in Guyana: Communicating Ritual and Personal Insults." *Journal of Black Studies* 10 (September, 1979), p. 21.

35. Herbert G. Gutman, *The Black Family in Slavery and Freedom, 1750-1925*. New York: Vintage Books, 1977, pp. 226-229.

36. Frank Tannenbaum, *Slave and Citizen: The Negro in the Americas*. New York: Vintage Books, 1946.

37. Jones, "Race Relations," provides an overview of this literature.

38. Franklin W. Knight, *Slave Society in Cuba During the Nineteenth Century*. Madison: University of Wisconsin Press, 1970, especially Chapters 1, 9; Leslie B. Rout Jr., *The African Experience in Spanish America: 1502 to the Present Day*. New York: Cambridge University Press, 1976, especially Chapters 3, 4.

39. Long, *Significations*, p. 178.

40. Carl N. Degler, *Neither Black nor White: Slavery and Race Relations in Brazil and the United States*, New York: Macmillan, 1971, pp. 226-232. Compare this view of the significance of the mulatto with that of Harmannus Hoetink, *The Two Variants in Caribbean Race Relations: A Contribution to Segmented Societies*. New York: Oxford University Press, 1969, pp. 164-190.

41. Abram Kardiner and Lionel Ovesey, *The Mark of Oppression: Explorations in the Personality of the American Negro*. Cleveland: Meridian Books, 1962, first published, 1951.

# 2

# THE AFROCENTRIC APPROACH: MEANING AND IMPLICATIONS

"When I discover who I am,
I'll be free."

*Ralph Ellison*

# AFROCENTRISM IN A MULTICULTURAL DEMOCRACY

*Phil Petrie*

Since the 17th century, the education of African-American children has been a matter of controversy. Today, depending on your source, this struggle is about integration, liberation or control. John Henrik Clarke, an astute African-American historian, contends that what is going on is nothing less than the "decolonization" of education.

In the antebellum South, education for black children--and adults, for that matter-was absolutely forbidden. In the free North, such education was not a burning issue, either. African Americans asserted themselves and received the fundamentals of education--reading, writing, and arithmetic--as best they could. In some cases it was clandestine, in other, as with Frederick Douglass, young black children learned from their white playmates. In New York City during the mid-1800s, a more organized effort was effected for the education of black children when African Americans organized the African Free School, the progenitor of the New York City public schools.

At that period in American history, just receiving an education was the crucial need. Years later, however, Carter G. Woodson, founder of the Association for the Study of Negro Life and History, injected a new demand. Woodson challenged what was being taught and referred to the education of African Americans as the "miseducation of the Negro."

The problem was one of both commission and omission. Textbooks were patently offensive in their use of racial stereotypes; just as offensive was the omission of black participation in national and international events.

After a continuous struggle, the problem of commission was reduced considerably, but not eliminated: There are now few stereotypes in our textbooks. The problem of omission, however, is still rampant.

It was this sin of omission that led the Southern Education Foundation in Atlanta to sponsor a

conference called "The Infusion of African and African-American Content in the School Curriculum." At the first conference, in 1989, there were 600 participants; the second conference, a year later, attracted 1,200. Dr. Herman Reese, a consultant at the foundation, estimates that the 1992 conference will have over 3,000 participants.

The infusion of the curriculum with African-American content is the latest battle being fought in the education of black children. The heavy munitions in this fight are the two buzzwords Afrocentrism and multiculturalism. Each is loaded with enough emotional weight to start yet another academic war.

Following are the opinions of eight scholars on this important subject. Remember that this isn't just another arcane exercise in education. Afrocentrism or multiculturalism will affect your child's education.

## MOLEFI KETE ASANTE

Multiculturalism in education is derived from several cultural perspectives; Afrocentricity is one of those perspectives, and it is one of the simplest and fastest growing ideas to have been developed in the African-American intellectual community. If you are African-American, placing yourself in the center of your analysis so that you are grounded in a historical and cultural context is to be Afrocentric. Without Afrocentricity, African Americans would not have a voice to add to multiculturalism.

Twelve years ago a friend of mine commented on the fact that I was wearing a piece of Ghanaian kente cloth. "I used to wear African fabrics, too, when I was in *my* ethnic phase," he said. I pointed out to him that he was then wearing a Scottish plaid scarf, Italian shoes, a French suit and an English tie. He never brings the subject up these days. But his comment underscored the need for African people to be Africa-centered. While Afrocentrism is not a call for Africans to accept everything our ancestors did, it does say that we should build upon their foundations.

I first articulated this view in the 1970s, aiming to reorient intellectual discussion around the future of African people in the United States. The key concept in any discussion of Afrocentricity is *place*--where you are standing culturally and psychologically when you act or make a statement about anything. The question "Do you like classical music?" usually elicits this response from me: "Whose classical?" Of course, if the person is Afrocentric, I respond, "Yes, I am particularly fond of John Coltrane, Wynton Marsalis and Charlie Parker."

Afrocentric theory does not pose a threat to multiculturalism; it does, however, pose a threat to Eurocentrism--the imposition of a European view that denigrates the experiences of others. European domination of Western culture over many years has resulted in the *dislocation* of Africans both physically and psychologically. To lose one's terms is to become a victim of the other's attitudes, models, disciplines and culture, and the ultimate effect of such a massive loss is the destruction of self-confidence, the distortion of history, and psychological marginality. Sanity will come only from a conscious *relocation* of ourselves from the margins of someone else's experience to the centrality of our own experience. "I love Harriet Tubman, because she first loved me," I tell my children.

Afrocentricity is not the opposite of Eurocentrism, nor does it seek to replace Eurocentrism. The beautiful thing about Afrocentricity is that it does not deny others their places. It is a totally different orientation to reality based on harmonious coexistence of an endless variety of cultures.

Conversely, there can be no true multiculturalism without Afrocentricity. These two ideas are complementary, not contradictory. What I have sought is pluralism without hierarchy. Afrocentricity should take its place not above but alongside other cultural and historical perspectives.

Molefi Kete Asante is chairman of African-American studies at Temple University in Philadelphia and author of Afrocentricity: The Theory of Social Change, The Afrocentric Idea and Kemet, Afrocentricity and Knowledge.

## KATRINA HAZZARD-GORDON

Afrocentricity is not a new concept. The idea of

empowerment through engaging a world view that confronts and challenges European-dominated thinking can be seen by the 1750s, in response to the emergence of white supremacy. Nor is the term Afrocentricity a recent formulation. My first encounter with the term was in a 1966 issue of *Africa Today* magazine.

Notwithstanding its operative origin or its coinage, Afrocentricity as a construct for empowerment raises more questions that it answers. I sometimes question whether some aspects of the discussion of Afrocentricity do not take us backward in the continuing dialogue on race.

Afrocentricity argues for an Africa-centered world view. It seeks to include African contributions to the world alongside, and sometimes in place of, those of Europe. It challenges the Western historical perception of European pre-eminence in art, culture, science, mathematics, religion and philosophy.

One component of the Afrocentric concept sees its approach as essential in ameliorating the economic and social condition of African Americans, whom it views as unwilling victims of psychological self-destruction brought on by a lack of "knowledge of self." The concept simultaneously challenges the sense of white supremacy, grounded on the myth that all significant contributions to human civilization have come from Europeans and their descendants. It is here, for me, that the debate becomes retrogressive.

As a sociologist and cultural artist who falls squarely in the materialist camp, I believe that material reality precedes and supports any psychological, perceptive or cultural reality. I do not believe that philosophy necessarily addresses economic realities. The maladies of African-American life, the ills that plague black communities are grounded on very real economic and social inequities that have existed since the founding of this nation. These inequities have, for the most part, gone unaddressed.

Afrocentricity does not account for the deleterious effect of post-industrial capitalism on the lives of working blacks. The local street corner drug dealer may know that he, as an African, is heir to a 6,000-year-old tradition that anyone would be proud of. But accepting that fact does not change the historical and economic circumstances under which he constructs his life. Nor does knowing that fact pay his rent or feed his children. He deals drugs not because of his lack of ethnic pride but because he needs money. Contribute to solving the problem of black male unemployment by gainfully employing all black males over the age of 18, and the positive psychological intent of Afrocentricity will be accomplished.

As I have observed the functional value of Afrocentricity--and I believe it has some--I would say that the concept is most useful and successful for, as well as understood by, blacks in academia. It helps black survive and meet the challenge to their ethnic integrity, social honor and cultural validity posed by the white academy. Ultimately, however, students of Afrocentric theory must confront the wider socioeconomic and racial realities of this nation and its ostrich-like ideology of denial.

Katrina Hazzard-Gordon, professor of sociology at Rutgers University in Camden, N.J., is author of Jookin': The Rise of Social Dance Formations in African-American Culture.

## WILSON J. MOSES

Edward W. Blyden, father of pan-Africanism and early advocate of Afrocentric thinking, made a pilgrimage to Egypt in 1866. "This is the work of my African progenitors," he mused while standing in the central hall of the Great Pyramid.

W.E.B. Du Bois wrote his first book on Africa, *The Negro*, in 1915, and endorsed Blyden's view that the African facial features of the Sphinx and other monuments revealed the race of the kings who built them. In *The World and Africa*, he wrote that Egypt was the source of civilization, and that the history of "its proudest triumphs" was merged with that of Ethiopia.

Cheikh Anta Diop reiterated the positions of Blyden and Du Bois in a series of works published between 1955 and 1967 and culminating in *The African Origin of Civilization*.

Ironically, the Afrocentric interpretation of civilization has sometimes been exploited by white supremacists. In 1839 Alexander Everett, a spokesman for the American Colonization Society, spoke with flattering hypocrisy of the African origins of civilization, to camouflage his racist goal of uprooting and deporting American citizens of African descent.

Today, as in the past, hypocritical white racists pay lip service to Afrocentric education, especially in its separatist applications, in order to serve their own segregationist agenda. It seems that we are never invulnerable. Whenever we attempt a program for self-help, racists will seize on the opportunity to play, once again, the old separate-but-equal joker. In recent years those students of Africana who reject the sentimental approach have been thankful for the publication of the late St. Clair Drake's two-volume work, *Black Folk Her and There: An Essay in History and Anthropology* (UCLA Center for Afro-American Studies, 1991). The title of his book, deriving from Du Bois' similar work, *Black Folk Then and Now;* makes clear his devotion to the memory of Du Bois. Drake's admiration for Blyden, evident in earlier writings, placed him within the "Blydenist" tradition of Afrocentrism and racial vindication.

Drake always acknowledged his sources and gave credit to the giants on whose shoulders he stood. Lesser minds claim victories that are not their own, or set up straw men and then knock them down. Drake is above such demagoguery. He vindicates the Africanity of Egypt, acknowledging and evaluating prior scholarship on the subject. In his second volume, he traces the origins of racism in the Christian, Jewish and Islamic worlds. Because he was a researcher, and not a rhetorician, Drake is able to expose hitherto unrevealed elements of racism in Eurocentric scholarship; he does not need to invent anything.

African Americans will profit greatly from acquaintance with all the work of St. Clair Drake. A humane scholar with a sense of irony, he gently teases the romantics, but he also teaches us to understand and appreciate our African heritage. Afrocentrism, as displayed in *Black Folk Here and There*, is the form of Afrocentrism that I embrace. Of course, there will be some who will reject Drake's approach, simply because he refuses to play the game of racial romanticism, so easily exploited by black demagogues and white supremacists. Others will admire his work because of its honesty and erudition.

Wilson J.Moses, professor of English and history and director of African-American studies at Boston University; is author of The Golden Age of Black Nationalism, Black Messiahs and Uncle Toms, Alexander Crummell and The Wings of Ethiopia.

## ASA G. HILLIARD III

Common components of slavery, colonialism, segregation, apartheid, racism and neo-racism have been and still are they systematic and pervasive defamation of blacks, the suppression of their history and the creation of an ideology of white supremacy, all by some of the most prestigious European and European-American scholars. Together, these components lead to a grandiose falsification of the human record, in a negative way for Africans and in a positive way for Europeans. There is massive valid academic literature to support these two assertions.

At the turn of the century, theologians in seminaries were debating whether African people had souls, psychologists were debating whether Africans were genetically inferior mentally, anthropologists were labeling Africans "primitive," historians were saying that Africans had no history, biologists were even debating the fundamental humanity of Africans. While the overt assertions of those positions are seldom heard today, the legacy of those beliefs lives on in camouflaged form.

The truth has yet to be told about Africa and its descendants world-wide. Yet there is a vast body of scholarly documentation that restores a more truthful picture of the history and culture of people of African descent, from ancient times to the present. Much of this scholarship is not new, just untapped.

The primary goal of curriculum change is to tell the truth, the whole truth. A truthful self- and group-image is a necessity for any people. No ethnic group can function appropriately with false images of itself. Some white supremacists scholars and media barons want to "stand in the schoolhouse door" to keep the academic content of schools segregated by keeping significant African and African-American content out of school curricula.

In the names of W.E.B. Du Bois, Carter G. Woodson, Drusilla Dunjee Houston, Edward W. Blyden, William Leo Hansberry, Cheikh Anta Diop and many other great historians, the work to engender a positive image of African Americans will go on.

Asa G. Hilliard III, professor of urban education at Georgia State University in Atlanta, organized the team that developed the "African-American Baseline Essays" as part of a multicultural curriculum resource project.

## JOHN BRACEY

When the movement for black studies made its first appearance, defenders of traditional white supremacists curricula argued long and loud that there was no such thing as black studies, that black studies was a hoax fostered by irrational black nationalists who were part of an anti-intellectual assault on an academy that they saw as character-

ized by universally shared standards of excellence.

Time has not been kind to those learned men and women who filled the pages of *Commentary* and he New York Times with their predictions of the imminent demise of black studies. In 1991 black studies is not only alive and well, but the fields of red (American Indian), brown (Hispanic and Puerto Rican) and yellow (Asian-American) studies are also making their impact.

Having lost the battle to keep the curriculum white, the old traditionalists have retreated to the posture of (1) trying to seize control of the definition of black studies, (2) trying to reduce black studies to the movements of a tiny galaxy of individual "stars" and (3) trying to bury it under an ill-defined multiculturalism.

Molefi Asante and other proponents of Afrocentrism are to be commended for carrying their critique of Eurocentrism to the very foundations of Western tradition. Drawing attention to the contributions of ancient African societies to the intellectual, social and political development of the "West" is a much needed corrective to the mystical view that every idea worth having originated in Athens in the fifth century B.C. Afrocentrists may overstate their case from time to time, but no matter. As W.E.B. Du Bois once wrote, "The champions of white folk are legion."

Though I am not convinced, intellectually, of the reality of a unified African cultural and cosmological view that stretches from ancient times to the present, I see no harm in teaching from an Afrocentric point of view. Why not? Afrocentrism at least has the virtue of making explicit its guiding assumptions, its biases nd its pedagogical goals, without parking behind some pious drivel about "universality" and "our common heritage." Afrocentrists put themselves out front, where you can see them and where they can be challenged. And if other non-white peoples offer analyses from their particular points of view, so much the better.

Eurocentrism has held the spotlight without competition long enough. Moreover, given the history of the relationship between whites and non-whites during the past 400 years and the way that many whites have been acting up lately in the United States, Eastern Europe and the Middle East, one is sorely tempted to agree with the reply attributed to Gandhi when asked what he thought about Western civilization: "Western civilization? That would be a good idea."

John Bracey, professor of Afro-American studies at the University of Massachusetts at Amherst, is co-editor of Black Nationalism in America and Black Protest in the 1960s.

## JAMES EARLY

Educational and cultural institutions in America have played pivotal roles in propagating disempowerment and denigration of non-European derived cultures. A 1990 survey conducted by the National Opinion Research Center at the University of Chicago found that a majority of whites still "retain negative beliefs about minorities."

Historically, black Americans have assumed a leadership role in challenging the ideological, social and economic foundations of racism in American education. Organized efforts to establish Negro history, Black History Month and black studies have made seminal contributions in overcoming miseducation in the nation's schools and cultural institutions.

The struggle against racism on all fronts has propelled the African-American community into the role of crucible for the expansion of democratic rights for all citizens and residents, irrespective of race, class, able-bodiedness or cultural background. Consider the worldwide adoption of "We Shall Overcome," the African-American freedom anthem, as the signature of resistance, hope and reconciliation by student movements, the women's movement and countless other groups striving for inclusion in the democratic ideal.

Afrocentricism, then, is an objective response, a democratic thrust attempting to overcome the monopoly of Eurocentric values, history and mythology over the lives of all people in the African diaspora.

While Afrocentrism reflects a particular cultural reaction to the egregious applications of Eurocentrism, multiculturalism brings into focus the democratic stirrings of other cultures in an ongoing renegotiation of civil, social, economic and cultural rights. Yet the strident criticism by the cultural and educational status quo against the variants of Afrocentrism reflects the continued importance of black/white relations in negotiation of rights and privileges for all.

Important and complex challenges still lie before us. Afrocentrism must guard against narrowing its outlook and content to African antiquity, environmental determinism, male superiority and perspectives that constrict the more expansive historical meaning of the black struggle: freedom and justice for all people. Simply highlighting the achievements of one oppressed group runs the risk of imposing the same kind of monocultural dominance over the other groups that are embattled against the grip of Eurocentrism.

Neither Afrocentrism nor multiculturalism yet outlines a sufficient strategy for re-educating Americans to a truer understanding of the nation's complex national history. For example, neither sufficiently addresses intra-group or inter-group dynamics of ethnicity, class or gender. Neither approach has worked out how best to balance direct participation in leadership of public-sector institutions, with the legitimate goals of "self-determination" for local or racial communities.

Nevertheless, Afrocentrism and multiculturalism are positive breaks from the stronghold of Eurocentrism. If they are pursued from this perspective, and if they guard against isolationist tendencies, the will continue to advance national debate and practice toward cultural equity, social stability and political and economic justice.

James Early is assistant secretary for public service at the Smithsonian Institution in Washington, D.C.

## ROBERT L. HARRIS, JR.

In many ways, the Afrocentrism vs. multiculturalism debate recalls the separation vs. integration controversy of the 1960s. Lerone Bennett Jr. in his book, *The Challenge of Blackness*, help put that schism to rest. He cogently writes that at issue was neither separation nor integration but liberation. The means, in other words, should not be confused with the end.

Afrocentrism, in my judgment, is a means to an end, rather than an end itself. It is a means to multiculturalism and awareness, understanding and appreciation of the roles that different people have played in the development of world civilization and in the growth of the United States. Multiculturalism, however, cannot be achieved without a perspective that centers the various cultures within their own history.

Otherwise, there is the danger of making the same mistake that the well-meaning white historian Kenneth Stampp made in the preface to his book, *The Peculiar Institution*. Stampp explained, "I have assumed that the slaves were merely ordinary human beings, that innately Negroes are, after all, only white men with black skins, nothing more, nothing less." The problems with that statement are too numerous for this commentary. Suffice it to say that it denied the existence of a viable African-American culture.

African Americans created a distinctive culture in the United States based, in large measure, on their African heritage. An Afrocentric perspective enables us to recognize and understand that culture from the inside out, rather than from the outside in. It thereby reveals a tradition in African-American letters, for example, that moves black literature beyond "protest writing," a characterization some white critics employ to dismiss its significance.

Afrocentrism places black people squarely on the stage of human drama. It rewrites the script to provide angles of vision that give new meaning to the story. It does not eliminate the other actors, who played their roles so well, but adds depth to their characters. It increases the size of the cast and poses more complex challenges, thereby transforming the plot.

Unfortunately, some actors cling desperately to their former roles and try to prevent others from sharing center stage. Such antagonism tempts some of the "outcasts" to form their own companies, write their own scripts, and mount their own productions. The danger here is one inherent in Afrocentrism, if the means is confused with the end. As an end itself, Afrocentrism abandons the main stage for a sideshow. As a means to an end, Afrocentrism fundamentally alters the productions, bringing it closer to reality. The human drama, if properly understood, is multicultural, with different actors playing lead roles at different times.

Robert L. Harris Jr. is president of the Association for the Study of Afro-American Life and History in Washington, D.C.

## RHETT S. JONES

An Afrocentric perspective is important not only for what it tells us about the black experience, but for the insight it provides unto people of other racial backgrounds. Surprisingly, a close study of the racial history of the United States reveals the history of black Americans to be more like that of white Americans than like that of groups now collectively called people of color.

The primary difference between Afro-Americans and Euro-Americans on the one hand and Native Americans, Asian Americans and Hispanic Americans on the other is the continuing impor-

tance of ethnicity among the latter. The term Indian was created by whites and for centuries has held little meaning for Native Americans. They continue to think of themselves as members of a specific tribe, defining themselves as Cherokee, Sioux or Hopi. Similarly, the term Asian American is a construct useful perhaps to census takers and political activists, but it masks cultural differences between, for example, third generation Chinese Americans and recently arrived Laotians.

The brutal cruelties of slavery eliminated ethnic distinctions among most black Americans, who, in one of history's most stunning achievements, have created a culture not only capable of enabling its people to survive and achieve, but to respect one another. African-American culture is truly the nation's first counterculture in that slaves creatively developed ways of honoring one another without money, property, political power or even full control over their own bodies. Ethnicity played no role in their struggle. Black Americans accomplished much as a race while at the same time forging a new racial identity to replace their lost West African ethnic identities.

Whites are the only other group to so completely lose their ethnic roots. While many Euro-Americans, particularly those who live in the East, think of themselves as Italo-Americans, Franco-Americans or Polish Americans, many others, particularly those who live in the South, Midwest and West, think of themselves only as whites or as Americans. Many have no idea of their ancestry. At the time their identity as a people was forged, ethnicity was no more important, or useful, to them than it was to African Americans.

The reasons for the absence of ethnicity among blacks and whites are certainly different. Black Americans were--with some rare exceptions-- unable to maintain any sense of African ethnicity. White Americans were--also with exceptions-- uninterested in maintaining any sense of European ethnicity. Moreover, ethnicity was not only useless to these pragmatic white folks, but often worked against a perceived need for white American unity.

In the 17th century, black and white Americans began building what was later to become the United States, and while they disagreed and continue to disagree over the meaning of race, they are generally agreed there is a white race and a black one. The other races have a different history. Their sense of self tends to be more ethnic than racial, a reality that has grave implications for any

proposed political alliance of people of color that
seeks to include blacks.

Rhett S. Jones, professor of history and Afro-American studies
at Brown University in Providence, R.I., is director of the
university's new Center on Race and Ethnicity.

# AFROCENTRIC SYSTEMATICS

*Molefi Kete Asante*

I offer this short essay as a contribution to clarity concerning of Afrocentricity. In two recent commentaries, one by the African American scholar Henry Louis Gates, Jr., on a Washington radio program; and another by the white writer Sidney Mintz, I have noticed confusion about the theory of Afrocentricity.

I certainly would not claim that the negative discussions of the idea are deliberate; they are nevertheless misleading and should be corrected. Gates' position is particularly troubling, because without defining Afrocentricity as it is used in the literature, he went on to say that there were certain Afrocentrists with whom he did not identify. That is fair enough if he had defined what he meant by Afrocentricity in the first place. However, he seemed to leave the impression that Afrocentricity was of a different intellectual order than, say, deconstruction.

Rather than engage the idea as I have explained it in three books, Gates attacks bogus arguments that have not been made by any Afrocentrists. Mintz, on the other hand, in advancing his theory of our culture, attacks Afrocentrists as disagreeing with something that, at least, I had never read. Both of these remarks suggest gratuitous commentary about the growing Afrocentric school of thought. There have been other such statements expressed mainly in press releases, public relations brochures and interviews in the white media.

Most of the comments proceed from ignorance of the concept.

Since my works (*Afrocentricity*, 1980; *The Afrocentric Idea*, 1987; and *Kete, Afrocentricity and Knowledge*, 1990) constitute the major corpus in the Afrocentric movement, I have accepted the challenge suggested by my colleagues to write an essay toward the systematics of Afrocentric theory to respond to some of the commentaries. For the

past two years I had hoped that the numerous publications in this emerging tradition would have been engaging enough, but it appears in many cases that those who have commented about Afrocentricity have not read the literature and have therefore reacted to the concept much like Europe reacted to Africa for nearly 500 years, that is, try to control it, trivialize it, or destroy it, but never study or learn from it.

The often flippant responses to Afrocentricity have underscored the point generally made by Afrocentric scholars, namely, that the imposition of the Eurocentric perspective on every subject and theme as if the Eurocentric position is the only human and universal view is the fundamental basis of a racist response to history. That it has affected and infected the academy should not come as a surprise, since it was in the academy where the ideas of white supremacy were propounded for centuries in Germany, France, England, and the United States by the likes of Hegel, Voltaire, Toynbee and others. If anything, our contemporary universities are the inheritors of this vicious virus that erodes the very nature of our seeing, our explanations, our methods of inquiry and our conclusions.

Sidney Mintz' conclusion about what Afrocentrists would agree with or not agree with in his article "The Birth of Afro-American Culture" is just such an example. He demonstrates no knowledge in his statement of the Afrocentric position on the question of the origin of African American culture. I can almost guarantee, however, that if his essay on Afro-American cultural origins does not proceed from an African American perspective he will be highly criticized by Afrocentrists. To study African Americans as sideshows to whites, as marginal to history, as detached from place and purpose--is to study amiss.

Afrocentricity is primarily an orientation to data. There are certainly data and facts which may be used by Afrocentrists in making analyses, but the principal component of the theoretical piece has to do with an orientation, a location, a position. Thus, I have explained in several books and articles that Afrocentricity is "a perspective which allows Africans to be subjects of historical experiences" rather than objects on the fringes of Europe. This means that the Afrocentrist is concerned with discovering in every case the centered place of the African. Of course, such a philosophical stance is not necessary for other disciplines; it is, however, the fundamental basis for African or African American studies. Otherwise, it seems to me that what is being done in African American studies at some institutions might successfully be challenged as duplicating in content, theory, and method the essentially Eurocentric enterprises that are undertaken in the traditional departments.

African American studies, however, is not simply the study and teaching about African people, but it is the Afrocentric study of African phenomena; otherwise, we would have had African American studies for a 100 years. But what existed before was not African American studies but rather a Eurocentric study of Africans. Some of these studies led to important findings and have been useful. So the Afrocentrists do not claim that historians, sociologists, literary critics, philosophers and others do not make valuable contributions. Our claim is that by using a Eurocentric approach, they often ignore an important interpretative key to the African experience in America and elsewhere.

This poses a special problem to those who teach in African American studies, because the field is not merely an aggregation of courses on African American history and literature. Without a fundamental orientation to the data that center on African people as subjects and agents of historical experiences, the African American studies programs are nothing more that extensions of the English, history or sociology departments. On the other hand, the Afrocentric study of phenomena asks questions about location, place, orientation and perspective. This means that the data could come from any field or place and be examined Afrocentrically. At Temple University, we experiment with materials as varied as literary texts, architectural designs, dance aesthetics, social institutions and management techniques to teach the concept of centeredness.

Like scholars in other disciplines, Afrocentrists are exposed to the hazards of place and position. We can never be sure that our place is as secure as we want it to be, but we do the best we can with the resources of mind at our disposal. The aim is to open fields of inquiry and to expand human dialogue around questions of social, economic, historical and cultural concern. Everything must be run through the sieve of doubt until one hits the bedrock of truth. Our methods, based on the idea of African centeredness, are meant to establish a clear pattern of discourse that may be followed by others.

Afrocentricity is not a matter of color but of perspective, that is, orientation to facts. The historian, sociologist, psychologist and political scientist may examine the Battle of Gettysburg and see different elements and aspects because of the different emphases of the disciplines. In a similar manner, the Afrocentrist would look at the Civil War or any phenomenon involving African people and raise different questions than the Eurocentrist. These questions are not more or less correct but better in an interpretative sense if the person doing the asking wants to understand African phenomena in context. Since the Afrocentric perspective is not a racial perspective, but an orientation to data, anyone willing to submit to the rigid discipline of the field might become an Afrocentrist.

There are two general fields in which the Afrocentrist works: cultural/aesthetics and social/behavioral. This means that the person who declares in an intellectual sense to be an Afrocentrist commits traditional discipline suicide because one cannot, to be consistent, remain a traditional Eurocentric intellectual and an Afrocentrist. Of course, three are those who might be bi-positional or multi-positional under given circumstances. In claiming this posture, I am not dismissing the work that has been done in other fields on Africans and African Americans; some of it has enlarged our understanding, particularly that work that might be considered pre-Afrocentric, such as the works of Melville Herskovits, Basil Davidson, Robert Farris Thompson, and other scholars who have sought to see through the eyes of Africans and to place Africans in a subject rather than object position.

Afrocentric theories are not about cultural separatism or racial chauvinism. Among those who have been quoted as making such a charge are Michele Wallace, Arthur Schlesinger, Miriam Lichtheim, Cornell West, Diane Ravitch and Henry Louis Gates, Jr. With such a stellar crew in the same bed, one is eager to discover the source of their offhanded remarks about Afrocentricity and separatism or chauvinism. Attempting to give them the benefit of the doubt, I have assumed that they sense in the Afrocentric perspective a pro-African and an anti-white posture. Apart from the fact that one can be pro-African and not anti-white, the concept of Afrocentricity has little to do with pros and cons; it is pre-eminently about how you view phenomena. Of course, I have always been unashamedly and unapologetically African. But this is no reason to condemn or dismiss the theory of Afrocentricity.

I believe that the white scholars who register a negative reaction to Afrocentricity do so out of fear. This fear is revealed on two levels. In the first place, Afrocentricity provides them with no grounds for authority unless they become students of Africans. This produces an existential fear: African scholars might have something to teach whites. The Afrocentric school of thought is the first contemporary intellectual movement initiated by African American scholars that has currency on a broad scale for renewal and renaissance. It did not emerge inside the traditional white academic bastions.

The second fear is not so much an existential one; it is rather a fear of the implications of the Afrocentric critique of Eurocentrism as an ethnocentric view posing as a universal view. Thus, we have opened the discussion of everything from the race theory, ancient civilizations, and African and European personalities to the impact of the glaciers on human behavior and dislocation in the writing of African American authors. We examine these topics with the eyes of African people as subjects of historical experiences. This is not the only human view. If anything, Afrocentrists have always said that our perspective on data is only one among many and, consequently, the viewpoint, if you will, seeks no advantage, no self-aggrandizement and no hegemony. The same cannot be said of Eurocentrism.

The African American and African Eurocentrists are a special problem. They represent two cases. The first case is represented by those who have been os well-trained in the Eurocentric perspective that they see themselves as copies of Europeans. These are the Africans who believe they came to America on the *Mayflower* or better yet that classical European music is the only real classical music in the world. Their rejection of Afrocentricity is tied to their rejection of themselves. Thus, the inability to see from their own centers or to posi-

tion their sights on phenomena from their own historical and cultural conditions is related to what Malcolm X used to call "the slave mentality," that is, the belief that their own views can never be divorced from the slave master's.

To a large degree these Africans tend to lack historical consciousness and find their own source of intellectual satisfaction in the approval of whites, not in the search for the interpretative key to their own history. I am not suggesting the stifling of this type of imitation in any politically correct way but rather I want to explain the response to Afrocentricity in an historical manner.

The second case is also historical, that is, Afrocentrists find evidences of it in our historical experiences. These are the Africans who seek to be appointed overseers on the plantation. They do not necessarily believe they are the same as whites. They recognize that they did not come here on the *Mayflower* but they aspire to universalism without references to particular experiences. For them, any emphasis on particular perspectives and experiences suggest separatism, and separatism suggest hostility. This is a fallacy because neither separatism nor difference suggests hostility except in the minds of those who fear.

In an intellectual sense, these African Eurocentrists feel inclined to disagree with any idea that has popular approval among the African American masses. Much like the overseers during the ante-bellum period, they are eager to demonstrate that they are not a part of the rebellion and that they distrust the ideas that are derived from the African masses. They might even consider themselves a part of the elite, almost white, separate from the rest of us. The progression of their *clarencization* is seen in the distance they seek to place between themselves and us. Indeed, they might even participate in what Louis Lomax once called "the fooling of white people" by telling white audiences that Afrocentrists represent a new and passing fad.

The point is that Afrocentricity is nothing more than what is congruent to the interpretative life of the African person. Why should an African American see himself or herself through the perspective of a Chinese or white American? Neither the Chinese nor the white American views phenomena from the perspective of the African American--nor should they. Historical and cultural experiences and traditions differ, and in order to understand the African American experience in dance, architecture, social work, art, science, psychology or communication, one has to avail one's self of the richly textured centered-ness of African Americans. In the end, you must ask yourself, why does such a simple rational position threaten so many people?

# AFROCENTRIC CURRICULUM

*Molefi Kete Asante*

Recently I spoke about Afrocentric teaching at a gathering of thousands of teachers in a large urban district. After my speech, I was pleased that two teachers wanted to share their classroom experiences with the audience.

After a trip to Africa, one teacher said, he returned to his classroom of mostly African-American students and began identifying them with various ethnic groups, "You look like a Fulani boy I saw in Northern Nigeria," he commented to a young man. "You're definitely Ibo," he said to a female student. "Yes, I have seen that face in the Ibo region." Turning to another student, he said, "I see Mandinka features in your face." Soon, all the children were clamoring for identification: "Me, who do I look like?" "Tell me my ethnic group," each one asked the teacher.

The other teacher remarked that she asks her students to write about their family's genealogy. The best way to approach the subject of identity and connectiveness, she suggested, is to begin with the family, because students have both personal and collective identities.

I applauded both teachers for doing precisely what all teachers should do: place children, or center them, within the context of familiar cultural and social references from their own historical settings.

## THE BREAKTHROUGH

The discovery of the centric idea was a major breakthrough in my educational conceptualization. It allowed me to explain what happens to white children who attend American schools, what happens to Asian children who are rooted in Asian culture and attend schools in their countries, what happens to children of the African continent who are grounded in their own culture

Kent, K. (1985). "A Successful Program of Teachers Assisting Teachers." *Educational Leadership* 43,3: 30-33. Reprinted with permission of the Association for Supervision and Curriculum Development. Copyriht © 1985 by ASCD. All rights reserved.

and attend their own schools.

In my 17 journeys to Africa during the past 20 years, I have visited schools and colleges in all parts of the continent and been impressed with the eagerness of the children to learn. Back home in Philadelphia, I wanted to explore why children in African seemed more motivated than African-American children here. Why did Africans on the continent learn four and five languages, when in some schools African-American children were often not encouraged to take even one foreign language? To say the least, I have been disturbed by the lack of direction and confidence that plague many African-American children. I believe it is because they are not culturally centered and empowered in their classrooms.

## EMPOWERING CHILDREN THROUGH THEIR CULTURE

One of the principal aspects of empowerment is respect. Students are empowered when information is presented in such a way that they can walk out of the classroom feeling that they are a part of the information.

The times I am able to relate a class topic to the background of a Native American, Chinese, Hispanic, or African child in a multicultural classroom make me very pleased, because I see the centering immediately register in the child's countenance. Self-perception and self-acceptance are the principle tools for communicating and receiving communication. And teaching is preeminently a communicating profession.

Most teachers do not have to think about using the white child's culture to empower the white child. The white child's language is the language of the classroom. Information that is being conveyed is "white" cultural information in most cases; indeed, the curriculum in most schools is a "white self-esteem curriculum"

Teachers are empowered if they walk into a class and there is an air of credibility. How do teachers empower themselves in a classroom with children of African-American or other heritages? They must use the same tools used to empower white children.

When I enter a classroom of white college students and demonstrate in the course of my lecture that I know not only words of Ogotommeli, Seti, and Ptahhotep but also Shakespeare, Homer, and Stephen J. Gould, I am usually empowered as a teacher with my white students. They understand that I have no problem centering them within their cultural framework. The reason they understand it is simple: this is the language of the dominant culture.

The fact that an African-American or an Hispanic person--in order to master the white cultural information--has had to experience the death of his or her own culture does not register with most teachers. The true "centric" curriculum seeks for the African, Asian, and Hispanic child in the same kind of experience that is provided for the white child.

## CENTERING THE AFRICAN-AMERICAN CHILD

The centric idea gave me some idea of what happened to African-American children whose culture has been ravaged by racism, discrimination, harassment, and the Great Enslavement. These children, with cultural handicaps, are forced to compete with students whose ancestors have not suffered such devastation.

What centers the African-American child? I began working with this question many years ago when I observed what happened to the African-American child in the large school systems of northern urban communities. Being brought up in Valdosta, Georgia, during the era of segregation, I had been nourished and nurtured by teachers who had mastered the nuances and idiosyncrasies of my culture. This is something that teachers often seem unable to do in many urban schools.

Of course, segregation was legally and morally wrong, but something was given to black children in those schools that was just as important in some senses as the new books, better educated teachers, and improved buildings of this era. The children were centered in cultural ways that made learning interesting and intimate.

African-American children who have never heard the Spirituals; never heard the names of African ethnic groups; never read Paul Laurence Dunbar, Langston Hughes, and Phillis Wheatley nor the stories of High John de Conqueror, Anansi, and the Signifying Monkey are severely injured in the most fragile parts of their psyches. Lacking reinforcement in their own historical experiences, they become psychologically crippled, hobbling along in the margins of the European experiences of most of the curriculum.

While I an not nostalgic for the era of segregated schools, we should remember what was best in those schools and use that knowledge to assist in centering African-American children. Through observations, inquiry, and discussions, I've found that children who are centered in their own cultural information are better students, more disciplined, and have greater motivation for schoolwork.

A neighbor of mine often speaks to elementary classes in one of the most economically devastated communities in Philadelphia. He tells the young children, "You're going to be somebody." Later, the children are often heard saying to their peers, "I am going to be somebody."

It sounds so ridiculously corny to say this, but many of these children have never been touched at their psychological centers, never been reached in their cultural homes. They see school as a foreign place because schools do foreign things. Of course, many students master the "alien" cultural information, but others have great difficulty getting beyond the margin in which they have been placed.

## A DISLOCATED CULTURE

When it comes to facing the reality of social and cultural dislocation, teachers are on the front lines. They are among the first in the society to see the devastation that has occurred to the African-American child's spirit. If they've been teaching for more than 20 years, they have seen more and more students who seem to have been dislocated culturally, socially, and psychologically.

I contend that the movement of Africans from the continent of Africa was the first massive dislocation. The African people was physically separated from place, from culture, and from traditions. In the Americas, the African person was punished for remembering Africa. Drums were outlawed in most of the colonies soon after the arrival of large numbers of Africans. And since the drum was an instrument intimate to the cultural transmission of values and traditions, its disappearance was one of the great losses in the African-American psyche. Physical movement became in reality a precursor to a more damaging dislocation and decentering.

Numerous educational, social, religious, and political structures and institutions have tried to minimize the dislocation. But the despair has intensified since the '60s, because of questions of equity and lack of economic opportunities. Schools affected inasmuch as their students are filled with the emptiness of their own self-dislocation.

Indeed, schools have often contributed to the dilemma by encouraging African-American children to concentrate on mastering only information about the majority culture. These children may learn, but, without cultural grounding, the learning will have destroyed their sense of place. Increasing numbers of children abandon, in their minds, their own cultures in order to become like others culturally, hoping this will bring them closer to the white norms.

Schools also reinforce feelings of limited self-worth and cultural dislocation by ignoring the historical contributions of African Americans or devaluing their culture. The teacher who teaches American literature and does not refer to one African-American writer is doing a disservice to students of all cultural backgrounds. Equally so, the teacher who teaches music and does not mention one composition by an African American is de-centering the African-American child and miseducating the rest of the children.

Certainly some schools and teachers do better than others. And, in some cases, the child will get a sense of the importance of African and African-American contributions to human knowledge. But, for the most part, the African-American child fails to find a sense of identification with the information being presented.

The rise of cultural manifestations in the clothing, concepts, and motifs of African Americans is a direct result of the Afrocentric movement. Growing from a sense of the necessity for relocation, the reawakening within the African-American community portends positive developments on the educational level.

## ACHIEVING SUCCESS THROUGH CONGRUENCE

The role of the teacher is to make the student's world and the classroom congruent. Language, examples, and concept must be relevant. As all teachers know, this is a risky maneuver because relating classroom experience to outside experience depends to a large degree on the teacher's ability to know the student's cultural location as well as the subject. One does not have to constantly maintain congruence to be successful, however; one needs only to have an openness to the possibility that the student who is not of European ancestry may need to be centered in a particular way. Such centering techniques as examples from history, from books, from real life situations may also be helpful to other students.

Of course, the choice of examples is as important as knowing that you should have some centering devices. I once knew a white teacher in California who thought that he was being aware of his Mexican-American students by referring to an incident with "wetbacks" along the Texas-Mexico border. He thought the students would understand that he was trying to bring them into his discussion on the politics of the third world. When the students complained to him and the principal, the teacher was shocked and still could not see his mistake.

Therefore, teachers must read information from the cultures of their students. Should teachers have Cambodian students, then they must know something about Cambodians. Should teachers teach African-American students, then they must read information from African-American studies. This means that teachers must examine their lessons to see that they do not contain pejoratives about African-Americans or other ethnic groups. Otherwise, they will not be empowered with the class.

Ideally, an Afrocentric program should be infused throughout the class period, not merely tagged on or added as a once-a-month feature. Resources for teaching with an Afrocentric approach are available from two major sources: Africa World Press of Trenton, New Jersey, and the GRIO publishing company of Philadelphia. Materials include books for all grades, informational packets, Afrocentric Kits, bibliographies, and sample lesson plans.[1]

## TOWARD MULTICULTURAL CLASSROOMS

What do the principles of an Afrocentric approach look like in the classroom? In the Hatch Middle School in Camden, New Jersey, Principal Jan Gillespie and her teachers have organized the

Molefi Asante Multicultural Academy. Utilizing the resources of the student's families, the academy's emphasis is on centering the children, treating each person's heritage with respect, and studying to learn about each other as a way to knowledge about self and the world.

Beyond raising the level of self-confidence among its students, the academy has become a training ground for teachers interested in building respect for cultural diversity as a way to empower teachers. Students often do what they see their teachers doing and, consequently, as the best teachers soar like eagles, their students soar with them.

Our society is a composite of many ethnic and racial groups, and all students should be able to converse about the cultural diversity of the nation. Thus, both content and process are important in an Afrocentric approach to teaching. By combining the best elements of the centering process reminiscent of the segregation era with the best of today's more sophisticated techniques and equipment, we might find a new synthesis in our ability to teach children.

## NOTES

1. For information on staff development, contact Don McNeely at the National Afrocentric Institute, Temple University. The institute prepares educational trainers to conduct inservice training on Afrocentric curriculum.

# 3

# RACE, RACISM, ETHNICITY AND THE AFRICAN AMERICAN EXPERIENCE: MYTHS AND REALITIES

"I would never be of service to
anyone as a slave."

*Nat Turner*

# GENETIC AND CULTURAL DEFICIT THEORIES: TWO SIDES OF THE SAME RACIST COIN

*Caroline Hodges Persell*

Many social science concepts could be examined for their racist content and consequences, but I will consider only two here--the concept of IQ and the concept of "cultural deprivation." These two are selected, first, because they dominate explanations of differential school achievement. Considerable behavioral and social science research and debate has centered on them, and they largely set the terms in which questions are posed. Their implications are not confined to academic debates, however, since they significantly influence educational practices and processes, thus pervading almost every school in the United States. They are central to both educational explanations and experiences.

## THE CONCEPT OF IQ

The concept of IQ rests heavily upon standardized aptitude testing procedures. These have been severely criticized on the grounds of their content and administration (Carver, 1975; Hobson v. Hansen, 1967; McClelland, 1974; Roth, 1974; Samuda, 1975). These criticisms are summarized in Persell (1977). The only reasonable conclusion to draw is that standardized IQ or aptitude tests are extremely inappropriate means of ascertaining the "ability" of lower-class and minority children. Yet they persist. The prevalent use of test scores for educational decisions has resulted in the misclassification and mislabeling of thousands of minority students, with the apparent additional consequences of undereducation, lower

AUTHOR'S NOTE: *This research was carried out through partial support from the National Science Foundation Institutional Grant to New York University, the Institute on Pluralism and Group Identity, and the National Institute of Education. A version of this article was presented at the 1977 American Sociological Association national meeting in Chicago, Illinois. Portions appear in the author's book.* Education and Inequality *1977 by The Free Press, a division of Macmillan Publishing Co., Inc.*

*Journal of Black Studies*, Vol. 12, No. 1, September 1981. Copyright© 1981 Sage Publications, Inc. Reprinted by permission of Sage Publications, Inc.

teacher expectations, diminished self-esteem, and increased rates of dropouts (see Persell, 1977).

Given the unexamined assumption of IQ and aptitude testing, problems or predictive validity, test content, and procedure, the contention of IQ heritability seems to rest on shaky ground. But the difficulties with a largely genetic explanation for differential IQ and achievement test scores go beyond these points. Jensen (1969) claims that 80% of the variation in intelligence is determined by heredity. He bases his assertion partly on (1) studies of identical twins reared apart, (2) studies of similarities between identical twins and fraternal twins reared in the same home, and (3) studies of adoptive children. Because identical twins have exactly the same genetic makeup, observed differences in their IQs should be due to environment. Hence if only small differences in their IQs are noted, the results suggest that heredity plays a large part in determining IQ. Such an inference is warranted, provided that the separate environments in which the twins are reared are totally uncorrelated and that the differences between those environments are as great as those between the homes of unrelated children.

In the available twin studies (Burt, 1966; Juel-Nielsen, 1965; Newman et al., 1937; Shields, 1962), these assumptions are unsupported. Kamin (1974), who has critically examined these four major twin studies, finds that Burt's work is filled with verbal contradictions and arithmetic inconsistencies, and that it is marked by utter failure to provide information about crucial procedural detail.[1] Shield's study provides an appendix rich in procedural detail, which shows that many of the presumably separated twins were actually reared in highly related environments. The Juel-Nielsen twin studies failed to standardize the IQ tests used on a Danish population, and Newman and co-workers' studies used procedures for selecting the sample that rewarded twins who could provide accounts of how widely separated they were from an early age, so such reports might well have been exaggerated. After careful documentation of the flaws, I have only briefly indicated here, Kamin (1974) concludes that what limited evidence we can believe from these studies makes the case stronger for environment than the researchers or secondary sources suggest.

Studies of identical and fraternal twins reared together assume the same environments for both types of twins, but recent work shows that parents tend to treat identical twins more similarly than fraternal twins (Scarr, 1968, cited in Bronfenbrenner, 1972: 121). Therefore, estimates of the heritability of IQ based upon such evidence are compounded by environmental differences.

Burks's (1928) study of adoptive families was used by both Herrnstein (1973) and Jensen (1972, 1973) to support their position that intelligence is largely inherited. Critical analysis by Goldberg, however, finds that Jensen "thoroughly misrepresented the content and implications of the Burks study" (1974b:i) while Herrnstein's report of it is "substantially inaccurate" (1974a:i). Contrary to Jensen's assertions, Burks's sample was highly selective, her measures of environmental factors were limited, and widely different estimates of heritability can be obtained from her data (Goldberg, 1974a, 1974b). Hence the study does not lend strong support to a predominantly hereditarian view of intelligence.

Earlier, Jensen (1968: 50-51) argued that since the correlation between unrelated children reared in the same home is only .24, the remaining 76% of the variance in IQ is due entirely to heredity. The possibility that differences exist in parental treatment, school experiences, peer influences, and so forth, is ignored. Jensen relies heavily upon Honzik's (1957) finding that the correlation between the IQs of adopted children and their true mothers was .40, but was unrelated to their adoptive mother's educational level (Bronfenbrenner, 1972: 120). But the study from which this figure was taken (Skodak and Skeels, 1949) revealed that the selective placement of children of more intelligent mothers in better foster homes significantly confounded this correlation. The mean IQ of true mothers was 86, while the mean IQ of the foster children at age 12 was 106. Skodak and Skeels attributed this to the "maternal stimulation. . .and optimum security" offered in the foster homes, particularly in those where children showed the most dramatic gains (cited in Bronfenbrenner, 1972: 120). Thus here, too, the original study differs from the interpretation Jensen gives to it, and

the evidence suggests the considerable importance of environment in developing IQ.

The importance of environment is also apparent in twin studies conducted by Scarr-Salapatek (1971). She reports greater similarity (and higher heritability coefficients) between twins form advantaged rather than disadvantaged socioeconomic groups and in white rather than black families. From this study we can envision environment as a necessary condition for the development of genetic potential. Further, the type of environment may condition the relative role played by environment and heredity. (Newman et al., 1937, cited in Bronfenbrenner, 1972: 123).

Can we draw any conclusions from these studies about the heritability of IQ? Confirmed behaviorist Kamin (1974: 1) concludes, "there exists no data which should lead a prudent man to accept the hypothesis that IQ test scores are in any degree heritable." Most other psychologists and geneticists do not share his conclusion. Biologist Lewontin (1970) sees the heritability of IQ as ranging from .6 to .8, and differs with Jensen's acceptance of the higher range. Bronfenbrenner (1972) rejects the figure of .8, but feels that "there can be no question that genetic factors play a substantial role in producing individual difference sin mental ability" (p. 124). Loehlin et al. (1975) think it safe to conclude that the heritability index is neither 0 nor 1. The evidence and reasoning presented above suggest that some portion of IQ is transmitted genetically from parents to children, but that we do not know exactly how much. Nor do we know very much about how heredity and environment interact, except to know that such interaction is likely and probably very significant. But even if IQ were totally heritable, what does it matter? Traits (such as height) which are highly heritable can change dramatically in greatly different environments (for examples see Bronfenbrenner, 1972); Gage, 1972; Lewontin, 1970). Hence, even very high heritability does not mean total determination.

A critical questions remains. If IQ is heritable to some degree, can IQ differences between blacks and whites be primarily attributed to genetic differences between the races, as Jensen (1969) suggests? Lewontin (1970) notes that there is absolutely no evidence on this question. One reason is that the black and white populations are not genetically distinct in the United States. Berreman (1972) concludes that "socially defined populations perform differently on socially defined tasks with socially acquired skills, and this is attributed by Jensen to biology." (p. 391).

In addition to the problem noted by Berreman, Bronfenbrenner (1972) stresses the importance of economic and social environments in facilitating the development of genetic potential, noting that blacks face more economic handicaps. If differences between the races are largely environmental, then when blacks and whites are reared in nearly identical environments, differences in their IQs should tend to disappear. Evidence addressing this issue has been presented by Scarr-Salapatek and Weinberg (1975). When they compared black and white children adopted by white parents, they found that the mean IQ of the black children was 106, while that of the white children was 111, a difference of only 5 points compared with the average national difference of about 15 points. The black children, on the average, had lived with their adoptive families for fewer years than the white children. Among those blacks who were adopted at a younger age, the average IQ was 100. It appears that the longer black children live in "advantaged" environments, the higher are their IQ scores. Regarding the small remaining differences, genetic proponents would say they are due to genes, while environmentalists would argue that the total environments (including past histories, school experiences, peer contacts, societal context, and so on) are not necessarily equal for members of different races even when both are adopted by white families. On the basis of my own observations of life in the United States, I concur with this latter position.

If IQ and achievement differences between the races are environmental rather than genetic, what features of the environment are responsible? Are the differences due to the "cultural deprivation" of certain ethnic and economic groups, or are there other environmental features which account for differential IQ and achievement?

## CULTURAL DEPRIVATION

Standing in apparent opposition to the genetic school of thought and stemming from progressive and liberal political and educational ideologies is the environmental-developmental view. This position argues that individual inequalities are not genetic in origin, but sociocultural.

At least four models have been developed: the deficient, depraved, different, and bicultural. Most social policy is based upon the first two. At one extreme--in the *deficit*, or absence of culture, model--some individuals and their families are so deprived that they are seen as actually having no culture.

This view as reflected in the introduction, by Mrs. Lyndon B. Johnson, to a brochure about Head Start in 1965. The brochure declared that these children are "lost in a gray world of poverty and neglect [and that the program would attempt to] lead them into the human family. Circumstance has stranded them on an island of nothingness" (quoted in Stein, 1971: 182).

In a similar vein, Wax and Wax (1971) report an Anglo educational administrator's explanation of the problems of educating the Sioux Indian child: "The school gets this child from a conservative home, brought up speaking the Indian language, and all he knows is Grandma. His home has no books, no magazines, radio, television, newspapers--it's empty! He comes into school and we have to teach him everything!. . .The Indian child has such a *meager* experience? (pp. 129-130). This "vacuum ideology" of the Indians' educators rationalizes the educator's roles in the schools. Wax and Wax (1971: 132) claim this attitude places responsibility for the lack of academic achievement on the Indian child and family:

> Since the child is entering the school with an empty head, then surely it is a triumph if he is taught anything whatsoever. Moreover, the ideology justifies almost any activity within the school as "educational" (just as it derogates any communal activity outside the school); for if the child is presumed deficient in almost every realm of experience, then the task of the educator can properly encompass anything and everything. Finally, the ideology justifies the educators in their social and cultural isolation form the lives of the parents of their students; if the child actually had a culture including knowledge and values, then the educators ought properly to learn about these and build upon them, but if, on entering school, he is merely a vacuum, then what need to give attention to his home and community?

In the second model, the child possesses a culture of some kind, but that culture is pathogenic, as in the *culture of poverty* view. Low-income or minority children do not achieve in school and in life, in this argument, because of deficiencies in their home environment: disorganization in their family structure; inadequate child-rearing patterns; undeveloped language use assumed to lead to deficient cognitive development; maladaptive values, including inability to defer impulse gratification; personal maladjustment; and low self-esteem.

In the *cultural difference* model, the lower-class or minority child possesses a distinct, separate culture that is as valid in its own right as the mainstream culture. This view is advocated by Baratz and Baratz (1970), who feel that educational programs should recognize the existence of distinct cultures or distinct subcultures and build upon those unique cultural features to bridge the two cultures, hence facilitating the learning of "mainstream" culture. This viewpoint may be seen as the basis of many bilingual educational programs. But, according to Valentine (1971), the central theoretical weakness of the difference model is "an implicit assumption that different cultures are necessarily competitive alternatives, that distinct cultural systems can enter human experience only as mutually exclusive alternatives, never as intertwined or simultaneously available repertoires" (p. 141). Moreover, this assumption contains a potential assimilationist bias. If cultures are mutually exclusive, then at some point children must choose which culture they are going to keep. Furthermore, since minority cultures are always at a power disadvantage, it seems inevitable, to me, that power differentials will creep into the interactions between members of the different cultures. Thus, when I hear New York City school officials talking about "mainstreaming" Spanish-speaking children in bilingual programs, I believe that the very choice of terminology connotes the superior power and position of the white Anglo culture. In the cultural-difference model there is one monolithic, homogeneous culture that all blacks or all members of any ethnic group share. But, in fact, there is rich variation within such cultural groupings (Valentine, 1971: 141).

Because of the difficulties he sees in the cultural deficit and cultural difference models, Valentine (1971) proposes a bicultural model, which he sees as helping to make better sense out of ethnicity:

the collective behavior and social life of the black community is bicultural in the sense that each Afro-American ethnic segment draws upon both a distinct repertoire of standardized Afro-American group behavior and, simultaneously, patterns derived from the mainstream cultural system of Euro-American derivation. Socialization into both systems begins at an early age, continues throughout life, and is generally of equal importance in most individual lives. . .The idea of

biculturation helps explain how people learn and practice both mainstream culture and ethnic cultures at the same time [p. 143].

Many social and educational politics are predicated on the deficit model, the principal themes of which include weaknesses in the home environment, family structure, child-rearing patterns, values and attitudes, linguistic capability, and cognitive development. These assumptions are refuted by evidence pressed by Baratz and Baratz (1970), Bridgeman and Shipman (1975), Carroll (1964), Labov (1973), Liebow (1967), and Wax and Wax (1971), and summarized in Persell (1977). Where differences do appear in children of different races and classes, they are not demonstrable causes of school failure. Finally, and most importantly, the differences which appear are rooted in the economic, political, and racial inequalities of the society, not in the failings of individuals. By locating the source of deficiency and failure in individuals, however, rather than in economic and racial inequalities, both researchers and reformers demonstrate the degree to which racist ideologies saturate our society.

Ideological saturation is perhaps even more apparent when we consider certain shared assumptions and consequences of the environmental and genetic deficit theories. While to me their commonalities outweigh their apparent differences, the conflict between them is perceived as very intense and meaningful by their adherents (see Valentine and Valentine, 1975). However, this conflict may itself serve positive functions for dominant groups in society (see Coser, 1956), by diverting attention from the premises and consequences that both approaches share. The vast, and somewhat technical, literature bearing on both these issues contributes to this smokescreen. Then nature-nurture controversy rests upon common assumptions about the importance and validity of test performance. Both the genetic and the cultural-deficit adherents assume that IQ is important for "success" in life, and appear to agree with the necessity for early selection in schools. Moreover, they both fail to deal with a number of apparently anomalous empirical findings.

The genetic-racial explanation is undermined by the analysis of Mayeske (1972), who found that the relationship between ethnicity and achievement disappeared when certain economic and social factors were controlled. If the effect of ethnicity can be explained by social and cultural factors, achievement differences cannot be due to genes.

Second, the genetic interpretation cannot explain the finding that socioeconomic status is more important for academic attainment than is IQ (Bowles and Gintis, 1976: 31).

Third, the achievement gap between high- and low-status students appears to increase over time (for example, Coleman et al., 1966; Douglas, 1967; Harlem Youth Opportunities Unlimited, 1964; Hobson v. Hansen, 1967). If the difference between social groups is due to cultural or genetic attributes groups bring with them to school, the gap should be greatest when they first enter school and then gradually narrow over time. Instead, the differences increase with each passing school year. Both genetic and cultural-deficit interpretations have attempted to handle this by saying that there is an *interaction* between what children bring to school and their educational experiences, but this interpretation has not yet specified the forms such interaction takes.

Fourth, some minority children show substantial cognitive gains when they are taught intensively (Bereiter, 1967; Hawkridge et al., 1968; Heber, 1972). Moreover, contrary to Jensen's (1969) global assertion that "compensatory education has been tried and it apparently has failed" (p. 2), a number of well-designed compensatory education programs demonstrate remarkable achievement gains (See Hawkridge et al., 1968; Kiesling, 1970). If genetic or cultural deficits impair the learning capacity of minority children, such children would never be able to learn successfully. But this is patently false.

A final difficulty with these deficit explanations rests on their unstated premise that intellectual and educational inequality are the causes of racial and economic inequality. This instrumental-meritocratic assumption is not supported by available evidence. If the assumption that education is related to life achievements were correct, we should find a reduction or elimination of occupational and economic inequality in situations where educational inequalities have disappeared. Has this happened? The absolute amount of inequality in educational attainment has declined in the last 50 years as the compulsory education age has risen and as educational opportunities have expanded, both in the United States and in Western Europe. But this reduction of educational inequality has not resulted in less economic inequality in the United States (according to Chiswick and Mincer, 1972, cited in Bowles and Gintis, 1976:

34), in England (Kelsall et al., 1972), nor in Western Europe (according to Boudon, 1973). Where equalization of schooling has occurred, it has not been accompanied by economic equality.

General trends, then, indicate little or no reduction of economic inequality in the face of increasing educational equality, and special educational programs in the "War on Poverty" have had an equally low impact. In this systematic survey of such programs, Ribich (1968) found that the economic benefits of compensatory education were generally low, with a few exceptions (cited in Bowles and Gintis, 1976: 35). Both Ribich (1968) and Averch et al. (1974) conclude that giving money directly to the poor would have accomplished more income equalization than the educational programs themselves have achieved.

Bowles and Gintis also consider the question of whether the reduction of the education gap between white and black males has equalized income. Citing U.S. Census Bureau figures, they note that by 1972 the education gap between white and black males 25-34 years old had shrunk to 4% (compared to the 38% gap between whites and blacks of all age groups in 1940). Nevertheless, the income gap between black and white young men is 30%. Bowles and Gintis (1976: 35) conclude that while blacks certainly suffer from educational inequality, the real source of their inequality lies in their unequal economic and racial power.

In brief, the genetic and cultural-deficit adherents are united in their support of the instrumental-meritocratic assumption that IQ determines life position. They do not question the need for performance on tests designed to differentiate. And they are alike in their inability to explain a number of anomalous empirical findings. Given these commonalities, it is no surprise that they have many similar consequences as well.

Supporters of both theories place the locus of blame of failure on children and their families. They divert attention from the entire educational system and how it operates to produce certain outcomes, including failure. Moreover, they absolve educators from the responsibility for children's failures. Accepting these theories justifies whatever educators do and rationalizes their isolation from the students they teach. A rationale is provided for intervention by trained experts who understand the "problem" and how to deal with it. For these reasons, it would be hard for educators not to believe in either genetic or cultural deficits or both.

These concepts also have self-fulfilling potency. As teachers, schools, the larger society, and perhaps children and their parents come to believe them, these assumptions begin to ensure that the child will not learn. (How this works with respect to educational structures and teachers' expectations is considered in Persell, 1977). These results, in turn, tend to corroborate the validity of the models.

In addition to diverting blame for educational failure from teachers and schools to students and families and having self-fulfilling potency, these concepts offer compensatory education as the solution to racial and class inequalities, thereby diverting attention from structural differences in power and wealth. Such a solution is likely to take generations. So, while the cultural-deficit view is not quite so immutable a view of poverty as the hereditarian view, the eradication of poverty is still seen as a long, slow process. However, the process is seen as being possible within the existing system (usually as a result of economic growth). Therefore, it has strong appeal for liberals who deplore existing inequalities but equally dislike the idea of radical changes to eliminate racism and poverty. Both views leave unchallenged the existing structure of inequalities, requiring only that the credo of equal opportunity be met. As Willhelm (1973) and Valentine and Valentine (1975) have noted, "equal opportunity" is another slogan (ideology) for denying equality and justice to the racially and economically dispossessed. "Equal opportunity" is offered instead of the equalization of wealth and power (Valentine and Valentine, 1975: 127).

By focusing so exclusively on deficiencies within the child or family, the revived nature-nurture debate has also diverted attention from questions and research about how different kinds of children do learn and what kinds of cognitive skills they possess. Finally, these models leave unexamined questions about the nature of knowledge to be taught and learned. Adherents of the cultural-deprivation, deficit, and difference models, as well as the genetic-deficit model, posit a certain view of knowledge. Individuals are seen as lacking the mental capacity or the conceptual tools for comprehending the "bodies" or "forms" of knowledge which have historically come to count as school knowledge, external to the knower, to be mastered, rather than as a series of possibilities for making sense of one's life-world.

In contrast to these views are those espoused by progressive educators, who think education should be child-centered, with children learning form experience. This perspective, carried to its extreme, limits children to the experiences they have already had, rather than building upon those experiences to add new insights and understanding. This approach also tends to deny that nay knowledge is essential for all to participate in a common life. In a society or a world in which some have more knowledge and power than others, those without such knowledge may find themselves subject to the greater power of those with it. This issue requires that the symbolic value of education be distinguished form its use value. While certain groups acquire certain kinds of education for its status value, clearly certain kinds of educational experience provide people with skills or qualities they value. If the concept of "mastery learning" (Bloom, 1971), with its attendant optimism about human potential, is going to be significant, we need to focus more on what it is important to learn. Issues such as these are rarely debated, perhaps because of nature-nurture controversies.

The foregoing does not imply that intellectual or cultural differences between individuals are nonexistent. But what is done with these differences, how they are regarded and treated, may contribute to the educational and social outcomes observed. It is not necessary to deny the existence of initial differences to suggest that such differences themselves are not an adequate explanation of differential school achievement. Bloom (1971) has convincingly argued that mastery learning of basic skills in reading and arithmetic is possible for 90% of all children, including all but severely brain-damaged youngsters. In China and the USSR, where quite different concepts of individual intellectual abilities and cultural variations prevail, visitors report that "slow learners" are worked with until they learn (Bronfenbrenner, 1972; Stein, 1975).

As Feinberg (1975: 204) notes, the Chinese accept differences in ability but emphasize the similarity of growth processes. He quotes Galtung and Nishima's (n.d.) interview with leading members of the Revolutionary committee of a middle school in Peking:

Of course people differ in ability. But a student who is weak in one field may be strong in another. And these abilities are not something innate and unchanging. Abilities grow when they are made use of, through practice. . . .As abilities grow by being used they are not constant, and it does not make any sense to say that a given individual has so and so much ability. Hence we do not have final examinations and diplomas with grades on them in our school. We do make use of examination during the school year, as a pedagogical method, as a check on students and teachers.

If virtually all children in other societies which have different conceptions of the meaning of intellectual and cultural differences learn the substantive material required, and if so-called disadvantaged groups of children in the United States can demonstrate "mastery learning," then an alternative explanation of differential achievement needs to be considered. Differences in intelligence or culture may be related to the speed with which certain things can be learned, or to what are more effective pedagogical approaches. But, as currently formulated, the concept of intellectual deficits, whether due to genes or culture, helps to depress the intellectual growth of some children. One way this happens is through the development of separate and different educational structures, where students receive decidedly different educations (see Persell, 1977).

To conclude, the differences between the seemingly warring genetic and cultural deficit explanations of different school achievements are more apparent than real. They share many premises and consequences and are both marred by serious evidentiary flaws. Why,then, do they persist--indeed, prevail? The shared assumptions and consequences of the concept of intellectual inadequacy (whether due to genes or culture) benefits all of the more powerful participants in the situation. This concept serves the interests of wealth owners by deflecting attention from their dominant positions, justifies the superior rewards of the occupationally privileged, legitimates racial inequalities, and rationalizes the unequal results of the educational system. Therefore, diverse interest groups are apparently united in their support of one or the other of these racist concepts.

## NOTE

1. Recently, even greater doubt has bene cast upon Burt's work. In the London Sunday *Times* of October 24, 1976, the newspaper's medical correspondent, Oliver Gillie, indicated that he had been unable to locate any evidence that the coauthors of Burt's later papers. (Margaret Howard and J. Conway) had ever existed (Wade, 1976). Two weeks later the *Times* reported that a Ms. Howard had been a faculty member at London University during the 1930s,

but doubts remain about the other coauthor and about Burt's data, which have numerous internal inconsistencies.

## REFERENCES

Averch, H. A. et al. (1974) *How Effective is Schooling? A Critical Review of Research.* Englewood Cliffs, NJ: Educational Technology Publications.

Baratz, J. and S. Baratz (1970) "Early childhood intervention: the social scientific basis of institutionalized racism." *Harvard Educ. Rev.* 39: 29-50.

Bereiter, C. (1967) *Acceleration of Intellectual Development in Early Childhood.* ERIC Document No. 014332.

Berreman, G. D. (1972) "Race, caste, and other invidious distinctions in social stratification." *Race.* 13: 385-414.

Bloom, B. S. (1971) "Mastery learning," in J. H. Block (ed.) *Mastery Learning: Theory and Practice.* New York: Holt, Rinehart & Winston.

Boudon, R. (1973) *Education, Opportunity, and Social Inequality.* New York: John Wiley.

Bowles, S. and H. Gintis (1976) *Schooling in Capitalist America.* Ne York: Basic Books.

Bridgeman, B. and V. Shipman (1975) *Predictive Value of Measures of Self-Esteem and Achievement Motivation in Four- to Nine-Year-Old Low-Income Children.* ETS-Head Start Longitudinal Study, Princeton, NJ: Educational Testing Service.

Bronfenbrenner, U. (1972) "Is 80% of intelligence genetically determined?" pp. 188-127 in U. Bronfenbrenner (ed.) *Influence on Human Development.* Hinsdale, Il: Dryden Press.

Burks, B. S. (1928) "The relative influence of nature and nurture upon mental development: a comparative study of foster parent-foster child resemblance and true parent-true child resemblance," pp. 219-316 in G. M. Whipple (ed.) *National Society for the Study of Education: Twenty-Seventh Yearbook: Nature and Nurture, Part I, Their Influence on Intelligence.* Bloomington, Indiana.

Burt, C. (1966) "The genetic determination of differences in intelligence: a study of monozygotic twins reared together and apart." *British J. of Psychology* 57: 137-153.

Carroll, J. (1964) *Language and Thought.* Englewood Cliffs, NJ: Prentice-Hall.

Carver, R. P. (1975) "The Coleman report: using inappropriately designed achievement tests." *Amer. Educ. Research J.* 12: 77-86.

Chiswick, B. and J. Mincer (1972) "Time series changes in personal income inequality in the U.S." *J. of Political Economy* 80, No. 3, Part II.

Coser, L. (1956) *The Functions of Social Conflict.* New York: Free Press.

Douglas, J.W.B. (1968) *All Our Future.* London: MacGibbon.

Feinberg, W. (1975) "Educational equality under two conflicting models of educational development." *Theory and Society* 2: 183-210.

Gage, N. L. (1972) "I. Q. heritability race differences, and educational research." *Phi Delta Kappan* 53: 308-312.

Galtung, J. and F. Nishima (n.d.) *Learning from the Chinese.* University of Oslo, Norway. (mimeo)

Goldberg, A. S. (1974a) *Mysteries of the Meritocracy.* Madison: Institute for Research on Poverty, University of Wisconsin.

--- (1974b) Professor Jensen, Meet Miss Burks. Madison: Institute for Research on Poverty, University of Wisconsin.

*Harlem Youth Opportunities Unlimited* (1964) *Youth in the Ghetto.* New York: Haryou Act.

Hawkridge, D. G., A. B. Chalupsky, and A.O.H. (1968) *A Study of Selected Exemplary Programs for the Education of Disadvantaged Children, Part II.* Palo Alto, CA: American Institute for Research.

Heber, R. (1972) "An experiment in the prevention of cultural-familial mental retardation." pp. 478-493 *Environment, Intelligence and Scholastic Achievement.* Testimony to the Senate Committee on Equal Educational Opportunity. Washington, DC: Government Printing Office.

Herrnstein, R. J. (1973) *IQ in the Meritocracy.* Boston: Atlantic Little, Brown.

Hobson v. Hansen (1967) *Congressional Record.* June 21, 1967, 16721-16766.

Honzik, M. P. (1957) "Developmental studies of parent-child resemblance in intelligence. *Child Development* 28: 215-228.

Jensen, A. R. (1973) *Educability and Group Differences.* New York: Harper & Row.

--- (1972) *Genetics and Education.* New York: Harper & Row.

--- (1969) "How much can we boost I.Q. and scholastic achievement?" *Harvard Educ. Rev.* 39: 1-123.

Juel-Nielsen, N. (1965) "Individual and environment: a psychiatric-psychological investigation of monozygotic twins reared apart." *Acta Psychiatrica et Neurologica Scandinavica* (monograph supplement).

Kamin, L. J. (1974) *The Science and Politics of I.Q.* Hillsdale, NJ: Lawrence Erlbaum.

Kelsall, R. K., A. Poole, and A. Kuhn (1972) *Graduates: The Sociology of an Elite.* London: Methuen.

Kiesling, H. J. (1970) *A Study of Successful Compensatory Education Projects in California.* Rand Report No. ED 059 174. Santa Monica, CA: Rand Corp.

Labov, W. (1973) "The logic of nonstandard English," pp. 21-66 in N. Keddie (ed.) *The Myth of Cultural Deprivation.* Harmondsworth, England: Penguin.

Lewontin, R. C. (1970) "Race and intelligence." *Bull. of the Atomic Scientists* 26: 2-8.

Liebow, Elliot. (1967) *Tally's Corner.* Boston: Little, Brown.

Loehlin, J. C., G. Lindzey, and J. N. Spuhler (1975) *Race Differences in Intelligence.* San Francisco: W.H. Freeman.

McClelland, D. C. (1974) "Testing for competence rather than for 'intelligence,'" pp. 163-197 in A. Gartner, C. Greer, and F. Riessman (eds.) *The New Assault on Equality.* New York: Social Policy.

Mayeske, G. W. (1972) "On the explanation of racial-ethnic group differences in achievement test scores," pp. 542-556 in *Environment, Intelligence, and Scholastic Achievement: A Compilation of Testimony to the Select Committee on Equal Educational Opportunity.* United States Senate. Washington, DC: Government Printing Office.

Newman, H. N., F. N. Freeman, and K. J. Holzinger (1937) *Twins: A Study of Heredity and Environment.* Chicago: Univ. of Chicago Press.

Persell, C. H. (1977) *Education and Inequality.* New York: Free Press.

Ribich, T. I. (1968) *Education and Poverty.* Washington, DC: Brookings Institution.

Roth, D. R. (1974) "Intelligence testing as a social activity," pp. 143-217 in A. V. Cicourel et al. (eds.) *Language Use and School Performance.* New York: Academic Press.

Samuda, R. J. (1975) *Psychological Testing of American Minorities.* New York: Dodd, Mead.

Scarr, S. (1968) "Environmental bias in twin studies." *Eugenics Q.* 15: 34-40.

Scarr-Salapatek, S. (9171) "Race social class and IQ. *Science* 174: 1285-1295.

--- and R. A. Weinberg (1975) "When black children grow up in white homes . . ." *Psychology Today* 9: 80-82.

Shields, J. (1962) *Monozygotic Twins Brought Up Apart and Brought Up Together.* London: Oxford Univ. Press.

Skodak, M. and H. M. Skeels (1949) "A final follow-up study of one hundred adopted children." *J. of Genetic Psychology* 75: 85-125.

A. Stein (1975) *Talk about Chinese educational system, to New York City Teachers,* New York University.

--- (1971) "Strategies of failure." *Harvard Educ.* Rev. 41: 158-204.

Valentine C. A. (1971) "Deficit, difference, and bicultural models of Afro-American behavior." *Harvard Educ.* Rev. 41: 137-157.

--- and B. L. Valentine (1975) "Brain damage and the intellectual defense of inequality." *Current Anthropology* 16: 117-50.

Wade, N. (1976) "IQ and heredity: suspicion of fraud beclouds classic experiment." *Science* 194: 916-919.

Wax, M. L. and R. Wax (1971) "Cultural deprivation as an educational ideology," pp. 127-139 in E. B. Leacock (ed.) *The Cultural of Poverty: A Critique.* New York: Simon and Schuster.

Willhelm, S. M. (1973) "Equality: America's racist ideology," in J. Ladner (ed.) *The Death of White Sociology.* New York: Vintage.

*Caroline Hodges Persell received her B.A. from Swarthmore College and her M.A. and Ph.D. in sociology from Columbia University. She worked for four years as a student counselor and scholarship scout at the National Scholarship Service and Fund for Negro Students. During that time she traveled around the United States visiting high schools and colleges. Dr. Persell is Associate Professor of Sociology at New York University, where she taches both graduate and undergraduate students. She is the author of numerous monographs, articles, and books, and is currently completing a book entitled* Understanding Society *aimed at introductory sociology students. She is also conducting research on differences between public and private schools.*

# ETHNICITY THE NEW IDEAL

*Itabari Njeri*

Back in what some think were the good old days, Henry Ford ran his company's English Melting Pot School.

Graduation was a public spectacle in which the automaker's foreign-born employees, dressed in Old World Costumes and carrying signs noting their birthplace, marched into a large, kettle-shaped prop labeled "Melting Pot." Moments later, they would emerge in business suits and waving American flags. - *America, circa 1916.*

## AMERICA, CIRCA 1991:

Jerry Yoshitomi, director of the Japanese-American Community Center, Stanford-educated and married to an Irish-Catholic American, recalls a recent family New Year's Day in Los Angeles.

"We woke up and went to mass at St. Brigid's, which has a black gospel choir. Before or after, we had coffee and doughnuts somewhere. Then we came (to the center) for the Japanese Oshogatsu New Year's program and saw Buddhist archers shoot arrows to ward off evil spirits for the year.

"Then we ate Japanese rice cakes as part of the service and listened to a young Japanese-American storyteller. On the way home, we stopped in Chinatown for a lunch at King Taco."

If you think what Yoshitomi described is another example of the melting pot, think again. Many Americans are. Blending in was once considered the ideal. But as the racial and ethnic nature of the nation has changed, so has the ideal.

Throughout the nation, multiculturalism--looking at the world through the eyes of more than one culture--is the new end-of-the-millennium buzzword.

The notion of the melting pot has seen "an astonishing repudiation," said historian Arthur Schlesinger Jr. in the Wall Street Journal last year.

"The contemporary ideal is not assimilation but ethnicity. We used to say *'e pluribus unum.'*

Now we glorify *'pluribus'* and belittle *'unum.'* The melting pot yields to the Tower of Babel.

We have heard about the demographic future--seen it in Los Angeles where 90 foreign languages are spoken in the public schools--but no one is sure how to define it.

Some say we should call it multiculturalism, or cultural pluralism--the politically correct term on many college campuses.

Or is it a salad? A mosaic? A patchwork quilt? Or is it possible to hold onto the beloved melting pot and just admit there are new ingredients in the stew?

The questions over how we define ourselves are triggered by population shifts that will lead us to what demographers say will be the new majority in 21st-century American: people of color.

A Time magazine article last year proclaimed: "By 2056, when someone born today will be 66 years old, the 'average' U.S. resident will trace his or her descent to Africa, Asia, the Hispanic world, the Pacific Islands, Arabia--almost anywhere but white Europe."

This already is a reality in Southern California, where ethnic and racial "minorities" compose the majority.

As 1991 begins, interpretations of multiculturalism vs. the melting pot are contentious and contradictory, especially among scholars on college campuses.

What must yield, said literary critic and historian Henry Louis Gates, is the "antebellum aesthetic position, where men were men, and men were white, when scholar-critics were white men, and when women and persons of color were voiceless, faceless servants and laborers, pouring tea and filling brandy snifters in the boardrooms of old boys' clubs.

The melting pot has its defenders.

"I subscribe to the notion of the melting pot," said Karen Klein, a professor of English literature at Brandeis University and the director of a Ford Foundation-funded project to diversify the university's curriculum. It is one of 19 such projects nationwide funded by the foundation. "But the melting pot concept has never meant that we give up our sense of pluralistic identity," she said.

But isn't that exactly what the concept represents?

"Yes," she said, "but I am trying to redefine it."

Melting pot salvagers seek to minimize what Harvard University professor Werner Sollors acknowledged is "sinister dominance."

But there is a flip side to the smelting notion, said Sollors, an expert on Afro-American literature and ethnic images in American literature as well as the author of "Beyond Ethnicity"--which provided the Ford Motor Co. Melting Pot School anecdote.

"What I like about the melting pot better than those other terms is the process that is implicit in it"--a culture constantly in change: "Japanese technology is sold by Hasidic Jews on 47th Street to imaginative artists who . . . living in Harlem or Brooklyn use this technology to create rap," which becomes a national music that is exported.

The questions being raised are new, but the fundamental issues have been central to American life for more than 200 years.

Independence, freedom, conformity, success, community, optimism, cynicism, idealism, materialism, technology, nature and work have been the pivotal issues in the nation's cultural dialogue, the Stanford University's George Spindler and his wife Louise conclude in their book, "The American Cultural Dialogue and Its Transmission."

"The balancing of assimilation and preservation of identity is constant and full of conflict," they write.

Those arguing against pluralism have to recognize the need to expand America's political, economic and social base with new blood, new ideas, new cultural styles.

However, no nation can survive if it is truly pluralistic.

"Large groups of people with really separate identities and languages . . . wouldn't be a nation," Spindler said. "The fact that the Soviet Union is breaking up right now is a case in point."

Said Spindler: "I have real questions as to whether we are going to survive as a society, because it is not just a matter of ethnic combat. It is combat between pro-lifers and pro-choicers, between environmentalist and exploiters and developers and so on. There isn't an area of American life where there isn't a polarized opposition."

Power implies access to economic, political and social resources, says sociologist Margaret L. Andersen of Newark. "By social resources I mean how people are perceived, how they are valued, what significance their culture is seen as having."

Linda Wong, a California Tomorrow executive, said she looked at affirmative action, diversity and cultural pluralism by turning to the civil rights movement.

"Clearly, that was the most coherent social movement to bring issues of race, ethnicity and cultural pluralism to the forefront of American life," she said. Laws were enacted "requiring equal opportunity and equal access for disenfranchised peoples in terms of gender, race, ethnicity, age and religion."

"We (tried to) eliminate differences based on gender, race or ethnicity," said Wong, a former practicing attorney. The philosophy then was "colorblindness."

But did colorblindness lead to equal opportunity, equal access? It seldom did, she said. Consequently, affirmative-action policies were developed and goals and timetables were created.

"And what we found," said Wong--even in cases where benchmarks were reached--"was that we could not keep the women, we could not keep the blacks or the Latinos hired under those affirmative-action programs."

Why? Because whether it was in the private or public sector "they had to accommodate themselves to a dominant culture"--Euro-Americans in general and Anglo, middle-class male sin particular--"with its own set of values and conduct deemed to be acceptable for success."

Women, blacks, Hispanics and Asians couldn't accommodate themselves to this environment and found they were hitting the proverbial glass ceiling.

"Many times, they found that their values, their conduct, their behavior was misinterpreted by those belonging to the dominant culture in those organizational settings. So they left (the organization)," she said.

Increasingly, "as we move into this third generation of understanding, people prefer to use the term diversity," Wong said. It doesn't automatically conjure associations with affirmative action, she pointed out.

Education equals participation and success, said George Spindler. "It's a simple equation. And if whites continue to have the best, the longest . . . the most professional kinds of educational experience," they are going to stay in control.

But, Spindler added: "If you have a large mass of blacks or Latinos who are educated, or even a smaller group who are superiorly educated, eventually this inequality is going to break down. But for most groups, it takes perhaps three generations to attain that competitive socioeconomic status."

Potentially the most significant phenomenon in the next decades will be the emergence of the multi-racial population.

The discussion generated by this new multi-ethnic generation is going to stimulate a decades-long debate--one that may force Americans to confront the myths that surround race and ethnicity in the United States.

What the coming multicultural, polyethnic, pluralistic--unarguably diverse--America will be no one knows for certain. There are no models anywhere for what is happening here.

# BLACKS SHOULD EMPHASIZE THEIR ETHNICITY

*Manning Marable*

America's society is more thoroughly integrated today in terms of race relations than at any point in its entire history. Since 1964, the number of black elected officials has increased from barely 100 to 7,000. The number of African Americans enrolled in colleges and universities has quadrupled; the number of black-owned banks and financial institutions has increased tenfold; the percentage of African Americans in the middle class and professions has significantly expanded.

Perhaps the most stringing changes in public perceptions of race have occurred in popular culture, social institutions, and the media. American music, theater, public education, sports, and the arts are now heavily influenced by the rhythms and patterns of African-American life. Black images in commercial advertisements are commonplace. Blacks remain underrepresented in the ownership and management of cultural and social institutions, but ware nearly omnipresent as employees and prominent public representatives, particularly in the state sector.

## PROBLEMS PERSIST

Despite these symbols of racial advancement, in recent years incidents of racist harassment, vigilante violence, and social disruption have escalated. Hundreds of African-American students have been victimized by intimidation or outright threats on university campuses across the country. White youth are forming "white student unions" at several institutions to push back affirmative action and the preferential recruitment of minorities as faculty and students.

Civil rights organizations point to a disturbing pattern of legal indictments and political harassment of black elected officials, and to the growth of violent incidents aimed against black-owned

Reprinted by permission from *Sojourners Magazine*, August/September 1990. "Blacks Should Emphasize Their Ethnicity," by Manning Marable. Sojourners, Box 29272, Washington, D.C. 20017. Suzanne Ascher Walker, Reprints Permissions.

property and individuals in urban areas. Racial tensions in cities such as New York have culminated in a series of massive public demonstrations by both blacks and whites, with both sides accusing the other of "racism." A quarter century removed from the historic Civil Rights Act of 1964, which abolished legal racial discrimination in public accommodations, and the Voting Rights Act of 1965, which extended the electoral franchise to all Americans regardless of race, the goal of racial harmony and integration seems more distant than ever before.

What explains the racial paradox, the emergence of a black middle class and acceptance of black cultural achievements within the context of a deepening crisis of race relations in the society as a whole? Any analysis of the contemporary status of African Americans in the United States must begin with analysis of the accomplishments and the contradictions of the civil rights movement of the 1950s and 1960s.

The leaders of the desegregation social protest movement a generation ago mobilized millions with one simple demand--"freedom." In the context of the "Jim Crow" or racially segregated society of the South in the post-World War II period, freedom meant the elimination of all social, political, legal, and economic barriers that forced black Americans into a subordinate status.

Implicit in the demand for desegregation were several assumptions. Desegregation would increase opportunities for blacks in business, government, and society overall. Desegregated educational institutions would promote greater racial harmony and understanding between young people from different ethnic communities, which in turn would promote residential integration. Affirmative action policies, the strategy of compensating for past discrimination against minorities, would gradually increase the numbers of African Americans, Hispanics, and other people of color in administrative and managerial positions.

It was assumed that as African Americans escaped the ghetto and were more broadly distributed across the social class structure and institutions of society, racial tensions and bigotry would decline in significance. As blacks were more thoroughly integrated into the economic system, it was thought, the basis for racial confrontation would diminish.

The thesis above was fundamentally flawed in several key respects. First, desegregation did not benefit the entire black community uniformly. Black professionals and managers, those who had attended colleges and technical schools, were the principal beneficiaries. Working-class African Americans also benefitted: Incomes increased as new opportunities were created in upper-income levels of the labor force, and their children for the first time had access to higher education.

## RACE AND CLASS

But opportunity in a capitalist society is always a function of social class position, which means ownership of capital, material resources, education, and access to power. For the unemployed, the poor, and those without marketable skills or resources, for those whose lives were circumscribed by illiteracy, disease, and desperation, "race" continued to occupy a central place as a factor in their marginal existence.

Legal desegregation contributed to the popular illusion that the basis for racial discrimination and conflict no longer existed. The abolition of racially separate residential districts, hotels, schools, and other public institutions convinced many white Americans that the "Negro question" had finally been firmly resolved. Black American leaders such as Martin Luther King Jr. had always insisted upon the achievement of a "colorblind society." The passage of antidiscriminatory legislation had eliminated all basic impediments to the socioeconomic and cultural advancement of African Americans, according to this view.

Thus, as many black leaders continued to speak out against current social injustices, or pointed to the growing economic disparities between blacks and the majority of middle-class whites, their complaints were easily dismissed as anachronistic, self-serving rhetoric. By raising the issue of racism, many whites no believed, blacks themselves must be "racist."

The American civil rights leadership and the black political establishment now find themselves in a quandary largely of their own making. Their failure to develop a body of politics representing a qualitative step beyond the discourse and strategies of the civil rights movement of a generation ago is directly linked to the poverty of their theoretical outlook.

## RACE AND ETHNICITY

The central theoretical and conceptual weakness of this largely middle-class, African-American leadership is its inability to distinguish between *ethnicity* and *race*, and to apply both terms to the realities of American capital, power, and the state. African-American people are both an ethnic group (or more precisely, a national minority) and a racial group. Our ethnicity is derived from the cultural synthesis of our African heritage and our experiences in American society, first as slaves and subsequently as sharecroppers, industrial laborers, the unemployed, and now as the core of the post-industrial urban underclass in the semi-destroyed central cities of North America.

### Integration and the Next Generation

Unlike the generation of blacks who reached maturity before, and during, the early '70s, my generation has no memory of credible black leaders, such as Malcolm X or Martin Luther King Jr. Nor do we have a relationship with those indigenous institutions, such as the black church, that developed as a consequence of racism and segregation. The debilitating effects of racism and segregation notwithstanding, blacks had been able to instill a sense of self and community. But the practice of integration created the illusion of equality with the wider culture, effectively wresting control of the black freedom movement by holding it hostage to federal good will and weakening or destroying those institutions that influenced blacks' worldview.

As black scholar W.E.B. DuBois observed nearly a century ago, black Americans are both African and American, "two souls, two thoughts, two unreconciled strivings; two warring ideals in one dark body, whose dogged strength alone keeps it from being torn asunder." This central duality is at the core of our ethnic consciousness, forming the fundamental matrix for all expressions of African-American music, art, language patterns, folklore, religious rituals, belief systems, the structure of our families, and other culture manifestations and social institutions. Blackness in the cultural context is the expression and affirmation of a set of traditional values, beliefs, rituals and social patterns, rather than physical appearance or social class position.

Race is a totally different dynamic, rooted in the structures of exploitation, power, privilege. "Race" is an artificial social construction that was deliberately imposed on various subordinated groups of people at the outset of the expansion of European capitalism into the Western Hemisphere five centuries ago. The "racial" consciousness and discourse of the West was forged above the bowels of slave ships, as they carted their human cargoes into the slave depots of the Caribbean and the Americas. The search for agricultural commodities and profits from the extreme exploitation of involuntary workers deemed less than human gave birth to the notion of racial inequality.

In the United States, a race is frequently defined as a group of individuals who share certain physical or biological traits, particularly phenotype (skin color), body structure, and facial features. But race has not scientific validity as a meaningful biological or genetic concept. Beyond this, the meaning of race shifts according to the power relations between the racial groups.

For instance, in apartheid South Africa, Japanese people were considered by the regime as "white," whereas Chinese were classified as being "colored." In Brazil, a person of color could be "white," "mulatto," or "black," depending upon the individual's vocation, income, family connections, and level of education . . .

## RACE IS SITUATIONAL

Race, therefore, is not an abstract thing, but an unequal relationship between social aggregates, which is also historically specific. The subordinated racial group finds itself divorced from the levers of power and authority within the socioeconomic order. The oppressed racial group's labor power, its ability to produce commodities, is systematically exploited, chiefly through abnormally low wage rates. It is denied ownership of the major means of production. It lacks full access to sources of capital and credit. The racial group's political status is marginal or peripheral, as full participation and legislative representation are blocked.

Finally, dominant and subordinate racial categories are constantly reinforced in the behaviors and social expectations of all groups by the manipulation of social stereotypes and through the utilization of the legal system to carry out methods of coercion. The popular American myth of the Negro's sexual promiscuity, prowess, and great physical attributes, for example, was designed to denigrate the intellectual abilities and the scientific and cultural accomplishments of blacks . . .

To be white in the United States says nothing directly about an individual's culture, ethnic heritage, or biological background. A society created to preserve "white culture" either would be very confused or tremendously disappointed. White culture does not exist. White power, privileges and prerogatives within capitalist society do exist.

## WHITENESS IS POWER

Whiteness is fundamentally a statement of the continued patterns of exploitation of subordinated racial groups which create economic surpluses for privileged groups. To be white means that one's "life chances," in the lexicon of American sociologists, improve dramatically. Any white person, regardless of personal appearance, income, or education, usually finds it much easier to establish credit, purchase better homes, and initiate businesses than the average non-white person.

To be white in the United States statistically means that police officers rarely harass you, that your life expectancy is significantly longer than non-whites, and that your children will probably inherit property and social position. Blackness in American racial terms has meant a hundred different insults, harassments, and liabilities experienced daily, living with the reality that a black university graduate will make less money in his or her lifetime than the average white graduate of secondary school; experiencing higher death rates due to the absence of adequate health care facilities in one's neighborhood; accepting the grim fact that, in 1990, a young white American male's statistical likelihood of becoming a victim of homicide is roughly one chance in 186, while a young black male's statistical chances are one in 20.

The ambiguity and confusion concerning the crucial differences between race and ethnicity within the United States are directly attributable to the uneven merger of the two concepts as they related to black Americans. People of African-American nationality, whose cultural patterns and social traditions were derived in part from Africa, were overdetermined externally as the subordinate racial category. Physical appearance and phenotype were convenient, if not always predictable, measures for isolating the members of the oppressed racial group, "the blacks."

For white Americans this racial-ethnic overdetermination did not occur for several reasons. White Americans originated from many different countries and cultures, ethnic intermarriage was frequent, and the rigid economic and legal barriers that confined blacks behind the walls of the ghetto usually did not exist. By the mid-20th century, millions of white Americans had no clear ethnic or cultural identity beyond vague generalization. Their sense of aesthetics was derived largely from the lowest cultural common denominator—the mass media and the entertainment industry.

Whites' racial identity was ruptured from ethnicity, and was only politically or socially relevant as it affected issues of direct personal interest—such as whether a Hispanic or African-American family intended to purchase a home in their neighborhood, or whether their employer planned to initiate an affirmative-action hiring program for minorities. Whiteness was fundamentally a measure of personal privilege and power, not a cultural statement.

## ABSORBING BLACK CULTURE

White capitalist America's cultural vacuity, its historical inability to nurture or sustain a vibrant "national culture," drawing upon the most creative elements of its various ethnic constituencies, helps to explain the present paradox of desegregation. Millions of white Americans, devoid of their own cultural compass, have absorbed critical elements of African-American music, dance, literature, and language. They now accept black participation in professional athletics and extend acclaim to African-American film stars and entertainers. In a desperate search for collective identity, whites have mimicked blacks in countless ways, from the black-faced minstrels of the 19th century to the contemporary white musical groups singing reggae and rap.

But white's affinity and tolerance for blackness are largely cultural, not racial. Many whites have learned to appreciate African-derived elements of music, dance, and religious rituals, but would not endorse the sharing of power or material privileges, which would undermine the stratification of race . . .

## INTEGRATION WITHOUT UNDERSTANDING

The central characteristic of race relations in the 1990s is "interaction without understanding." White students purchase the latest taped recordings of black singers and cheer the latest exploits of black athletes, while they bitterly reject the imposition of course requirements mandating classes in African-American politics, history, or literature. White employers encourage the recruitment of black junior executives in their firms, but would shudder at the prospect of minorities moving into their exclusive neighborhoods or joining their elite private clubs. White religious leaders espouse pious platitudes about ethnic understanding and racial reconciliation, while doing relatively little to bring their white, upper-class congregations into close contact with the gritty problems of the ghetto. Racial integration, within the framework of capitalism, has produced the symbols of progress and the rhetoric of racial harmony without the substance of empowerment for the oppressed.

Perhaps the greatest irony in this post-civil rights situation is that African Americans born after 1960 frequently have great difficulty identifying the realities of contemporary oppressive race and class structures because of the transformation of white racial etiquette. No white politician, corporate executive, or religious leader now uses the term "nigger" in public. African Americans coming to maturity in the 1980s and 1990s have never personally experience Jim Crow segregation. They cannot express how they feel to be denied the right to vote because their electoral rights are guaranteed by law. They have never personally participated in street demonstrations, boycotts, picket lines, and seizures of government and academic buildings. Few have tasted the pungent fumes of tear gas or felt the fiery hatred of racist mobs. The absence of a personal background of struggle casts a troubled shadow over the current generation of black Americans who are poorly equipped to grapple with the current complexities of racial and class domination.

## CULTURAL LITERACY

Integration also crippled African Americans in the context of their "cultural literacy." Under traditional racial segregation, the strict barriers that were established forced a wide variety of professions and social classes into intimate interaction. Black physicians had to look for patients in the black community. African-American attorneys depended upon black clients. Black storeowners looked to blacks for patronage.

Black social organizations, civic associations, and religious institutions reflected the broad spectrum of social class, from custodians and sanitation workers to school teachers and civil servants. The sense of shared suffering and collective cooperation provided the basis for an appreciation for the community's racial identity and heritage. African-American history was taught in segregated schools and churches, and pictures of prominent black leaders were frequently displayed.

Denied access to the white media, blacks established their own network of race-oriented publications. A separate cultural and artistic underground developed in the cities, creative enclaves that produced the classical legacy of modern jazz and the urban blues.

But as the racial boundaries were liberalized and as white public discourse became largely race-neutral, the terrain for black cultural awareness diminished. Young African-Americans no longer were forced to confront their ethnicity or cultural history. In effect, we are witnessing the development of a substantial segment of the African-American population, which is "post-black-"without any cultural awareness, historical appreciation, or political commitment to the traditions, customs, values and networks that have been the basis for black identity in America . . .

The challenges of race, class, and power confronting black Americans are far more complicated than Martin Luther King Jr. every anticipated when he stood on the steps of the Lincoln Memorial at the August 1963 March on Washington, D.C., delivering his "I Have a Dream" speech. The objective should not be the realization of a utopian, colorblind society, but a democratic social order that seeks to achieve several goals.

## Integration into What?

Integration begs the question--integration into what? What kind of society prefers selective assimilation to transformation? The answer is one which still seeks to cover-over the fundamental questions of justice and compassion. Integration has served that cover-up.

The reign of insatiable materialism over human dignity in American society destroys the souls of rich and poor alike. And the acceptance of an economic system based on theft from the poor at home and around the world will continue to keep masses of people at the bottom. In a white-controlled society, a disproportionate number of those will be people of color.

First, democratic principles must be extended from the electoral system into the structures of the economy and social order, making a job or guaranteed income a human right. Also, public health-care facilities, housing, and access to transportation must be available to all. Finally, ethnicity must be distinctly separated from race, which would preserve America's diverse cultural and ethnic heritages while abolishing all forms of institutional discrimination that are justified by the perpetuation of racial categories. We must destroy "race" without uprooting culture and ethnicity.

# SOCIALIZATION AND RACISM: THE WHITE EXPERIENCE

*Rutledge M. Dennis*

✳ READ ✳

One of the first researchers to lament the paucity of studies on the effects of racism on the white majority was Clark (1955). Given the absence of data on this problem, he suggested that we make use of "the available findings as a basis for further research into the likely effects of discrimination on the personality of members of the dominant or privileged group." Young (1969: 87) said essentially the same thing, in a voice that reflected the atmosphere of urgency during the late 1960s, when he stated that "perhaps sociologists will oblige us by dropping their preoccupation with the alleged pathologists of black America and study the very real, corroding sickness of white America."

Despite the urgings of Clark and Young, we have not yet made a dent in this area. This chapter uses what little information is available to analyze the consequences of racism for white children and the white population. It relies mainly, though not exclusively, on autobiographical writings. I am aware of the problems of using autobiographical accounts, but believe that recollections of personal odysseys provide us with an especially vivid view of the peculiarities of race mirrored in the accounts of those who have sought to explain its impact on them. I also believe that information from any and all sources must be exploited if we are to foster breakthroughs of comprehension in areas as obviously undeveloped as this.

## RACISM AND SOCIETY

The socialization of children is designed to inculcate values, traditions, standards, and codes of behavior. It tells the child what "mommy and daddy like or don't like" and what is "good" and what is "bad." he major question posed in this chapter is this: What happens to families and children, and the white population in general,

Dennis, Ruthledge M., *Socialization and Racism: The White Experience Impacts of Racism on White America*, 1989 pg. 71-85. Copyright © 1981 by Sage Publications, Inc. Reprinted by permission.

when an ideology of racial supremacy becomes a main socializing motif in person-to-person and group-to-group interaction in multiracial and multicultural societies?

In order to understand the dynamics and the impact of racism, we must view it as a faith--and, for the American society, a permanent belief system rather than a transient apparition. Its longevity has been tried and tested. It now occupies a place in the American value pantheon alongside such concepts as democracy and liberty, though one would ordinarily view this combination as contradictory.

Important in any assessment of racism in the United States is the degree to which it fills the interstices of the society. Historic legal restraints to social equality, and the ensuing encapsulation of Blacks as "social" as well as "biological" beings, meant that early in the American experience the stage was set to look at the possible impact of racism on the majority. Any evaluation of the impact of racism on Whites must consider the economics of slavery and Jim Crowism (materialism), as well as the ideology and ethos of racism (idealism), and combinations of the two. Racism is diffused and generalized throughout the American society. It both helps to shape and is shaped by social institutions. Obviously Afro-Americans and other racial groups have been negatively affected by racism, but the effects of racism for Whites may well be no less devastating and debilitating, both individually and institutionally.

People engage in racist behavior because they are reasonably sure that there is support for it within their society. In the second section of this chapter I will discuss how racism (1) supports irrationality, (2) inhibits intellectual growth, and (3) negates democracy. I shall emphasize again and again the degree to which racism not only distorts the personal vision of the individual White, but likewise distorts a larger collective vision. As autobiographical sketches on race and racism show, the almost complete immersion of individuals in a social network of racism makes it difficult for any White to avoid its influence.

## THE FAMILY AND EARLY RACIAL EDUCATION--THE RITES OF PASSAGE

> From the time little Southern (white) children take their first step they learn their ritual, for Southern tradition leads them through its intricate movements . . . These ceremonials in honor of white supremacy, performed from babyhood, slip from the conscious mind down deep into muscles and glands and become difficult to tear out . . . Southern tradition taught well: we learned our way of life by doing. You never considered arguing with the teacher, because you could never see her. You only felt the iron grip of her hand and knew you must go where all the other children were going. And you learned never, never, to get out of step (Smith, 1961: 96).

Given the importance of the family in the life cycles of individuals, it is informative to view the process by which negative racial values and attitudes become manifest there. A dissection of the *process* by which families teach children the "proper" racial behavior highlights the degree to which group antagonisms, rather than being "natural" and "normal," are, to the contrary, taught by parents and relatives.

According to Clark (1955; 25-26), children's attitudes toward Blacks are determined chiefly "not by contact with Negroes but by contacts with the prevailing attitudes toward Negroes." Clark concludes that it is the *idea* of Blacks, rather than any particular characteristics of Blacks, that evokes hostility toward them. He adds that American parents "rarely . . . deliberately teach their children to hate members of another racial . . . group," but racist views are transferred in "subtle and sometimes unconscious ways." Finally, Clark asserts that the process by which racial intolerance is transmitted from parents to children "is frequently forgotten by parents." But if Clark is correct about parents forgetting the racial rituals they force upon their children, the testimonies of their children reveal that they (the children) often have not forgotten.

## EFFECTS OF RACISM ON WHITE CHILDREN

I wish now to explore autobiographical sources to illustrate four effects of racist socialization on white children: (1) ignorance of other people; (2) development of a double social psychological consciousness; (3) group conformity; and (4) moral confusion and social ambivalence.

*Ignorance of other people.* Many years ago the sociologist W.E.B. DuBois (Dennis, 1979( used such words as "behind the veil," "looking out from a dark cave," and "entombed souls" to describe the effects of segregation on Blacks. These same terms apply equally well to the white population. One of the myths governing racial inequality in American society is the idea that Whites "know" Blacks. But, as we noted, Clark maintains that Whites "know" and understand an "idea" of the Black. They themselves have carefully constructed and nurtured this idea--or these ideas. Hence, they have felt little need to critically analyze assumptions about Blacks--"The answers were already in."

DuBois's (1966) proposal to negate the ideas commonly held by Whites about Blacks constituted the core of his proposal to launch a systematic study of black life.

Speaking of his childhood, Canzoneri (1965) said that after being schooled in the mythology of race, Whites were sure that they had the inside dope on Blacks and their place in the society. As Canzoneri described it: "Nobody had to say so, everybody *knew* it, and accepted it" (italics added). "*Knowing*" Blacks thus displaced any search to understand the complexities of black life. It allowed Whites to simply *fill in the blanks* about Blacks.

Boyle (1962: 30) wrote of what she and her young peers "knew" of Blacks: "Their virtues as well as their faults were fixed and exaggerated in my mind. Blacks were artistic and creative, content in hardship and ill fortune, loyal, faithful, and warm." Zinn (1964) expressed a similar sentiment when he indicated that this "knowledge" of Blacks was the knowledge passed on to him by his grandmother. Had he been asked, he said, to expand about Blacks, he would "probably have quoted verbatim remarks about 'niggers' made by my grandmother."

Ovington (1947) gave us yet another example of the blindness that racism fosters in white children. Citing her experience as a settlement worker in New York City, she described taking fifteen boys representing eight nationalities on a park tour where a black woman sat and talked. "Suddenly, as at a signal every boy jumped on is feet and yelled, 'Nigger, Nigger, Nigger!'" She does not attribute this behavior to the racism of the boys, but rather to the fact that "their yelling was a ritual that they had learned."

Finally, Smith (1961) wrote of the lies about skin color and culture that 'nice" white people propagated, lies calculated to sow fear and deepened ignorance about Blacks by young Whites. But the lies were also intended to be building blocks in the construction of a self-sustaining racial mythology that would be a constant reminder to Whites of their "superiority" and to Black so their "inferiority." As Whites reveal the processes by which they *overcame* their ignorance, one sees them moving from "knowing" Blacks to knowing Blacks, from deracialization to reracialization, toward a more "objective" approach to race with a clearer understanding of the role of race and culture in society. Halsey (1946) analyzed this ignorance that is the child of racism, and she also dissected one of the consequences of it: Racism deprives Whites of getting to know Blacks and further increases their ignorance of the many-sidedness of the black population that would move Whites beyond racial stereotypes. Halsey, and later Clark (1955: 121), contended that the interdependency of people of variety of religious and social systems in the world make it not only stupid, but dangerous for ignorance of other races and cultures to exist.

*The double social and psychological consciousness.* One of the first to raise the question of a potential psychological and sociological duality resulting from racial divisiveness in the United States was W.E.B. DuBois (Dennis and Henderson, 1980, Dennis, 1977a, 1977b). In his now familiar concept of the double conscious, he was referring to this duality as it confronts Blacks, but the term is appropriate to intraracial as well as interracial references (Dennis and Henderson, 1980). Myrdal (1962) speaks to the same duality with his thesis of the American "dilemma"; later Merton (1976) posed similar ideas under the rubric of "sociological ambivalence." What DuBois, Myrdal, and Merton are talking about is an indeterminacy and fluctuation people manifest toward themselves, others, and social values.

Smith (1961: 27) writes of this duality with such poignancy that her description of it deserves to be quoted at length:

> The mother who taught me what I know of tenderness and love and compassion taught me also the bleak rituals of keeping Negroes in their "place." The father who . . . reminding me that "all men are brothers," trained me int he steel-rigid decorums I must demand of every colored male. They who so gravely taught me to split my

body form my mind and both from my "soul" taught me also to split my conscience from my acts and Christianity from Southern tradition.

Since children must be taught to hate and fear others, the process of driving white children into racial conformity must be at least partially attributable to parental socializers. Contrary to his own assumption that racial training is haphazard, Clark (1955) quotes a study by Horowitz in which a group of Southern white children told Horowitz that they were punished often by their parents when they played with black children who lived in their neighborhood. And Hyman (1969) quotes a study by Valien to the effect that parents do in fact attempt to guide their children in matters of race.

Boyle (1962) writes at length about the impact of racist education on her own social and psychological development. Writing of the joys she had experienced from playing with black youngsters and the moment when she was asked to give up those friendships, she lamented the fact that "all that had been best in my life was branded WRONG. It was RIGHT to do what I dimly sensed was contrary to the laws of love and loyalty." It is this splitting of the mind and of the individual's social existence by parental desires to create a racial environment to force children into a bewildering world of their own alleged racial superiority that often confuses the children who are obliged to go through the ritual. Boyle (1962: 22) shares her reaction to her own racial "coming of age":

> I remember running in to the house heartsick after snubbing the advances of a child of whom I was particularly fond. He had skipped up to me, suggesting that I come along on some small adventure . . . Crushing back my desire both for his company and for fund, I answered stiffly, "No, I can't." Then I added with proper Southern-lady courtesy, "How are you?" My mother had watched the exchange . . . she said, "Mother saw and heard everything. That was a good girl." A strange combination of depression and pride swept me. I was a GOOD GIRL. But, oh, what had I *done*!

The social and psychic split is evident in this scene. On sees the compartmentalization of many "selves," for the solution was to reach an accommodation between the racial contradictions that existed within the society and the individual's response to those contributions. Boyle (1962: 29) describes the process that went on within herself: "When my training period, 'racial indoctrination,' was over, I was as close to a typical Southern lady as anyone . . . My mind had many partitions and my heart many levels. I was a mixture of high idealism and contradictory practice, of rigid snobbery and genuine human warmth."

Myrdal has suggested that people learn to adjust to a lack of correspondence between deed and creed. There comes a time when there is no longer a dilemma because the creed-deed discrepancy has been placed on the back burner for so long that it is no longer a social or personal issue to be dealt with or confronted by most people. However, as the recollections above suggest, the early stages of racial indoctrination can be traumatic for children who are taught to love everyone, but not Blacks, or to respect older people, but not Blacks. This final quote by Smith (1961: 29) again points to the depth of the personal and social duality:

> From the day I was born, I began to learn my lesson . . . I learned it is possible to be a Christian and a white southerner simultaneously; to be a gentlewoman and an arrogant callous creature in the same moment...I learned to believe in freedom, to glow when the word democracy was used, and to practice slavery from morning to night. I learned it . . . by closing door after door until one's mind and heart and conscience are blocked off from each other and from reality.

*Group conformity.* Reference group and role theories have been presented by social scientists as explanations of the determinants of behavior (Warner and Dennis, 1970; Dennis, 1979). They describe the expectations generated by the group and the degree to which individuals look to the group for support. These expectations are often accompanied by community pressures on individuals to conform to prevailing social norms. In no other sector of American life has the pressure to conform been greater than it has been in matters of race. In matters of race, America has been a "closed society." It has sought to keep tight control over the ideology presented to its young; and its young learn early that racial conformity is required and expected. Those brought up under the racial etiquette of "white superiority--black inferiority are either sympathetic to it or are impressed by the healthy wisdom of not rocking the boat" (Silver, 1964). It is virtually impossible for the young white child to escape the pressures to conform to the racial etiquette. How a young white girl raised to expect deference from Blacks reacted to the growing familiarity of a young black college student who worked as a domestic

worker in the author's home is shown in the following passage.

> One day we talked she suddenly called me Patty instead of Miss Patton. I felt my entire interior congeal. A Negro had failed to call me Miss! . . . I said nothing to her at the time but my sleep was tormented by a frighteningly dark and ugly cloud of guilt. I felt trapped . . . She must suffer because I had permitted familiarity . . . Tinglingly, heavily, my heart sank down. I straightened my back and faced her. Evelyn . . . you mustn't call me that (Patty) people might not understand (Boyle, 1962: 40).

Smith's (1961) ideas about racial rites of passage bear on this discussion, for we must ultimately view the ideology of white supremacy as a belief system like any other "ism" and not simply as a rationale to exploit the black, brown, or red population. Her remarks suggest that the idea of racism, and the public ceremonies that pay homage to it, "performed from babyhood, slip from the conscious mind down deep into muscles and glands and become difficult to tear out."

The young are no more immune from the pressure to conform than their parents and elders. Note the actions of the youngsters in Ovington's autobiography or the account by the Rosens (1962) of a seven-year-old Deerfield, Illinois, boy who, after having heard his young friends discuss the fact that a black family had moved into the neighborhood, ran yelling to his mother, crying, "Niggers are moving here! And we're going to get rid of 'em!" This story recalls another part of Smith's commentary on the process by which children learn the rituals of racism: "You only felt the iron grip of her (Southern Tradition) hand *and knew you must go where all the other children were going. And you learned never, never, to get out of step*" (italics added).

Evident in the adult effort to force racist values on children is the portrayal of Blacks as collectively abominable. The ceremonial cycle of racism repeats itself over and over as the child becomes the adult and his or her memory conjures up all the early indoctrination (Boyle, 1962: 13): "that blacks cannot be trusted, smell bad, carry diseases, were repulsive, and dangerous." Once certain concepts and people are coupled, despite all evidence to the contrary, the relationship tends to stick. As Boyle states it: "Ignorant-Negro was practically one word. Ignorance was a racial trait." It is little wonder, then, that white children and youth carry their racial ignorance and social fears into adulthood and pass them on to their own children, thus completing the generational cycle. White adults' efforts to force conformity upon young Whites eventually restricts the world view of the young and hinders their search for "truth." It also encourages whites to view Blacks only as abstractions, "the Blacks," and impersonal, "they"' it is easy to dismiss the abstract and the impersonal as being of no importance to one's existence.

*Moral ambivalence.* Moral ambivalence refers to the moral dilemmas that result from divergent norms and values that pull individuals and groups in contradictory directions. Examples of the contradictory values that create ambivalence in the young are these:

1. the desire to be a Christian versus the desire to be a traditional white Southerner;
2. the belief in freedom and democracy versus the belief in racial inequality;
3. the desire to show love and compassion versus the desire to keep Blacks in their place at all costs;
4. the belief in the Southern tradition of respect for the old versus the belief that older Blacks are not worthy of the highest respect;
5. the belief that each person should be treated according to his or her individual merits versus the belief that Blacks should be evaluated as a group without regard to individual merits an talents.

Autobiographical accounts by white authors of their socialization into American racial mores provide us with ample evidence of the contradictory moral values that are inherent in a society in which race is an important social determinant on one hand, and in which legalistic ideals, on the other hand, tend to support nonracist orientations. Evident in examples of moral ambivalence is the anxiety and frustration that permeate the lives of young Whites confronted with these crisscrossing values. One part of them demands loyalty to a "universal community of values" and another to a "particularistic white brotherhood." The problem i unsolvable without the complete disappearance of racism from the American society.

What authors Smith, Canzoneri, Silver, Zinn and Boyle articulate is the desired by the young to understand the ideology that is shaping their racial and group identity. They feel the pains of guilt or moral outrage, yet they remain trapped as youngsters in a world they did not make, a world in which it was expected that they wold follow the orders of their parents without question. When Lillian Smith questioned her mother's assertion that she could not play with a young black girl, her mother answered with a typical non sequitur designed to end such inquiries: Smith--"I don't understand."; Mother--"You're too young to understand. And don't ask me again, ever again, about this."

Dabbs (1962), too, speaks of the explanations and whippings he received from his father when the latter insisted that the young James address Whites with "Sir" and "Ma'am" and Blacks with "uncle" and "aunt." He recalls having infuriated his father during one of those race "lessons" with the comment: "But he's a man, isn't he?"

## OTHER SPECIFIC EFFECTS OF RACISM

Continuing to focus on the impact of racism on Whites, as revealed in autobiographical writings, I now shift from an emphasis on white children to the impact of racism on the white population in general. I shall review three specific implications of racism for the white population: (1) it engenders irrationality,; (2) it inhibits intellectual growth; and (3) it negates democracy.

*Irrationality.* Clark's suggestion that it is the *idea* of Blacks rather than the specific behavioral attributes of Blacks the generate white hostility, and Smith's observation that this ideas has slipped from consciousness and has become embedded into the white population's "muscles and glands," bears noting again. It means that we cannot readily probe white hostility from a traditionally logical or rational vantage point. In their analyses of the emergence of Nazi ideology in Germany, both Reich (1970) and Alexander (1942) center the ideological currents of Nazism in the psychic structure of the German masses. In an observation that has relevance for our analysis of race in America, Reich (1970: 18) notes that

> the basic traits of the character structures corresponding to a definite historical situation are formed in early childhood, and are far more conservative than the forces of technical production. It results from this that, as time goes on, the psychic structures lag behind the rapid changes of the social conditions form which the derived, and later come into conflict with new forms of life.

Reich's analysis helps us understand why it is difficult to change ideological orientations after certain values have bene ingrained. It is this that explains resistance to change lingering within a population long after any initial reason for hostility has vanished. The irrationality sinks deep and becomes, in Reich's term, a part of the character structures of individuals. The difficulty of uprooting decades of racial indoctrination was expressed by Boyle (1962), who said that she had a constant struggle with those deeply entrenched *ideas* she had been taught about Blacks long after her outer habits had ceased to segregationist. The problem is how to bridge the gap between the mythic and the rational.

It is obvious that Whites suffer and pay a price for this irrational response to race. Halsey (1946: 41) sees this suffering as the result of "a mounting sense of suffocation because blacks refuse to recognize their place . . . Any sense of 'progress' for black is to give whites with racist feelings (the idea) that the world is becoming unhinged and that a new unbearable world is on the horizon." Some of this "suffering" is seen in Griffin's (1961: 53) account of the irrationality of the white response to Blacks when he darkened his skin and posed as Black:

> I walked up to the ticket counter. When the lady ticket-seller saw me, her otherwise attractive face turned sour, violently so . . ."What do you want?" she snapped. She answered rudely and glared at me with such loathing I knew I was receiving what the Negroes call "the hate stare." . . . She reappeared to hurl my change and the ticket on the counter with such force most of it fell ont he floor at my feet. I was truly dumbfounded . . . Her performance was so venomous . . . you feel lost, sick at heart before such unmasked hatred . . . you see a kind of insanity, something so obscene . . . *I felt like saying: "What in God's name are you doing to yourself?"*

White Americans have been fed such a heavy dose of legends, fantasies, and myths about Blacks that even individuals who pride themselves on applying logic and reason to all aspects of their lives are quite willing to forgo them in matters of race. To seek to understand the irrational response to race is to delve into a subterranean world that transposes logic and turns it on its head.

Griffin's question--"What in God's name are you doing to yourself?"--speaks to the dehumanization of the white majority, which is evident, too, in "the jeers, the profane shouts, and the sullen bitter undertones" when a black family integrates a neighborhood in Chicago (Johnson, 19650, and in the reaction when a Black integrates Ole Miss (Silver, 1964: vii): "The pounding of the bricks on the cars and the screams, 'We'll kill the bastards'-- plus shrill cries of filth and obscenity, proved that eighteen and nineteen year-old students have suddenly been turned into wild animals." Another description of the Ole Miss disturbance has been given by Canzoneri(1965: 147): "They (the coeds) did not act like young ladies. They literally stood around James Meredith and shouted 'Nigger' like common Northern slumbred viragos . . . I wanted by some means to discredit the television pictures . . . Those nice girls just wouldn't act that way." Some whites looked at this collective irrationality of the white population and equated the condition to an insane asylum. As Evans Harrington (Canzoneri, 1965) noted: "Our way of life is based on keeping the Negro downtrodden . . .TThis is where the psychic damage to our state appears . . . How much shock, shame, and dismay can we whites endure without turning the state into a psychiatric ward."

Further evidence of how racism evokes irrational responses from Whites is provided by Cohn (1948: 40). He writes of a white physician in the Delta who regularly assisted black patients, often without pay: "But whenever a black was accused of raping a white woman or killing a white man, the soft-spoken doctor would assist the lynching mob."

What seems clear is that the irrationality of the white response to the *idea* of Blacks goes deeper than simply the attempt by Whites to rationalize their power over Blacks. It is as if they psyche of the white population, after feeding so long the mythology of white supremacy, cannot tolerate the psychic void that would inevitably ensue if Blacks were released from their mythic position. Thus, the ideology of black inferiority persists in the psyche of the white population despite studies and empirical findings that refute these myths.

Young (1969: 86) speaks to the ideological structure of racism in the psyche of white Americans when he says that the task of the American social scientists is to find out "why so many whites are psychologically dependent on identifying with a privileged caste system, even when the reap no economic benefits form it themselves." A similar thought was expressed by DuBois (1940: 6), who was to lament the fact that he only came to appreciate the psychology of racism late in his academic life:

> I saw that the color bar could not be broken by a series of brilliant assaults. Secondly, I saw defending this bar not simply ignorance and will; these to be sure; but also *certain more powerful motives less open to reason or appeal.* There were economic motives, urges to build wealth on the backs of black slave and colored serfs; *there followed those unconscious acts and irrational reactions, unpierced by reason, whose current form depended on the long history of relation and contact between thought and idea* [italics added].

*Inhibition of intellectual growth.* This particular consequence of racism is a counterpart to irrationality. Racism not only stalls and kills growth for individual Whites, but also for entire nations. Myrdal summed up the costs intellectual energy spent on the Negro problem in America should, if concentrated in a single direction, have moved mountains." But liberating minds from racism will prove impossible if the logic of one columnist who opposed college integration prevails: "We didn't send our children to college to hear both sides; we sent them to learn what is right." It is this desire to close the mind and seek the shelter of the narrowest of spheres that debilitates and allows racism to feed upon its already closed intellectual world. Thus, the mental poverty that results form racism must inevitably create minds that are nonreflective, minds that, indeed, fear reflection. Racists may perceive the scars they place upon the black population, even sometimes with pleasure, but they do not view themselves as emotionally disfigured and intellectually stunted by their racial arrogance. They may not see the damage their racism inflicts upon the very things they claim to uphold. Thus, though many Southerners claimed to be resisting Blacks in order to help the South, the results of their fight to exclude Blacks were basically negative. One can state a case to explain the educational and economic poverty of the South, for example, by looking at the monumental efforts most Southern sates expended trying to prohibit black advances (Dennis and Sartain, 1980). Conversely, much of the energy of the black population has likewise been diverted toward fighting for greater economic, educational, and political rights.

Smith's comment that white supremacy grips and clings to the psyche of white children with tenacity and continues on into adulthood, accounts for what Silver sees as the basic immaturity of the white population and the inability of Whites

"to grow up, to accept the judgements of civilization." The ability to accept change and "the judgement of civilization" would mean tearing the white population away from a past many Whites would like to see as frozen and suspended in time. And because so many whites see the racial hierarchy as fixed and permanent, they are unable to understand the strivings and frustrations of Blacks, since almost all institutions within the white world tend to support the prevailing racial configuration. This is why it proved necessary to focus on changing the *behavior* of Whites rather than their *attitudes* during the litigations in the 1950s and 1960s (Warner and Dennis, 1970). The logic of stressing a change in behavior over a change in attitude was that racism was so deeply lodged in the white mind that forcing Whites to behave toward Blacks in nondiscriminatory ways would be easier than trying to change white attitudes, beliefs, and emotional responses to Blacks.

*Negation of democracy.* The white response to democracy in American has been to limit its extension to the black population; the black response has been to interpret the idea of democracy and the constitution in its widest sense to support the political, social, and economic aspirations of Blacks. When Myrdal wrote his highly acclaimed critique of American democracy, he was following a tradition already set in motion by, among others, William Highland Garnett, Sojourner Truth, Martin Delaney, and Frederick Douglass. What these activists and thinkers sought was a democratic order that would eliminate class and sex, as well as racial oppression.

The repudiation of democracy by Whites (for Blacks at least), and their cheating and hedging to insure that the white population enjoys an edge in the political, social, and economic marketplace, is seen everywhere in the United States. Racism prompts rejection of the idea of fair play and the sense of justice, themes that are important to the very survival of a democracy. The responsibility of one citizen toward another or one group toward another, if seen in a categorical laissez-faire manner, may come down to "no one owes anything to anybody. Each pot has to sit on its own bottom in the economic and social marketplace." Fine. But why then must the spirit of this credo be broken by denying one group access to valued goods and positions? Democracy, as Brown (1949) explains, depends upon the interdependency of individuals and groups. White society would perhaps feel a keener sense of the consequences of the negation of democracy if it understood, as DuBois suggested, that the antidemocrat is a menace to his neighbor and the entire society.

What is to be done when the entire body political takes the stance of the antidemocrat? The frustration of this condition was brought home to Smith (1961: 52) by a young white girl after a summer retreat in which racial justice and democracy were discussed:

> you have made us want to be good . . . you've talked of love . . . human rights . . . bridging chasms between people . . . when I go back to my town, how can I live these ideals! Tell me, if you can--but you can't! That's what I have realized.

What the young girl asked was, "Where can I go to begin the quest to break down racial barriers?" Silver (1964: 15) explained that there were few places one could go that were not already infected with racism. As he explained it:

> Racism has created an institutional support network. Every lawmaking body and every law enforcing agency is completely in the hands of whites who are faithful to the orthodoxy. The white man is educated to believe in his superiority . . . the civic and service clubs, the educated institutions, the churches, the business and labor organizations, the patriotic, social, and professional fraternities all individuals who would advance themselves in any of these are oriented from infancy in the direction of loyalty to the accepted (racial) code.

This network of racism forms a chain, both physical and psychological, around the neck of social democracy. It holds it captive to group emotions and the irrationalities of short-term rather than long-term advantages. Booker T. Washington (19110 said it long ago and present critics of racial oppression agree: It is a grave mistake for the vast majority of Whites to assume that they can remain free and enjoy democracy while they are denying it to Blacks. The antidemocrat not only wants to ensure that Blacks do not enjoy certain rights, he also want to ensure that no White is free to question or challenge this denial. The statement in the Kerner Commission Report (National Advisory Commission on Civil Disorders, 1968) that the nation was moving toward two permanently separated societies, one black, the other white, is till true more than ten years later--and for the same reason. The antidemocratic thrust has scarcely abated; the network of racism continues to thrive.

## CONCLUSION

The evidence presented here supports the contention that we can scarcely speak of a "happy racist." From the early years of indoctrination by parents on, one finds racists backed against the wall, angry and afraid, bursting with rage at the very thought that their racial views might shift. I am now more convinced than ever of the need to probe the roots of the irrational, to ascertain the *process* by which myths, legends, and fantasies become embedded in the psyche as "ideological imperatives" that seemingly resist all efforts to dislodge them. Such an approach might be viewed as a complement of materialistic approaches to analysis of the ways one's position within a social structure permits or disallows the entrenchment of certain values within the psyche. Now may be the time to consider DuBois's racial studies in reverse: Instead of organizing a hundred years of study to systematically analyze black life and the black world, as DuBois suggested, perhaps we should commit ourselves to a systematic study of the psychological, ideological, and material reasons that Whites accept the mythology of white supremacy and deny Blacks equal opportunity to participate in the American society.

# DEFUSING RACE: DEVELOPMENTS SINCE THE KERNER REPORT

*Joyce A. Ladner*
*Walter W. Stafford*

The Kerner Commission Report was issued over twelve years ago. Since that time there has been considerable interest in its impact, or lack thereof, on the condition of Blacks. A decade after the Report was released the New York *Times* published a series of articles examining the critical issues, then and now, that affected Blacks. Scholars, human relations experts, and civil rights organizations engaged in similar retrospective analyses. The Report's startling thesis that "our nation is moving toward two societies, one Black, one White--separate and unequal" was unprecedented (National Advisory Commission on Civil Disorders, 1968: 1). Although it had been issued as a result of the civil unrest of the sixties, when riots in Los Angeles, Detroit, Newark, and elsewhere were thought to have threatened the stability of the nation, still Americans had not expected this government panel, appointed by President Lyndon B. Johnson, to be so declarative and radical in its assessment of the problem.

The National Advisory Commission on Civil Disorders, headed by Otto Kerner, then Governor of Illinois, was formed largely in response to the mounting racial disorders that occurred during the summer of 1967. During a two-week period in July, race riots occurred in Newark and Detroit, setting off a chain reaction in neighboring communities. President Johnson established the Commission on July 28, 1967, and directed it to provide answers to three questions:

1. What happened?
2. Why did it happen?
3. What can be done to prevent it from happening again? (National Advisory Commission on Civil Disorders, 1968: 1.)

The president's charge to the Commission, on the surface, appeared to be an easy task. However,

Ladner, Joyce A., Stafford, Walter W., *Defusing Race: Developments Since the Kerner Report*, "Impacts of Racism on White America," 1989 pp. 51-69. Copyright © 1981 by Sage Publications, Inc. reprinted with permission.

the violence and disruption that had occurred in the early summer of 1967 had been devastating. Some 68 persons had been killed in Newark and Detroit alone. A total of 83 had died in riots in these two cities and in surrounding areas. Hundreds were injured and property damage was estimated to be about 55 million dollars. The first riot occurred in the summer of 1965 and cost 32 lives, in the Watts area of Los Angeles. There were also riots in other cities in the summer of 1966, but the Newark and Detroit disruptions were so devastating that the president felt compelled to devote major attention to uncovering the underlying causes.

Other commissions had been formed to study facial disorders in the past: the Chicago Commission on Race Relations in 1922; the New York City Mayor's Commission to Inquire into Conditions in Harlem in 1935; and the McCone Commission, which studied the Watts riots in Los Angeles in 1965 (Edwards and Jones, 1969: 529). However, none of these commissions, including the one headed by McCone, had gone as far as the Kerner Commission did in placing the major blame upon "white racism," and attributing the causes to the fact that whites control ghetto institutions. The Report stated:

> Certain fundamental matters are clear. Of these, the most fundamental is the racial attitude and behavior of white Americans toward black Americans. Race prejudice has shaped our history decisively . . . White racism is essentially responsible for the explosive mixture which has been accumulating in our cities [Edwards and Jones, 1969: 529, 532].

The Report also called attention to "a new mood of racial pride . . . the growing concentration of Blacks in the urban ghettoes and the unfulfilled expectations aroused by the judicial and legislative victories of the Civil Rights Movement" (Glenn, 1969: 515).

Finally, the recommendations of the Kerner

Commission Report were disturbing to some of its critics, who considered the recommendations too radical. The Report recommended "a national system of income supplementation based strictly on need (a negative income tax) to provide a minimum standard of decent living for all citizens. And it recommends that the federal government provide at least ninety percent of all welfare costs, make available six million new and existing housing units to low-income families within five years, and provide funds for year-around compensatory education programs in disadvantaged neighborhoods" (Glenn, 1969: 515-516). The Report recommended costly reform measures that have not been implemented more than a decade later.

The Kerner Commission Report did not represent the attitudes and opinions existing within the mainstream of American society. A majority of white Americans in 1967 were not likely to regard themselves as the major cause of the riots in Newark and Detroit. The riots occurred during a period of prosperity and rising expectations among Americans in general. Even the poor were beneficiaries of the Great Society programs (Head Start, Neighborhood Youth Corp., and so on). White Americans were not sympathetic to the idea that their taxes should be used to solve the problems of the nation's ghettoes. While the Kerner Commission could state in a forthright manner that "white racism" was the major contributing factor to the civil unrest, white Americans were totally unaccustomed to being targeted as "racists," especially within the above-mentioned context. The recommendations "add to the emerging consensus that only drastic reform in our community and institutional life will eliminate the costly failure of the society to provide opportunities for all of its members and thus forestall disorders" (Edwards and Jones, 1969: 532).

Another important factor is that the Report was issued in February 1968, when the country was deeply involved in the Vietnam war. Antiwar protests, campus disturbances, inflation, and the presidential campaign had begun to take priority over the issue of civil rights for Blacks. By the end of the decade, other issues, including energy, the recession, women's rights, and the growing demand of other ethnic minorities for an equal share in America's scarce rewards and resources, had almost completely replaced the initial concern that led to the formation of the Kerner Commission. The civil rights movement that had dominated the decade of the sixties would take a lesser and minor role in the seventies. By the early seventies, social analysts had begun to predict that this would be a decade of apathy, when the "silent majority," as Richard Nixon labeled them, would replace the protesters of the sixties.

It is very interesting to note that as the 1980s began and the riots in Miami and Wrightsville, Georgia, occurred, no one called for a national commission, and few organizations or persons even pretended to have the answers to the difficult problems of the black community. What happened? Had the nation moved toward a greater recognition as represented by the media--that the statistical profile of the black community was devastating, but the solutions were beyond the nation? Had the nation moved to another level of conservatism and anxiety, in which the problems of Blacks were insignificant when compare to those of the economy, moralism, and shrinking resources? We will explore these questions further below.

One of the most significant characteristics of the Kerner Commission Report was its radical departure from tradition, focusing on "white racism" as a causative factor. Traditional analyses in race and ethnic relations have placed the burden on the victim by emphasizing the "costs" of racism to those affected by it. Rarely have social scientists and policy makers attempted to assess the "costs" of racism to those who inflict it. Hence, the literature is replete with studies on the costs and consequences of racism to Blacks, while very little has been written on the implications of racism for Whites. This reflects a fundamental bias in the social sciences, a bias that reflects the relative power of the white-dominated professions to *define* and articulate the problems of race from their own perspective, instead of from the perspective of the oppressed. Indeed, we would argue that most race relations experts do not perceive racism to have consequences for Whites, yet there are victims of racism on both sides of the color line. Those who promote racism also deny themselves the full range of choices, experiences, and resources that could be theirs. Of course, the costs to the victims--the denial of equal access to educational, economic, and political power--have been amply documented.

## A FRAMEWORK FOR
## INTERPRETATION
## OF THE CHANGES

The excitement and hope associated with the release of the Kerner Commission Report in 1968 had been mitigated by the loss of economic status among Blacks and their low priority in the determination of rewards in the political economy. This was not accidental; there were many forces set in motion prior to the riots and the release of the Report that now appear to have created false hopes for many Blacks and their supporters. It should be remembered that at the time of the release of the Report the nation was undergoing a relatively good period of economic growth. This growth, however, was an illusion. The Great Society programs provided a grand dream that was intricately associated with the economic boom. This was also the period of the Vietnam war, which tore at many of the dream's moral underpinnings and set in motion the division between the radical left (liberals) and the Blacks who had to support domestic programs. It is important to recall that the Report did not deal with many of the emerging issues of the time, including the growth of females in the labor force, the demands of the service society for a growing number of technical and replacement lower-level occupations, or the profound economic changes occurring in the nation due to its new role in the economic order. The Report gave official legitimacy to the two societies, but failed to provide new definitions or interpretations of the racial inequities.

In all fairness, at the time the Report was released, or since that time, none of these factors could be seen in their entirety. Segregation and discrimination were analyzed in the Report with a high degree of emphasis on new avenues for improvement by the state, but with few interpretations of the potential limitations. Ironically, the Report and social analyses during this period were unable to predict the wide array of new demands on the state that were to lessen the prospects for Blacks, and which eventually accentuated a growing conservative sentiment which a crisis of authority and excessive demands caused to weaken the nation's political and economic structures. In many ways, the Kerner Report was symbolic of many of the "ills" that conservatives were to choose later as rationales for their positions (see Nash, 1976). As we show, the emerging

neoconservative positions about race were not antiblack, but often antistate when it came to the demands of the underclass, and when it came to educational and occupational changes.

To understand fully the perspective of the trends, it is necessary to place several forces in historical and projected molds. The thesis is straightforward, yet requires detailed explanation. Simply stated, *many of the more recognized symbols and legislative achievements of Blacks came at a period when the political and economic views of race and minorities were being given new interpretations.* The symbols often came into conflict with groups whose power depended on the new service society. The best example was the conflict in New York City in Ocean-Hill Brownsville. There was an uneasy and uncomfortable feeling among white groups in the Northern service cities about the symbols which had been used by Blacks in the South.

In many respects, the basis for the symbols--greater economic and political power--were probably in line with the changes that were occurring in the nation; however, it put on guard many white professional and ethnic groups that were made to feel powerless by the contours of the economic forces of postindustrial capitalism. At the base of these forces were the economic, cultural, and political arrangements being shaped by postindustrial capitalism. Since we are referring to a period that had begun in the early 1950s, it is clear that many of the symbols attached to black progress had little basis in reality. The framework of these changes included the fact that the nation had been under constant pressure since World War II to adjust to the changing economic order in the world. As the most advanced postindustrial state, America had little time to fine tune the political economy to meet consumer demands and the demands of a growing array of interest in groups.

From a sociological perspective, the lack of stability had been key to racial attitudes and the low priority the society assigned to Blacks. Consider, for example, that following World War II there were ten years of recession, twelve years of recovery, and seven years under the influence of wartime pressures. Of the six recovery periods, four turned into recessions before full employment was reached; the other two merged into the Korean and Vietnam wars. The postindustrial period of the nation had been synonymous with recessions. The "typical" middle-class way of life had not been stable, and the uncertainty had been reflected in political and social attitudes that reflected sensitivities to racial change (see Magdoff and Sweezy, 1977).

Another factor concerning the economy had been the continual growth of the service sector and white-collar employment in comparison with the traditional manufacturing sector. The so-called service society was a reality at the time of the Kerner Report, although the prevalent thinking was still of a type of industrial recovery for Blacks. This perception was dangerous and unreal. White-collar workers had increased from less than 45 percent of the labor force in the 1950s to over 50 percent by the early 1970s. The female participation rate had increased to 43.4 percent by 1970. The signs of a new economic and cultural framework were evident.

In addition to these factors, the manner of interpreting the key racial elements was also changing. The unions, as bastions of racism, certainly remained, but not in their former state. As the industrial sector changed, the membership among blue-collar workers declined, as did union membership. Lower-level white-collar workers, including Blacks, became the new interpretations of organizational racism. Stated in another way, many of the traditionally "racist" institutions were now incorporating Blacks or symbols of black progress that required new interpretations.

A third aspect of change in the economy relates to the political role. Postindustrial capitalism is, indeed, a political economy. This can be demonstrated in several respects; however, for the purpose of this chapter, it is best seen in the tremendous rise in the role of local-state governments, as well as the federal government, in providing services. The protest that is occurring now regarding fiscal management and conservatism is a reaction against these trends. The expenditures of states and local governments have grown more rapidly than the Gross National Product, while revenues have been limited by statutory requirements. Transfer payments made up only 21 percent of the federal expenditures in 1955; in 1970 they were 37 percent. Clearly, as pressures to reduce the rapid expenditures increased, groups had to take on a certain legitimacy if they were (or are) to receive some of the scarce rewards.

There were other considerations basic to the emerging trends that provided social legitimacy. The first of these factors was the rising tide of educational expectations. By 1968, 12.4 percent of the adult population had completed college, and the demand for credentials was reaching an all-time high. Although a large number of private colleges were to fail in later years, the demand brought into being a system of highly educated persons, although education alone could not suffice as a basis for legitimacy (clearly, however, the opposite was true without an education). A second factor was the dissemination of "cultures" as educational achievement increased (see Germani, 1973: 3-58; Abu-Lughod, 1974: 68-85) new employment centers proliferated throughout the nation, and outmigration from the older industrial centers reached its peak (see Long and Boerstein, n.d.). A basic feature of postindustrial capitalist society is that culture became more diffuse.

This diffusion gave credence to the growing ethnic and religious pluralism that was often sharpened by regions. The great increase in credentials of the population and the creation of new employment centers in the South and West created a balance among regions that encouraged pluralistic forces. A new competition was created that meant that the old industrial North no longer dominated the shaping of educational, social, and cultural values. What emerged during this period was a highly educated and mobile population that could shift allegiance to status and rights based on the needs of the place and the particular social or economic needs at a given time.

The outline of the above trends incorporates most of the ideas for the new legitimacy to rewards for minority status. In a maturing postindustrial society undergoing highly complex transitional (demographic, economic and social) stages, minority status had emerged as a *right* and not necessarily a factor to be disdained. Blacks, through their civil rights efforts, had opened up the institutionalizing of a series of statutory and constitutional rights that invited new forms of participation and definitions. Certain necessities were almost guaranteed by the state (food, some health care, and perhaps a few others). However, in a society in which an infinite number of rights were emerging concomitant with a recognition of increasingly limited resources, the issue became not only *who* benefits, but how much. Stated from another perspective, once the statutory and constitutional decisions of the 1960s were in place, everyone had a right to be a member of a minority group. The key issue was defining the dimensions of these rights.

The dimensions of rights raised serious ideological questions that were opened in the Bakke and Weber cases and in the diverse rights of immigrants, undocumented workers, and other groups. Clearly, as the nation suffered through the pains of defining the latter stages of postindustrialism, groups could now be defined as minorities for traditional, ideological, political, and economic reasons. The acceptance of any of these rights by the state became dependent upon the ability of groups to define themselves within legislation,[1] by the needs of the political economy (for example, undocumented workers), or by ideological-legalistic arguments (white males, white females, Italian Americans, and so on).

By the late 1970s race alone was insufficient as a criteria for minority status, because it could not be defined per se as a need or benefit for the economy or the state. The tide had turned. American society was confronted with the difficult challenge of defining minority status in economic and political terms. Several examples are clear. One is the Cuban influx during the summer of 1980 and the decision about what their rights were as opposed to those of Haitians; other examples are the resettlement policies for groups from Southeast Asia. Probably the most perplexing challenges were the issues of white women and Blacks. Society had to decide who was most deserving among the minorities, and the fact that the government *did not* move to establish commissions on the riots during the 1980s may have been a signal.

## THE NEW MINORITIES: WOMEN AND OTHERS

The civil rights movement of the sixties, with its emphasis on racial pride and racial consciousness, encourages the development of ethnic consciousness and women's consciousness that have been parlayed into social movements. Evans (1978) argues that the civil rights movement and the new left movement provided the foundation upon which women began to redefine their roles, eventually to form the feminist movement. Traditionally the emphasis has been placed on those racial, ethnic, or religious groups that have suffered discrimination. They were often nonwhite, relatively powerless, and politically, economically, and socially disadvantaged. However, the sixties changed this traditional conceptualization of what it meant to be a member of a minority group. Women, who constitute over half of the American population, are now considered this nation's largest minority group. Proponents of this redefinition of women's status argue that sexism is akin to racism because it is rooted in a philosophy based on the systematic denial of equal rights because of special characteristics. Prejudice and discrimination are key components of sexism in much the same way they are components of racism. The second-class citizenship and low status that women occupy give legitimacy to the claim for minority status and benefits.

Therefore, women are protected by affirmative action guidelines. Affirmative action laws give protection to women and minorities by removing those barriers that systematically deprived them of equal opportunities in education, employment, and housing. These guidelines are based on Title VI and Title VII of the Civil Rights Act of 1964, and Title IX of the Education Amendments of 1972. The Department of Health, Education, and Welfare established the guidelines for implementing affirmative action that are applied to all employers with fifty or more employees who receive federal funds or contracts. They are required to set aside a given number of jobs or places (as in the case of a university) for women and minorities.

Affirmative action has been far-reaching in its interpretations. In the City University of New York, Italian Americans are accorded minority status. Hasidic Jews in Brooklyn and Italian Americans in Newark, New Jersey, have made use of the same redefinition of minority status to acquire federal grants to improve their neighborhoods and to launch employment and school lunch programs for members of their ethnic groups. Michael Novak has been one of the leading advocates of a "white ethnic" movement, and the resurgence of ethnic pride and consciousness among Americans of European descent:

> Those Poles of Buffalo and Milwaukee--so notoriously taciturn, sullen, nearly speechless. Who has ever understood them? . . . But where in America is there any where a language for voicing what a Christian Pole in this nation feels? He has no Polish culture left him, no Polish tongue. Yet Polish feelings do not go easily into the idiom of happy America, the America of the Anglo-Saxons, and, yes, in the arts, the Jews. (The Jews have long been a culture of the world, accustomed to exile, skilled in scholarship and in reflection. The Christian Poles are largely of Peasant origin, free men for hardly more than a hundred years.) Of what shall the man of Buffalo

think, on his way to work in the mills departing from his relatively dreary home and street? What roots does he have? What language of the heart is available to him? [Novak, 1971: 44.]

The resurgence of European ethnicity, as advocated by Novak, stirred the interest of the federal government, which sought ways to exploit this new phenomenon. Senator Schweiker and Representative Pucinski introduced bills in the Congress that established "ethnic heritage studies" in the public schools using federal funds. The National Confederation of American Ethnic Groups, a Washington-based association that claimed a membership of 67 groups and 18.6 million individuals, pushed for white ethnic representation on such federal panels as the Equal Employment Opportunity Commission. It also lobbied to become a conduit for federal grants to white ethnic groups. White ethnics who had been silent during the black revolt of the sixties began to demand their fair share of the federal monies and cultural resources that had previously been limited to Blacks and Hispanics. Ethnic studies programs and departments were established in some major universities, largely in response to the formation of black studies academic programs. Ethnic minorities sought and gained legitimacy and thus established their claims for the same types of preferential treatment that had been accorded racial minorities in the sixties.

Other "new minorities" include homosexuals, the elderly, the handicapped, ex-convicts, drug addicts and alcoholics, and white ethnics. Moreover, nonwhite ethnic minorities, including Mexican Americans, Puerto Ricans, and Native Americans have gained even greater visibility in recent years as a result of the intense focus on minorities. The end result has been a dilution (and diminution) of what Americans have traditionally understood "minority" to mean. In the past, minorities have been viewed as categories of people in the society that have been subjected to systematic discrimination because of some trait or attribute they possess. They have usually been in the numerical minority, although not always. (For example, non-Whites in South Africa constitute a numerical majority but are assigned inferior minority status. Moreover, the nation of South Africa has ample resources to provide more equitable treatment for Blacks, yet the repressive apartheid system brutally subjugates this numerical majority, which is also that nation's indigenous population.) In the United States minorities have

usually been defined within the context of power. Therefore, the concept has most frequently been applied to nonwhite, powerless, oppressed groups in American society.

Today, however, the concept of minority has assumed, as demonstrated above, a more inclusive interpretation. No longer does it apply solely to those groups who are victims of systematic prejudice and discrimination based on race, ethnicity, or religion. Virtually any group that perceives itself to have relatively fewer scarce resources and less power than other groups in the society can possibly redefine itself as a minority and assert its legitimacy. This indicates that there has been a manipulation and, indeed, a transformation of one of the nation's historic cultural symbols. It can apply, as recent history as shown, to any group that seizes the opportunity to redefine itself in relationship to scarcity. It is within this context that groups who advocate anything from "Polish Power" to "Gay Pride" have captured the minority status and symbols.

The sixties opened up this new era. The civil rights movement illustrated to Americans all over that they could redefine the rules of the game and capture the cultural symbols for their own use. Today it matters less to women, white ethnics, homosexual activists, and the like that the recommendations of the Kerner Commission were not fulfilled, leaving what some civil rights advocates have called an "unfinished agenda." Some thirteen years later the problems of poverty, black unemployment, and inadequate education and medical care remain critical for the underclass.

Thus it would appear that some elementary distinctions should be made among the different groups' claims to minority status. Perhaps there should be some minimal requirements as to what constitutes, in a functional sense, minority status and group membership. In effect, does the definition apply equally to impoverished families in the Mississippi Delta or the Appalachians, to middle-class professional women, and to homosexual activists? It would appear that finite distinctions are necessary, distinctions that are based on objective socioeconomic criteria that would provide some more *deserving* minorities with greater access to the scarce resources than would be required of others. Such a basic determination may be made by using the Department of Labor's statistics regarding the income necessary to provide for a family of four. Family units falling short of this requirement could be accorded the "most deserving" minority status. Of course, various alternatives can be used to make this determination.

## WHY IT HAPPENED

The new agenda that gave rise to the emergence of the wide variety of "new minorities" had its genesis in the above-mentioned factors. However, the enduring characteristic of the black population to consistently adjust to economic and political setbacks was put to the test in the seventies. The apparent dream of gaining an economic foundation in the nation was completely reversed for a significant number of Blacks, most notably in family income. In 1969 the family income of Blacks rose to 61 percent of that of Whites. By 1978, this figure was approaching 55 percent.[2] Unemployment levels for Blacks in the 1970s reached their highest peak since World War II. Black joblessness was but one problem; a new type of leadership and participation was also being demanded by postindustrial society. Thus Blacks were confronted with a dual dilemma: the inability to adjust to economic changes, and declining mass political participation. By the late 1960s the National Urban League and the National Association for the Advancement of Colored People were the only broad-based organizations that were effectively addressing the problems of Blacks. The Student Nonviolent Coordinating Committee (SNCC) was defunct, the Southern Christian Leadership Conference (SCLC) that had faltered since the assassination of Martin Luther King, Jr., was undergoing serious reorganizational problems, and the Congress of Racial Equality (CORE) was confronted with issues of financial mismanagement. Even the NAACP, with branches throughout the nation, was over $800,000 in debt, a factor which limited its effectiveness. A Gallup public opinion poll, conducted in 1973, found that fewer than half the Blacks interviewed voiced a sense of contentment about the future.[3]

The uneasiness of Blacks was symptomatic of the larger society. Two recessions and continuing inflation had also changed the manner in which the white population approached and viewed change within the nation. The rapid social and political changes of the 1960s had left a substantial segment of the white population isolated in terms of its understanding of the fabric of society. The strong votes for George Wallace and the election of Richard Nixon reflected this mood. Nixon prom-

ised stability and a return to greatness (Richey and Jones, 1974), but, while he reversed some of the centralization by the national government with the institution of revenue sharing, and dismantled the Office of Economic Opportunity, the Republican administration had little effective control of economic changes. Even before Nixon's eventual downfall, a large segment of the white population was seeking new leadership.

For both Blacks and Whites, but particularly Whites, the 1970s was a confusing period. The traditional faith that the middle-class white community had in the private sector was severely shaken by several factors. Private industry clearly showed up as a major contributor to the political subterfuge of the Nixon administration, and the industrial sector often evidenced a lack of commitment to communities and workers. Many Northern cities such as Akron, Ohio, were left defenseless by the changing needs of industry. This city represented in many respects the white middle class of the industrial North, yet in the period of 1950-1978 the city lost over 25,000 jobs. Finally, in 1978, the giant tire companies moved their operations out of the city.[4]

Akron, Ohio, was a reflection of the rapid changes which had quietly been taking place. A silent revolution had occurred for much of the white middle class at a time when their focus was often on Blacks. Included, but not limited to the changes, were the facts that women constituted over 40 percent of the labor force, and much of the base of the service society by 1977. The political tempo was being set by the growing industrial regions of the South and West. These two regions accounted for over 50 percent of the nation's population in 1978, and their congressional delegations often proved to be insensitive to the economic concerns and vital interests of the urban North. The critical point in our interpretation is that a major segment of the white population was ill prepared for the economic, social, and geographical changes which had altered the fabric of the nation in the decades after World War II. The white population was ripe for new interpretations of societal change. Their crisis became the new economic problems that he nation had to try to resolve. High interest rates, declining competitive advantage with other industrial nations, productivity, and so on, set the tone for the new industrial order in which lower-middle-class Whites as well as Blacks would have to suffer as adjustments were made. Many Blacks were confronted with a new economic and political order, for which they were ill prepared.

## THE FOUNDATION OF
## THE NEW CONSERVATISM

The inability of a major segment of the population to control or interpret the changes in the nation contributed to an inward-looking middle class seeking new answers and alternatives. There were many paradoxes in the trends. Politically, the 1950s had witnessed a gradual growth in activity by a major segment of the population. The 1960s continued these trends, with an outburst of groups of all types demanding increased representation and benefits. In the views of several political scientists, services provided by government at all levels, particularly the national, were overextended.[5] In our over view, this overextension combined with the rapid economic changes to set the base for challenges to the major institutions in the nation. Studies show that over the twenty-year period from 1958 to 1978 voters dramatically shifted their views of who benefitted from government and the leadership of the major institutions in the nation. In the 1950s the feeling was that government was run to benefit the interests of the people. By the 1970s fewer than one-third of those surveyed shared this view. At the time of the latter survey, over half of the respondents identified government as serving the interests of big business (Huntington, 1975). These views appeared to be dominant in the 1970s. Thus, despite the fact that the United States faced a major energy crisis in the 1970s, polls showed that one of every two persons surveyed did not believe that there was a crisis (Coughlin, 1977). Neither business nor government was to be believed.

A crisis of leadership was also evident. The Vietnam war and the Nixon Watergate scandal contributed to the crisis. However, the symptoms were much deeper than the war and Watergate. A Louis Harris study in 1973 showed interesting contrasts between 1966 and 1973 in the ranking of institutions by confidence levels by the public. In 1966, a dominant period of social unrest, confidence in the leadership of institutions was highest in medicine, the military, higher education, the major companies, and the Supreme Court. The executive branch of the national government ranked seventh on a list of ten institutions. By 1973 the highest confidence levels were expressed for leadership in medicine, higher education, televi-

sion, news, the military, and organized religion (Huntington, 1975). Leadership by these institutions represented an apolitical, authority--respecting view. The major companies and the federal executive branch dropped to ninth and tenth on the list. It cannot be overlooked that this was a recession period with international consequences. Leadership in government and business was losing its efficacy at a time when the nation was being drawn more deeply into international events.

The third trend was an outgrowth of the confidence levels. As the views of governmental institutions declined, voter apathy increased. Jimmy Carter, in 1976, appealed to a key element of the population because he promised new organizational patterns at a the national level, and he appealed to the inward seeking who respected his religious candor. He was the man of the shifting tides of uneasiness. Public opinion polls showed that public confidence had risen significantly regarding the future, with the key exception of Blacks.[6] The Carter victory, however, was a personalized view for many voters, thus it was not easily translated into institutional changes. Carter won with 46 percent of the Protestant vote, the largest percentage since the election of Lyndon Johnson. By this time, however, the religious activity of a substantial number of Protestants was individualized and fundamentalist. One survey showed that two-thirds of the Protestants in the nation considered themselves to be evangelical in 1976.[7] There existed an atmosphere for the emergence of religiopolitical causes, which were not geared to the major parties. Participation in political parties drastically declined, with special-interest groups filling the vacuum. Thus, although these special-interest groups involved only about 6 percent of the population, they wielded strong power in the political arena.[8] Voter participation increased only on specialized or antiestablishment issues, and the Democratic and Republican parties were losing their bases of organization. The ultimate apathy was evidenced in the 1978 congressional elections, which had the lowest midterm voter turnout since 1942.[9] One of the best examples of special-interest group power in the 1970s was the Right to Life Party, which involved a group of Long Island, New York, housewives. By the end of the 1970s this party was powerful enough to be a major force in New York State politics, and was listed on the ballot in the elections. Nevertheless, the fact that only 35 percent of the voting age population participated in the elections illustrates our point that the individualized views of the world and American society remained a major challenge to the institutional framework of the nation.

The fourth aspect of the changing trend was the decline in liberalism and the reflection of this trend on state and national levels. Given the changes outlined above, the lack of liberal identification could be expected. The magnitude of the changes, however, was noteworthy. Within the Democratic Party the number of adherents who identified themselves as liberal declined from 30 percent in 1968 to 26 percent in 1976. Within the Republican Party the decline was from 16 percent to 6 percent. Overall, the number of persons who identified themselves as liberal declined from 24 percent to 19 percent in the period of 1968-1976.[10]

Much of the change had a moderating effect at the state and local levels. It meant that moderates could be elected at the state level on regional issues. It also meant that the lack of party discipline allowed liberals and Blacks to be elected at the local level. The total effect nevertheless could not be negated. Many liberal congressmen were electing to retire prematurely (in terms of age) by the 1980s, and others were moving toward more conservative identifications. Liberal organization and magazines had also shifted their focus (Jones et al., 1977). This resulted, in part, from the liberals' problems with the issues surrounding the Bakke case and related affirmative action issues. However, in the context in which we describe the changes, it was not simply a rift between the Jewish and labor communities and Black,s but a need for reaffirmation of what many felt were control mechanisms. Liberalism was not dead. Nevertheless, it had become a dying victim of its inability to address the fact of declining governmental and business confidence without distinctly separating liberals and conservatives. What in the 1960s appeared radical was often conservative--for example, local control, neighborhood government, and controls on spending. By the late 1970s, with an open split between Blacks and many liberals on racial issues, there was a return to the conservative camp with little challenge from the adherents of the 1960s.

The results of the four factors identified above were a growing trend of personalized individualism and an emphasis on political issues which lead to religiopolitical control. The issues that were place don state ballots in the late 1970s reflected this individualized religious scarcity

(commonly known as Proposition 13) in California, which limited spending based on use of property taxes. This idea spread rapidly during this period, with mixed results. However, the idea was spread to such an extent that over 30 states by 1979 were demanding a constitutional convention dedicated to seeking ways to balance the budget.

The limitations on spending perspectives were not the only ideas that fell into the religious control philosophy. In 1978 the New York State Legislature passed a law for juvenile prosecution, several states banned textbooks or other reading material, in Missouri the right to work laws were included on the ballot, an din numerous other states a variety of measures indicated the ability of special interest groups to fill the vacuum left by the majority will. During this period there were ballot issues in California, Idaho, and Oregon for restoration of the death penalty (all of which were passed in 1978), an initiative in California which would have permitted schools to fire homosexuals (it was defeated), and death penalty concerns. Crime rose as the most dominant concern in many states, and these issues carried the largest voter support. California expanded the use of the death penalty with 71.8 percent voter support; Idaho established minimum sentences for crimes with 69.6 percent of the vote; Oklahoma established mandatory minimum sentences for habitual criminals with 71 percent of the vote; and Oregon restored the death penalty with over 60 percent of the voters' support.[11]

The magnitude of the changes was evolving over a ten-year period. While the middle class could not control and did not trust business and governmental institutions, it was using its rights under an ill-defined Republican government to revolt against recent history. Thus, the issues were not new. What was new--and the real paradox--was that the conservatives had become the planners for the future. Rigid definitions of conservatism had declined. Senator Charles George Mathias of Maryland noted that the new test was the fine tuning being exerted by what we identify as the conservatism element.[12] The question was, how strong was conservatism and what was its long-term base?

## CONCLUSION

Several forces merged during the late 1960s and 1970s which constituted the basis for the "new minorities." First, there was a dissemination of rights which were guaranteed or opened up by the civil rights movement. Being a minority was a *right* that accorded certain rewards if a group could manipulate the political system to its advantage. Many groups gained by including their specific needs in legislation, or because they were needed by the economy. Blacks tended to lose because they were defined loosely in legislation and programs as disadvantaged and were not looked upon as a single interest group.

Second, postindustrial capitalism encouraged a new individualism type of politics that strained the system but invited new ideological dimensions of rights and freedoms. Women were active in these discussions because they could show how they benefitted the system, and how the system had great need for their skills. Other groups attempted to do the same, including undocumented workers, Italian Americans, and others. The key framework was the ability to define group needs and relate them to the needs of the state and the economy. Blacks clearly lost in many respects because they did not set forth this type of framework. The ideological basis that blacks had so successfully used in the 1960s dealt with constitutional rights and legislative mandates. The rights of the 1970s dealt with scarcity and the ability to manipulate symbols (such as the definition of minority) and ideas. Too often, Blacks had defined minority status solely in "negative" terms. The ideological framework of the 1970s was the opposite. To be a minority could mean greater access to scarce goods and rewards. Minority status had been transformed from a negative to a positive attribute.

Third, many of the forces contributing to the definitions of the "new minorities" dovetailed with the neoconservative tide. What appeared radical in the 1960s was no longer out of line when scarcity as an ideology was the issue. This can be shown to some degree by the neighborhood control movement, which by the 1970s incorporated many of the conservative principles adhered to by radicals of the prior decade. The same is the case for many of the other social movements of the 1970s. The right to be a minority has been defended by some of the leading intellectuals in the nation, while the 1960s-style liberals have continued to wage basically the same argument in defense of minorities.

In many respects, the conservatives won the battle to guide the state of the economy and the changing role of the nation in the world political economy. The election of Ronald Reagan in 1980 was the culmination of the collective efforts of the conservative forces discussed in this article. The religious groups were represented by loosely knit organizations such as the Moral Majority, while the conservative political action committees (PACs) took responsibility for defeating many liberal congressmen and senators. The intellectuals who had inspired change through articles and books also began to move into the vanguard. Although none of them joined Reagan's cabinet, there had emerged a more visible network of universities and foundations dedicated to the neoconservative principles, (for example, the Hoover Institute, the American Enterprise Institute, and the Heritage Foundation).

The merger of the political, religious, and intellectual adherents of the new right was far from cohesive. The Reagan administration did not appoint many of the candidates promoted by the Moral Majority or the neoconservative PACs. Moreover, it was not clear that the ideas of the neoconservatives could easily be translated into governmental and political action. It was abundantly clear, however, that Blacks were not prepared for the events that culminated in the election of Reagan and the victories of the neoconservatives. The traditional civil rights groups had not incorporated the black and white intellectuals on the left who probably could develop the most forceful arguments against the neoconservatives; and much of their strategy still emphasized intervention approaches or training options which were not in keeping with the downward economic trends. Moreover, Blacks as a group faced tremendous competition as one of the many "minority" or constituent groups competing for limited resources.

The economic and social needs were clear. However, in a nation where special-interest political groups set the norms of society, Blacks were emerging as one of the least influential groups. The Kerner Report had validated the problems of Blacks and helped sanction the right of minorities to claim redress from the state. The issue for the 1980s and the future was that the pre-1960s classification of minority based solely on race was no longer sufficient. The rewards in times of scarcity went to those who could combine their intellectual and political resources into institutions which supported the goals of the major economic leaders. It was the old game, which had taken a turn that was excluding Blacks from any meaningful participation.

## NOTES

1. Many groups, following the revolt of the 1960s, took advantage of the right to define themselves as minorities indirectly in legislation. Those with a specific problem, such as the handicapped, were cited directly. Hispanics benefitted by legislation that cited bilingual or bicultural needs. Blacks lost to a great degree because they were beneficiaries only of terms specifying "disadvantaged."
2. These figures are from *Social and Economic Status of the Black Population in the United Stated, 1974,* U.S. Government Printing Office.
3. See *Religion in America,* the Gallup Opinion Index 1977-1978, Princeton, New Jersey.
4. From the Washington *Post,* March 4, 1979.
5. See the special issue of *The Public Interest,* "The Great Society: Lessons for the Future," Winter 1974.
6. See note 3.
7. See note 3.
8. From the New York *Times,* November 14, 1978, p. B14.
9. From the *Congressional Quarterly,* March 31, 1979, p. 574.
10. From the New York *Times,* January 7, 1979, p. 20. The data cited in the newspaper article were from a survey conducted by the University of Michigan's Center for Political Studies.
11. From the *Congressional Quarterly,* November 18, 1978, p. 3300.
12. See note 10.

# RACISM AND RESEARCH: THE CASE OF THE TUSKEGEE SYPHILIS STUDY

*Read #*

*Allan M. Brandt*

The Tuskegee study of untreated syphilis was one of the most sordid episodes in American race relations and American medicine in this century. For a period of forty years, until 1972, doctors and public health officials held a deathwatch over some 400 syphilitic black sharecroppers in Alabama, in a "scientific" experiment that was riddled with invalid methods and in any case could produce no new useful information about syphilis.

The subjects of the study were never told they were participating in an "experiment"; treatment that could easily have cured them was deliberately withheld; and they were systematically deceived about the purpose of this "health program." As a result, scores of people died of the disease; others became permanently blind or insane; and the children of several were born with congenital syphilis.

How could this extraordinary episode, requiring the collaboration of doctors, county and state health departments, draft boards, and the U.S. Public Health Service, ever have occurred? As Allan Brandt suggests, the Tuskegee study can be understood only in terms of racism. It had its roots in pseudoscientific theories about race and about black sexuality. The study's willingness to treat people as less than human merely reflected the deep, irrational prejudice that permeated the rest of American life.

In 1932 the U.S. Public Health Service (USPHS) initiated an experiment in Macon County, Alabama, to determine the natural course of untreated, latent syphilis in black males. The test comprised 400 syphilitic men, as well as 200 uninfected men who served as controls. The first published report of the study appeared in 1936 with subsequent papers issued every four to six years, through the 1960s. When penicillin became widely available

by the early 1950s as the preferred treatment for syphilis, the men did not receive therapy. In fact, on several occasions, the USPHS actually sought to prevent treatment. Moreover, a committee at the federally operated Center for Disease Control decided in 1969 that the study should be continued. Only in 1972, when accounts of the study first appeared in the national press, did the Department of Health, Education and Welfare halt the experiment. At that time seventy four of the test subjects were still alive; at least twenty eight, but perhaps more than 100, had died directly from advanced syphilitic lesions.[1] In August 1972, HEW appointed an investigatory panel which issued a report the following year. The panel found the study to have been "ethically unjustified," and argued that penicillin should have been provided to the men.[2]

This articles attempts to place the Tuskegee Study in a historical context and to asses its ethical implications. Despite the media attention which the study received, the HEW *Final Report*, and the criticism expressed by several professional organizations, the experiment has been largely misunderstood. The most basic questions of *how* the study was undertaken in the first place and *why* it continued for forty years were never addressed by the HEW investigation. Moreover, the panel misconstrued the nature of the experiment, failing to consult important documents available at the National Archives which bear significantly on its ethical assessment. Only be examining the specific ways in which values are engaged in scientific research can the study be understood.

## RACISM AND MEDICAL OPINION

A brief review of the prevailing scientific thought regarding race and heredity in the early twentieth century is fundamental for an understanding of the Tuskegee Study. By the turn of the century, Darwinism had provided a new rationale for American racism.[3] Essentially primitive peoples, it was argued, could not be assimilated into a complex, white civilization. Scientists speculated that in the struggle for survival the Negro in American was doomed. Particularly prone to disease, vice, and crime, black Americans could not be helped by education or philanthropy. Social Darwinists analyzed census data to predict the virtual extinction of the Negro in the twentieth century, for they believed the Negro race in American was in the throes of a degenerative evolutionary process.[4]

The medical profession supported these findings of late nineteenth and early twentieth century anthropologists, ethnologists, and biologists. Physicians studying the effects of emancipation on health concluded almost universally that freedom had caused the mental, oral, and physical deterioration of the black population.[5] They substantiated this argument by citing examples in the comparative anatomy of the black and white races. As Dr. W. T. English wrote: "A careful inspection reveals the body of the negro a mass of minor defects and imperfections from the crown of the head to the soles of the feet . . . "[6] Cranial structures, wide nasal apertures, receding chins, projecting jaws, all typed the Negro as the lowest species in the Darwinian hierarchy.[7]

Interest in racial differences centered on the sexual nature of blacks. The Negro, doctors explained, possessed an excessive sexual desire, which threatened the very foundations of white society. As one physician noted in the *Journal of the American Medical Association*, "The negro springs from a southern race, and as such his sexual appetite is strong; all of his environments stimulate this appetite, and as a general rule his emotional type of religion certainly does not decrease it."[8] Doctors reported a complete lack of morality on the part of the blacks.

> Virtue in the negro race is like angels' visits few and far between. In a practice of sixteen years I have never examined a virgin negro over fourteen years of age.[9]

A particularly ominous feature of this overzealous sexuality, doctors argued, was the black males' desire for white women. "A perversion from which most races are exempt," wrote Dr. English, "prompts the negro's inclination toward white women . . . "[10] Though English estimated the "gray matter of the negro brain" to be at least a thousand years behind that of the white races, his genital organs were overdeveloped. As

Dr. William Lee Howard noted:

> The attacks on defenseless white women are evidences of racial instincts that are about as amenable to ethical culture as is the inherent odor of the race . . . When education will reduce the size of the negro's penis as well as bring about the sensitiveness of the terminal fibers which exist in the caucasian, then will it also be able to prevent the African's birthright to sexual madness and excess.[11]

One southern medical journal proposed "Castration Instead of Lynching," as retribution for black sexual crimes. "An impressive trial by a ghostlike kuklux klan [sic] and a 'ghost' physician or surgeon to perform the operation would make it an event the 'patient' would never forget," noted the editorial.[12]

According to these physicians, lust and immorality, unstable families, and reversion to barbaric tendencies made blacks especially prone to venereal diseases. One doctor estimated that over 50 percent of the Negroes over the age of twenty-five were syphilitic.[13] Virtually free of disease as slaves, they were now overwhelmed by it, according to informed medical opinion. Moreover, doctors believed that treatment for venereal disease among blacks was impossible, particularly because in its latent stage the symptoms of syphilis become quiescent. As Dr. Thomas W. Murrell wrote:

> They come for treatment at the beginning and at the end. When there are visible manifestations or when harried by pain, they readily come, for as a race they are not averse to physic; but tell them not, thought they look well and feel well, that are still diseased. Here ignorance rates science a fool . . .[14]

Even the best educated black, according to Murrell, could not be convinced to seek treatment for syphilis.[15] Venereal disease, according to some doctors, threatened the future of the race. The medical profession attributed the low birth rate among blacks to the high prevalence of venereal disease which caused stillbirths and miscarriages. Moreover, the high rates of syphilis were thought to lead to increased insanity and crime. One doctor writing at the turn of the century estimated that the number of insane Negroes had increased thirteen-fold since the end of the Civil War.[16] Dr. Murrell's conclusion echoed the most informed anthropological and ethnological data:

> So the scourge sweeps among them. Those that

are treated are only half cured, and the effort to assimilate a complex civilization drives their diseased minds until the results are criminal records. Perhaps here, in conjunction with tuberculosis, will be the end of the negro problem. Disease will accomplish what man cannot do.[17]

This particular configuration of ideas formed the core of medical opinion concerning, blacks, sex, and disease in the early twentieth century. Doctors generally discounted socioeconomic explanations of the state of black health, arguing that better medical care could not alter the evolutionary scheme.[18] These assumptions provide the backdrop for examining the Tuskegee Syphilis Study.

## THE ORIGINS OF THE EXPERIMENT

In 1929, under a grant from the Julius Rosenwald Fund, the USPHS conducted studies in the rural South to determine the prevalence of syphilis among blacks and explore the possibilities for mass treatment. The USPHS found Macon County, Alabama, in which the town of Tuskegee is located, to have the highest syphilis rate of the six counties surveyed. The Rosenwald Study concluded that mass treatment could be successfully implemented among rural blacks.[19] Although it is doubtful that the necessary funds would have been allocated even in the best economic conditions, after the economy collapsed in 1929, the findings were ignored. It is, however, ironic that the Tuskegee Study came to be based on findings of the Rosenwald Study that demonstrated the possibilities of mass treatment.

Three years later, in 1932, Dr. Taliaferro Clark, Chief of the USPHS Venereal Disease Division and author of the Rosenwald Study report, decided that conditions in Macon County merited renewed attention. Clark believed the high prevalence of syphilis offered an "unusual opportunity" for observation. Form its inception, the USPHS regarded the Tuskegee Study as a classic "study in nature," rather than an experiment.[20] As long as syphilis was so prevalent in Macon and most of the blacks went untreated throughout life, it seemed only natural to Clark that it would be valuable to observe the consequences. He described it as a "ready made situation."[21] Surgeon General H. S. Cumming wrote to R. R. Moton, Director of the Tuskegee Institute:

The recent syphilis control demonstration carried out in Macon County, with the financial assistance of the Julius Rosenwald Fund, revealed the presence of an unusually high rate in this county and, what is more remarkable, the fact that 99 per cent of this group was entirely without previous treatment. This combination, together with the expected cooperation of your hospital, offers an unparalleled opportunity for carrying on this piece of scientific research which probably cannot be duplicated anywhere else in the world.[22]

Although no formal protocol appears to have been written, several letters of Clark and Cumming suggest what the USPHS hoped to find. Clark indicated that it would be important to see how disease affected the daily lives of the men:

The results of these studies of case records suggest the desirability of making a further study of the effect of untreated syphilis on the human economy among people now living and engaged in their daily pursuits.[23]

It also seems that the USPHS believed the experiment might demonstrate that antisyphilitic treatment was unnecessary. As Cumming noted: "It is expected the results of this study may have a marked bearing on the treatment, or conversely the nonnecessity of treatment, of cases of latent syphilis."[24]

The immediate source of Cumming's hypothesis appears to have been the famous Oslo Study of untreated syphilis. Between 1890 and 1910, Professor C. Boeck, the chief of the Oslo Venereal Clinic, withheld treatment from almost two thousand patients infected with syphilis. He was convinced that therapies then available, primarily mercurial ointment, were of no value. When arsenic therapy became widely available by 1910, after Paul Ehrlich's historic discovery of "606," the study was abandoned. E. Bruusgaard, Boeck's successor, conducted a follow-up study of 473 of the untreated patients from 1925 to 1927. He found that 27.9 percent of these patients had undergone a "spontaneous cure," and now manifested no symptoms of the disease. Moreover, he estimated that as many as 70 percent of all syphilitics went through life without inconvenience from the disease.[25] His study, however, clearly acknowledged the dangers of untreated syphilis for the remaining 30 percent.

Thus every major textbook of syphilis at the time of the Tuskegee Study's inception strongly advocated treating syphilis even in its latent stages, which follow the initial inflammatory reaction. In discussing the Oslo Study, Dr. J.E. Moore, one of the nation's leading venereologists wrote, "This summary of Bruusgaard's study is by no means intended to suggest that syphilis be allowed to pass untreated.[26] If a complete cure could not be effected, at least the most devastating effects of the disease could be avoided. Although the standard therapies of the time, arsenical compounds and bismuth injection, involved certain dangers because of their toxicity, the alternatives were much worse. As the Oslo Study had shown, untreated syphilis could lead to cardiovascular disease, insanity, and premature death.[27] Moore wrote in his 1933 textbook:

> Though it imposes a slight though measurable risk of its own, treatment markedly diminishes the risk from syphilis. In latent syphilis, as I shall show, the probability of progression, relapse, or death is reduced from a probable 2530 percent without treatment to about 5 percent with it; and the gravity of the relapse if it occurs, is markedly diminished.[28]

"Another compelling reason for treatment," noted Moore, "exists in the fact that every patient with latent syphilis may be, and perhaps is, infectious, for others.[29] In 1932, the year in which the Tuskegee Study began, the USPHS sponsored and published a paper by Moore and six other syphilis experts that strongly argued for treating latent syphilis.[30]

The Oslo Study, therefore, could not have been provided justification for the USPHS to undertake a study that did not entail treatment. Rather, the suppositions that conditions in Tuskegee existed "naturally" and that men would not be treated anyway provided the experiment's rationale. In turn, these two assumptions rested on the prevailing medical attitudes concerning blacks, sex, and disease. For example, Clark explained the prevalence of venereal disease in Macon County by emphasizing promiscuity among blacks:

> This state of affairs is due to the paucity of doctors, rather low intelligence of the Negro population in this section, depressed economic conditions, and the very common promiscuous sex relations of this population group which not only contribute to the spread of syphilis but also contribute to the prevailing indifference with regard to treatment.[31]

In fact, Moore, who had written so persuasively in favor of treating latent syphilis, suggested that

existing knowledge did not apply to Negroes. Although he had called the Oslo Study "a never-to-be-repeated human experiment,"[32] he served as an expert consultant to the Tuskegee Study:

> I think that such a study as you have contemplated would be of immense value. It will be necessary of course in the consideration of the results to evaluate the special factors introduced by a selection of the material from negro males. Syphilis in the negro is in many respects almost a different disease from syphilis in the white.[33]

Dr. O.C. Wenger, chief of the federally operated venereal disease clinic at Hot Springs, Arkansas, praised Moore's judgment, adding, "This study will emphasize those differences."[34] On another occasion he advised Clark, "We must remember we are dealing with a group of people who are illiterate, have no conception of time, and whose personal history is always indefinite."[35]

The doctors who devised and directed the Tuskegee Study accepted the mainstream assumptions regarding blacks and venereal disease. The premise that blacks, promiscuous and lustful, would not seek or continue treatment, shaped the study. A test of untreated syphilis seemed "natural" because the USPHS presumed the men would never be treated; the Tuskegee Study made that a self-fulfilling prophecy.

## SELECTING THE SUBJECTS

Clark sent Dr. Raymond Vonderlehr to Tuskegee in September 1932 to assemble a sample of men with latent syphilis for the experiment. The basic design of the study called for the selections of syphilitic black males between the ages of twenty-five and sixty, thorough physical examination including x-rays, and finally, a spinal tap to determine the incidence of neurosyphilis.[36] They had no intention of providing any treatment for the infected men.[37] The USPHS originally scheduled the whole experiment to last six months, it seemed to be both a simple and inexpensive project.

The task of collecting the sample, however, proved to be more difficult than the USPHS had supposed. Vonderlehr canvassed the largely illiterate, poverty-stricken population of sharecroppers and tenant farmers in search of test subjects. If his circulars requested only men over twenty-five to attend his clinics, non would appear, suspecting he was conducting draft physicals. Therefore, he was forced to test large numbers of women and men who did not fit the experiment's specifications. This involved considerable expense since the USPHS had promised Macon County Board of Health that it would treat those who were infected, but not included in the study.[38] Clark wrote to Vonderlehr about the situation: "It never once occurred to me that we would be called upon to treat a large part of the county as return for the privilege of making this study . . . I am anxious to keep the expenditures for treatment down to the lowest possible point because it is the one item of expenditure in connection with the study most difficult to defend despite our knowledge of the need therefor."[39] Vonderlehr responded: "If we could find from 100 to 200 cases . . . we would not have to do another Wassermann on useless individuals . . ."[40]

Significantly, the attempt to develop the sample contradicted the prediction the USPHS had made initially regarding the prevalence of the disease in Macon County. Overall rates of syphilis fell well below expectations; as opposed to the USPHS projection of 35 percent, 20 percent of those treated were actually diseased.[41] Moreover, those who had sought and received previous treatment far exceeded the expectations of the USPHS. Clark noted in a letter to Vonderlehr:

> I find your report of March 6th quite interesting but regret the necessity for Wassermanning [sic] . . . such a large number of individuals in order to uncover this relatively limited number of untreated cases.[42]

Further difficulties arose in enlisting the subjects to participate in the experiment, to be "Wassermanned," and to return for a subsequent series of examinations. Vonderlehr found that only the offer of treatment elicited the cooperation of the men. They were told they were ill and were promised free care. Offered therapy, they became willing subjects.[43] The USPHS did not tell the men that they were participants in an experiment; on the contrary, the subjects believed they were being treated for "bad blood" the rural South's colloquialism for syphilis. They thought they were participating in a public health demonstration similar to the one that had been conducted by the Julius Rosenwald Fund in Tuskegee several years earlier. In the end, the men were so eager for medical care that the number of defaulters in the experiment proved to be insignificant.[44]

To preserve the subjects' interest, Vonderlehr gave most of the men mercurial ointment, a non-effective drug, while some of the younger men apparently received inadequate dosages of neoarsphenamine.[45] This required Vonderlehr to write frequently to Clark requesting supplies. He feared the experiment would fail if the men were not offered treatment.

> It is desirable and essential if the study is to be a success to maintain the interest of each of the cases examined by me through to the time when the spinal puncture can be completed. Expenditure of several hundred dollars for drugs for these men would be well worth while if their interest and cooperation would be maintained in so doing . . . It is my desire to keep the main purpose of the work from the negroes in the county and continue their interest in treatment. That is what the vast majority wants and the examination seems relatively unimportant to them in comparison. It would probably cause the entire experiment to collapse if the clinics were stopped before the work is completed.[46]

On another occasion he explained:

> Dozens of patients have been sent away without treatment during the past two weeks and it would have been impossible to continue without the free distribution of drugs because of the unfavorable impression made on the negro.[47]

The readiness of the test subjects to participate of course contradicted the notion that blacks would not seek or continue therapy.

The final procedure of the experiment was to be a spinal tap to test for evidence of neurosyphilis. The USPHS presented this purely diagnostic exam, which often entails considerable pain and complications, to the men as a "special treatment." Clark explained to Moore:

> We have not yet commenced the spinal punctures. This operation will be deferred to the last in order not to unduly disturb our field work by any adverse reports by the patients subjected to spinal puncture because of some disagreeable sensations following this procedure. These negroes are very ignorant and easily influenced by things that would be of minor significance in a more intelligent group.[48]

The letter to the subjects announcing the spinal tap read:

> Some time ago you were given a thorough examination and since that time we hope you have

gotten a great deal of treatment for bad blood. You will now be given your last chance to get a second examination. This examination is a very special one and after it is finished you will be given a special treatment if it is believed you are in a condition to stand it . . .

REMEMBER THIS IS YOUR LAST CHANCE FOR SPECIAL FREE TREATMENT. BE SURE TO MEET THE NURSE.[49]

The HEW investigation did not uncover this crucial fact: the men participated in the study under the guise of treatment.

Despite the fact that their assumption regarding prevalence and black attitudes toward treatment had proved wrong, the USPHS decided in the summer of 1933 to continue the study. Once again, it seemed only "natural" to pursue the research since the sample already existed, and with a depressed economy, the cost of treatment appeared prohibitive although there is no indication it was ever considered. Vonderlehr first suggested extending the study in letters to Clark and Wenger:

> At the end of this project we shall have a considerable number of cases presenting various complications of syphilis, who have received only mercury and may still be considered untreated in the modern sense of therapy. Should these cases be followed over a period of from five to ten years many interesting facts could be learned regarding the course and complications of untreated syphilis.[50]

"As I see it," responded Wenger, "we have no further interest in these patients *until they die.*"[51] Apparently, the physicians engaged in the experiment believed that only autopsies could scientifically confirm the findings of the study. Surgeon General Cumming explained this in a letter to R. R. Moton, requesting the continued cooperation of the Tuskegee Institute Hospital:

> This study which was predominantly clinical in character points to the frequent occurrence of severe complications involving the various vital organs of the body and indicates that syphilis as a disease does a great deal of damage. since clinical observations are not considered final in the medical world, it is our desire to continue observation on the cases selected for the recent study and if possible to bring a percentage of these cases to autopsy so that pathological confirmation may be made of the disease processes.[52]

Bringing the men to autopsy required the USPHS to devise a further series of deceptions and in-

ducements. Wenger warned Vonderlehr that the men must not realize that they would be autopsied:

> There is one danger in the latter plan and that is if the colored population become aware that accepting free hospital care means a postmortem every darkey will leave Macon County and it will hurt [Dr. Eugene] Dibble's hospital.[53]

"Naturally," responded Vonderlehr, "it is not my intention to let it be generally known that the main object of the present activities is the bringing of the men to necropsy."[54] The subjects' trust in the USPHS made the plan viable. The USPHS gave Dr. Dibble, the Director of the Tuskegee Institute Hospital, an interim appointment to the Public Health Service. As Wenger noted:

> One thing is certain. They only way we are going to get postmortems is to have the demise take place in Dibble's hospital and when these colored folks are told that Doctor Dibble is now a Government doctor too they will have more confidence.[55]

After the USPHS approved the continuation of the experiment in 1933, Vonderlehr decided that it would be necessary to select a group of healthy, uninfected men to serve as controls. Vonderlehr, who had succeeded Clark as Chief of the Venereal Disease Division, sent Dr. J.R. Heller to Tuskegee to gather the control group. Heller distributed drugs (noneffective) to these men, which suggests that they also believed they were undergoing treatment.[56] Control subjects who became syphilitic were simply transferred to the test group a strikingly inept violation of standard research procedure.[57]

The USPHS offered several inducements to maintain contact and to procure the continued cooperation of the men. Eunice Rivers, a black nurse, was hired to follow their health and to secure approval for autopsies. She gave the men noneffective medicines "spring tonic" and aspirin as well as transportation and hot meals on the days of their examinations.[58] More important, Nurse Rivers provided continuity to the project over the entire forty year period. By supplying "medicinals," the USPHS was able to continue to deceive the participants, who believed that they were receiving therapy from the government doctors. Deceit was integral to the study. When the test subjects complained about spinal taps one doctor wrote:

> They simply do not like spinal punctures. A few

of those who were tapped are enthusiastic over the results but to most, the suggestion causes violent shaking of the head; others claim they were robbed of their procreative powers (regardless of the fact that I claim it simulates them).[59]

Letters to the subjects announcing an impending USPHS visit to Tuskegee explained: "[The doctor] wants to make a special examination to find out how you have been feeling and whether the treatment has improved your health."[60] In fact, after the first six months of the study, the USPHS had furnished no treatment whatsoever.

Finally, because it proved difficult to persuade the men to come to the hospital when they became severely ill, the USPHS promised to cover their burial expenses. The Milbank Memorial Fund provided approximately $50 per man for this purpose beginning in 1935. This was a particularly strong inducement as funeral rites constituted an important component of the cultural life of rural blacks.[61] One report of the study concluded, "Without this suasion it would, we believe, have been impossible to secure the cooperation of the group and their families.[62]

Reports of the study's findings, which appeared regularly in the medical press beginning in 1936, consistently cited the ravages of untreated syphilis. The first paper, read at the 1936 American Medical Association annual meeting, found "that syphilis in this period [latency] tends to greatly increase the frequency of manifestations of cardiovascular disease."[63] Only 16 percent of the subjects gave no sign of morbidity as opposed to 61 percent of the controls. Ten years later, a report noted coldly, "The fact that nearly twice as large a proportion of the syphilitic individuals as of the control group has died is a very striking one." Life expectancy, concluded the doctors, is reduced by about 20 percent.[64]

A 1955 article found that slightly more than 30 percent of the test group autopsied had died *directly* from advance syphilitic lesions of either the cardiovascular or the central nervous system.[65] Another published account stated, "Review of those still living reveals that an appreciable number have late complications of syphilis which probably will result, for some at least, in contributing materially to the ultimate cause of death."[66] In 1950, Dr. Wenger had concluded, "We now know, where we could only surmise before, that we have contributed to their ailments and shortened their lives."[67] As black physician Vernal Cave, a member of the HEW panel, later wrote, "They

proved a point, then proved a point, then proved a point."[68]

During the forty years of the experiment the USPHS had sought on several occasions to ensure that the subjects did not receive treatment from other sources. To this end, Vonderlehr met with groups of local black doctors in 1934, to ask their cooperation in not treating the men. Lists of subjects were distributed to Macon County physicians along with letters requesting them to refer these men back to the USPHS if they sought care.[69] The USPHS warned the Alabama Health Department not to treat the test subjects when they took a mobile VD unit into Tuskegee in the early 1940s.[70] In 1941, the Army drafted several subjects and told them to begin antisyphilitic treatment immediately. The USPHS supplied the draft board with a list of 256 names they desired to have excluded from the treatment, and the board complied.[71]

In spite of these efforts, by the early 1950s many of the men had secured some treatment on their own. By 1952, almost 30 percent of the test subjects had received some penicillin, although only 7.5 percent had received what could be considered adequate doses.[72] Vonderlehr wrote to one of the participating physicians, "I hope that the availability of antibiotics has not interfered too much with this project."[73] A report published in 1955 considered whether the treatment that some of the men had obtained had "defeated" the study. The article attempted to explain the relatively low exposure to penicillin in an age of antibiotics, suggesting as a reason: "the stoicism of these men as a group; they still regard hospitals and medicines with suspicion and prefer an occasional dose of time-honored herbs or tonics to modern drugs."[74] The authors failed to note that the men believed they already were under the care of the government doctors and thus saw no need to seek treatment elsewhere. Any treatment which the men might have received, concluded the report, had been insufficient to compromise the experiment.

When the USPHS evaluated the status of the study in the 1960s they continued to rationalize the racial aspects of the experiment. For example, the minutes of a 1965 meeting at the Center for Disease Control recorded:

> Racial issue was mentioned briefly. Will not affect the study. Any questions can be handled by saying these people were at the point that therapy would no longer help them. They are getting better medical care than they would under any other circumstances.[75]

A group of physicians met again at the CDC in 1960 to decide whether or not to terminate the study. Although one doctor argued that the study should be stopped and the men treated, the consensus was to continue. Dr. J. Lawton Smith remarked, "You will never have another study like this; take advantage of it."[76] A memo prepared by Dr. James B. Lucas, Assistant Chief of the Venereal Disease Branch, stated: "Nothing learned will prevent, find, or cure a single case of infectious syphilis or bring us closer to your basic mission of controlling venereal disease in the United States."[77] He concluded, however, that the study should be continued "along its present lines." When the first accounts of the experiment appeared in the national press in July 1972, data were still being collected and autopsies performed.[78]

## THE HEW FINAL REPORT

HEW finally formed the Tuskegee Syphilis Study Ad Hoc Advisory Panel on August 28, 1972, in response to criticism that the press descriptions of the experiment had triggered. The panel, composed of nine members, five of them black, concentrated on two issues. First, was the study justified in 1932 and had the men given their informed consent? Second, should penicillin have been provided when it became available in the early 1950s? The panel was also charged with determining if the study should be terminated and assessing current policies regarding experimentation with human subjects.9 The group issued their report in June 1973.

By focusing on the issues of penicillin therapy and informed consent, the *Final Report* and the investigation betrayed a basic misunderstanding of the experiment's purposes and design. The HEW report implied that the failure to provide penicillin constituted the study's major ethical misjudgment; implicit was the assumption that no adequate therapy existed prior to penicillin. Nonetheless medical authorities firmly believed in the efficacy of arsenotherapy for treating syphilis at the time of the experiment's inception in 1932. The panel further failed to recognize that the entire study had been predicated on non-treatment. Provision of effective medication would have violated the rationale of the experiment to study the natural course of the disease until death. On several occasions, in fact, the USPHS had prevented the men from receiving proper treatment. Indeed, there is no evidence that the USPHS

ever considered providing penicillin.

The other focus of the *Final Report* informed consent also served to obscure the historical facts of the experiment. In light of the deceptions and exploitations which the experiment perpetrated, it is an understatement to declare, as the *Report* did, that the experiment was "ethically unjustified," because it failed to obtain informed consent from the subjects. The *Final Report's* statement, "Submitting voluntarily is not informed consent," indicated that the panel believed that the men had volunteered *for the experiment*.[80] The records in the National Archives make clear that the men did not submit voluntarily to an experiment; they were told and they believed that they were getting free treatment from expert government doctors for a serious disease. The failure of the HEW *Final Report* to expose this critical fact that the USPHS lied to the subjects calls into question the thoroughness and credibility of their investigation.

Failure to place the study in a historical context also made it impossible for the investigation to deal with the essentially racist nature of the experiment. The panel treated the study as an aberration, well-intentioned but misguided.[81] Moreover, concern that the *Final Report* might be viewed as a critique of human experimentation in general seems to have severely limited the scope of the inquiry. The *Final Report* is quick to remind the reader on two occasions: "The position of the Panel must not be construed to be a general repudiation of scientific research with human subjects."[82] The *Report* assures us that a better designed experiment could have been justified:

> It is possible that a scientific study in 1932 of untreated syphilis, properly conceived with a clear protocol and conducted with suitable subjects who fully understood the implications of their involvement, might have been justified in the pre-penicillin era. This is especially true when one considers the uncertain nature of the results of treatment of late latent syphilis and the highly toxic nature of therapeutic agents then available.[83]

This statement is questionable in view of the proven dangers of untreated syphilis known in 1932.

Since the publication of the HEW *Final Report*, a defense system of the Tuskegee Study has emerged. These arguments, most clearly articulated by Dr. R. H. Kampmeier in the *Southern Medical Journal*, center on the limited knowledge of effective therapy for latent syphilis when the experiment began. Kampmeier argues that by 1950, penicillin would have been of no value for these men.[84] Others have suggested that the men were fortunate to have been spared the highly toxic treatment of the earlier period.[85] Moreover, even these contemporary defenses assume that the men never would have been treated anyway. As Dr. Charles Barnett of Stanford University wrote in 1974, "The lack of treatment was not contrived the USPHS but was an established fact of which they proposed to take advantage."[86] Several doctors who participate din the study continued to justify the experiment. Dr. J. R. Heller, who on one occasion had referred to the test subjects as the "Ethiopian population," told reporters in 1972:

> I don't see why they should be shocked or horrified. There was no racial side to this. It just happened to be in a black community. I feel this was a perfectly straightforward study, perfectly ethical, with controls. Part of our mission as physicians is to find out what happens to individuals with disease and without disease.[87]

These apologies, as well as the HEW *Final Report*, ignore many of the essential ethical issues which the study poses. The Tuskegee Study reveals the persistence of beliefs within the medical profession about the nature of blacks, sex, and disease belies that had tragic repercussions long after their alleged "scientific" bases were known to be incorrect. Most strikingly, the entire health of a community was jeopardized by leaving a communicable disease untreated.[88] As a result, the ethical canons of experimenting on human subjects were completely disregarded.

The study also raises significant questions about professional self-regulation and scientific bureaucracy. Once the USPHS decided to extend the experiment in the summer of 1933, it was unlikely that the test would be halted short of the men's deaths. The experiment was widely reported for forty years without evoking any significant protest within the medical community. Nor did any bureaucratic mechanism exist within the government for the periodic reassessment of the Tuskegee experiment's ethics and scientific value. The USPHS sent physicians to Tuskegee every several years to check on the study's progress, but never subjected the morality or usefulness of the experiment to serious scrutiny. Only the press accounts of 1972 finally punctured the continued rationalizations of the USPHS and brought the study to an end.

Even the HEW investigation was compromised by fear that it would be considered a threat to future human experimentation.

In retrospect the Tuskegee Study revealed more about the pathology of racism than it did about the pathology of syphilis; more about the nature of scientific inquiry than the nature of the disease process. The injustice committed by the experiment went well beyond the facts outlined in the press and the HEW *Final Report*. The degree of deception and damages have been seriously underestimated. As this history of the study suggests, the notion that science is a value free discipline must be rejected. The need for greater vigilance in assessing the specific ways in which social values and attitudes affect professional behavior is clearly indicted.

## NOTES

1. The best general accounts of the study are "The 40-Year Death Watch," *Medical World News* (August 18, 1972), pp. 15-17; and Dolores Katz, "Why 430 Blacks with Syphilis Went Uncured for 40 Years," Detroit *Free Press* (November 5, 1972). The mortality figure is based on a published report of the study which appeared in 1955. See Jesse J. Peters, James H, Peers, Sidney Olansky, John C. Cutler, and Geraldine Gleeson, "Untreated Syphilis in the Male Negro: Pathological Findings in Syphilitic and Nonsyphilitic Patents," *Journal of Chronic Diseases* 1 (February 1955), 127-48. The articles estimated that 30.4 percent of the untreated men would die from syphilitic lesions.
2. *Final Report* of the Tuskegee Syphilis Study Ad Hoc Advisory Panel, Department of Health, Education, and Welfare (Washington, D.C.: GPO, 1973). (Hereafter, HEW *Final Report*.)
3. See George M. Frederickson, *The Black Image in the White Mind* (New York: Harper and Row, 1971), pp. 228-55. Also, John H. Haller, *Outcasts From Evolution* (Urbana, Ill.: University of Illinois Press, 1971), pp. 40-68.
4. Frederickson, pp. 247-49.
5. "Deterioration of the American Negro," *Atlanta Journal Record of Medicine* 5 (July 1903), 287-88. See also, J. A. Rodgers, "The Effect of Freedom upon the Psychological Development of the Negro," *Proceedings* of the American Medico-Psychological Association 7 (1900), 88-99. "From the most healthy race in the country forty years ago," concluded Dr. Henry McHatton, "he is today the most diseased." "The Sexual Status of the Negro--Past and Present," *American Journal of Dermatology and Genito-Urinary Diseases* 10 (January 1906), 7-9.
6. W. T. English, "The Negro Problem from the Physician's Point of View, *Atlanta Journal-Record of Medicine* 5 (October 1903), 461. See also, "Racial Anatomical Peculiarities," *New York Medical Journal* 63 (April 1896), 500-01.
7. "Racial Anatomical Peculiarities," p. 501. Also, Charles S. Bacon, "The Race Problem," *Medicine* (Detroit) 9 (May 1903), 338-43.
8. H. H. Hazen, "Syphilis in the American Negro," *Journal of the American Medical Association* 63 (August 8, 1914), 463. For deeper background into the historical relationship of racism and sexuality see Winthrop D. Jordan, *White Over Black* (Chapel Hill: University of North Carolina Press, 1968; Pelican Books, 1969), pp. 32-40.
9. Daniel David Quillian, "Racial Peculiarities: A Cause of

the Prevalence of Syphilis in Negroes," *American Journal of Dermatology and Genito-Urinary Diseases* 10 (July 1906), p. 277.

10. English, p. 463.

11. William Lee Howard, "The Negro as a Distinct Ethnic Factor in Civilization," *Medicine* (Detroit) 9 (June 1903), 424. See also, Thomas W. Murrell, "Syphilis in the American Negro," *Journal of the American Medical Association* 54 (March 12, 1910), 848.

12. "Castration Instead of Lynching," *Atlanta Journal-Record of Medicine* 8 (October 1906), 457. The editorial added: "The badge of disgrace and emasculation might be branded upon the face or forehead, as a warning, in the form of an 'R,' emblematic of the crime for which this punishment was and will be inflicted."

13. Searle Harris, "The Future of the Negro from the Standpoint of the Southern Physician," *Alabama Medical Journal* 14 (January 1902), 62. Other articles on the prevalence of venereal disease among blacks are: H.L. McNeil, "Syphilis in the Southern Negro," *Journal of the American Medical Association* 67 (September 30, 1916), 1001-04; Ernest Philip Boas, "The Relative Prevalence of Syphilis Among Negroes and Whites," *Social Hygiene* 1 (September 1915), 610-16. Doctors went to considerable trouble to distinguish the morbidity and mortality of various diseases among blacks and whites. See, for example, Marion M. Torchia, "Tuberculosis Among American Negroes: Medical Research on a Racial Disease, 1930-1950," *Journal of the History of Medicine and Allied Sciences*, 32 (July 1977), 252-79.

14. Thomas W. Murrell, "Syphilis in the Negro: Its Bearing on the Race Problem," *American Journal of Dermatology and Genito-Urinary Diseases* 10 (August 1906), 307.

15. "Even among the educated, only a very few will carry out the most elementary instructions as to personal hygiene. One thing you cannot do, and that is to convince the negro that he has a disease that he cannot see or feel. This is due to lack of concentration rather than lack of faith; even if he does believe, he does not care; a child of fancy, the sensations of the passing hour are his only guides to the future," Murrell, "Syphilis in the American Negro," p. 847.

16. "Deterioration of the American Negro," *Atlanta Journal-Record of Medicine* 5 (July 1903), 288.

17. Murrell, "Syphilis in the Negro; Its Bearing on the Race Problem," p. 307.

18. "The anatomical and physiological conditions of the African must be understood, his place in the anthropological scale realized, and his biological basis accepted as being unchangeable by man, before we shall be able to govern his natural uncontrollable sexual passions." See, "As Ye Sow That Shall Ye Also Reap," *Atlanta Journal-Record of Medicine* 1 (June 1899), 266.

19. Taliaferro Clark, *The Control of Syphilis in Southern Rural Areas* (Chicago: Julius Rosenwald Fund, 1932), 53-48. Approximately 35 percent of the inhabitants of Macon County who were examined were found to be syphilitic.

20. See Claude Bernard, *An Introduction to the Study of Experimental Medicine* (New York: Dover, 1865, 1957), pp. 5-26. (In 1865, Claude Bernard, the famous French physiologist, outlined the distinction between a "study in nature" and experimentation. A study in nature required simple observation, an essentially passive act, while experimentation demanded intervention which altered the original condition. The Tuskegee Study was thus clearly not a study in nature. The very act of diagnosis altered the original conditions. "It is on this very possibility of acting or not acting on a body," wrote Bernard, "that the distinction will exclusively rest between sciences called sciences of observation and sciences called experimental.")

21. Taliaferro Clark to M. M. Davis, October 29, 1932. Records of the USPHS Venereal Disease Division, Record Group 90, Box 239, National Archives, Washington National Record

Center, Suitland, Maryland. (Hereafter, NA-WNRC). Materials in this collection which relate to the early history of the study were apparently never consulted by the HEW investigation. Included are letters, reports, and memoranda written by the physicians engaged in the study.

22. H. S. Cumming to R. R. Moton, September 20, 1932. NA-WNRC.

23. Clark to Davis, October 29, 1932, NA-WNRC.

24. Cumming to Moton, September 20, 1932, NA-WNRC.

25. Bruusgaard was able to locate 309 living patients, as well as records from 164 who were diseased. His findings were published as *"Ueber das Schicksal der nicht specifizch behandelten Luctiken,"* *Archives of Dermatology and Syphilis* 157 (1929), 309-32. The best discussion of the Boeck-Bruusgaard data is E. Gurney Clark and Niels Danbolt, "The Oslo Study of the Natural History of Untreated Syphilis," *Journal of Chronic Diseases* 2 (September 1955), 311-44.

26. Joseph Earle Moore, *The Modern Treatment of Syphilis* (Baltimore: Charles C. Thomas, 1933), p. 24.

27. Moore, pp. 231-47; see also John H. Stokes, *Modern Clinical Syphilology* (Philadelphia: W.B. Saunders, 1928), pp. 231-39.

28. Moore, p. 237.

29. Moore, p. 236.

30. J.E. Moore, H.N. Cole, P.A. O'Leary, J.H. Stokes, U.J. Wile, T. Clark, T. Parran, J.H. Usilton, "Cooperative Clinical Studies in the Treatment of Syphilis: Latent Syphilis," *Venereal Disease Information* 13 (September 20, 1932), 351. The authors also concluded that the latently syphilitic were potential carriers of the disease, thus meriting treatment.

31. Clark to Paul A. O'Leary, September 27, 1932, NA-WNRC. O'Leary, of the Mayo Clinic, misunderstood the design of the study, replying: "The investigation which you are planning in Alabama is indeed an intriguing one, particularly because of the opportunity it affords of observing treatment in a previously untreated group. I assure you such a study is of interest to me, and I shall look forward to its report in the future." O'Leary to Clark, October 3, 1932, NA-WNRC.

32. Joseph Earle Moore, "Latent Syphilis," unpublished typescript (n.d.), p. 7. American Social Hygiene Association Papers, Social Welfare History Archives Center, University of Minnesota, Minneapolis, Minnesota.

33. Moore to Clark, September 28, 1932, NA-WNRC. Moore had written in his textbook, "In late syphilis the negro is particularly prone to the development of bone or cardiovascular lesions." See Moore, *The Modern Treatment of Syphilis*, p. 35.

34. O. C. Wenger to Clark, October 3, 1932, NA-WNRC.

35. Wenger to Clark, September 29, 1932, NA-WNRC.

36. Clark Memorandum, September 26, 1932, NA-WNRC. See also, Clark to Davis, October 29, 1932, NA-WNRC.

37. As Clark wrote: "You will observe that our plan has nothing to do with treatment. It is purely a diagnostic procedure carried out to determine what has happened to the syphilitic Negro who has had no treatment." Clark to Paul A. O'Leary, September 27, 1932, NA-WNRC.

38. D. G. Gill to O. C. Wenger, October 10, 1932, NA-WNRC.

39. Clark to Vonderlehr, January 25, 1935, NA-WNRC.

40. Vonderlehr to Clark, February 28, 1933, NA-WNRC.

41. Vonderlehr to Clark, November 2, 1932, NA-WNRC. Also, Vonderlehr to Clark, February 6, 1933, NA-WNRC.

42. Clark to Vonderlehr, March 9, 1933, NA-WNRC.

43. Vonderlehr later explained: "The reason treatment was given to many of these men was twofold: First, when the study was started in the fall of 1932, no plans had been made for it continuation and a few of the patients were treated before we fully realized the need for continuing the project on a permanent basis. Second it was difficult to

hold the interest of the group of Negroes to Macon County unless some treatment was given." Vonderlehr to Austin V. Diebert, December 5, 1938, Tuskegee Syphilis Study Ad Hoc Advisory Panel Papers, Box 1, National Library of Medicine, Bethesda, Maryland. (Hereafter, TSS-NLM.) This collection contains the materials assembled by the HEW investigation in 1972.

44. Vonderlehr to Clark, February 6, 1933, NA-WNRC.
45. H. S. Cumming to J. N. Baker, August 5, 1933, NA-WNRC.
46. January 22, 1933; January 12, 1933, NA-WNRC.
47. Vonderlehr to Clark, January 28, 1933, NA-WNRC.
48. Clark to Moore, March 25, 1933, NA-WNRC.
49. Macon County Health Department, "Letter to Subjects," n.d., NA-WNRC.
50. Vonderlehr to Clark, April 8, 1933, NA-WNRC. See also, Vonderlehr to Wenger, July 18, 1933, NA-WNRC.
51. Wenger to Vonderlehr, July 21, 1933, NA-WNRC. The italics are Wenger's.
52. Cumming to Moton, July 27, 1933, NA-WNRC.
53. Wenger to Vonderlehr, July 21, 1933, NA-WNRC.
54. Vonderlehr to Murray Smith, July 27, 1933, NA-WNRC.
55. Wenger to Vonderlehr, August 5, 1933, NA-WNRC. (The degree of black cooperation in conducting the study remains unclear and would be impossible to properly asses sin an article of this length. It seems certain that some members of the Tuskegee Institute staff such as R. R. Moton and Eugene Dibble understood the nature of the experiment and gave their support to it. There is, however, evidence that some blacks who assisted the USPHS physicians were not aware of the deceptive nature of the experiment. Dr. Joshua Williams, an intern at the John A. Andrew Memorial Hospital [Tuskegee Institute] in 1932, assisted Vonderlehr in taking blood samples of the test subjects. In 1973 he told the HEW panel: "I know we thought it was merely a service group organized to help the people in the area. We didn't know it was a research project at all at the time." [See, "Transcript of Proceedings," Tuskegee Syphilis Study Ad Hoc Advisory Panel, February 23, 1973, Unpublished typescript. National Library of Medicine, Bethesda, Maryland.] It is also apparent that Eunice Rivers, the black nurse who had primary responsibility for maintaining contact with the men over the forty years, did not fully understand the dangers of the experiment. In any event, black involvement in the study in no way mitigates the racial assumptions of the experiment, but rather demonstrates their power.)
56. Vonderlehr to Wenger, October 24, 1933, NA-WNRC. Controls were given salicylates.
57. Austin V. Diebert and Martha C. Bruyere, "Untreated Syphilis in the Male Negro, III," *Venereal Disease Information* 27 (December 1946), 301-14.
58. Eunice Rivers, Stanley Schuman, Lloyd Simpson, Sidney Olansky, "Twenty-Years of Followup Experience In a Long-Range Medical Study," *Public Health Reports* 68 (April 1953), 391-95. In this article Nurse Rivers explains her role in the experiment. She wrote: "Because of the low educational status of the majority of the patients, it was impossible to appeal to them from a purely scientific approach. Therefore, various methods were used to maintain their interest. Free medicines, burial assistance or insurance (the project being referred to as 'Miss Rivers' Lodge'), free hot meals on the days of examination, transportation to and from the hospital, and an opportunity to stop in town on the return trip to shop or visit with their friends on the streets all helped. In spite of these attractions, there were some who refused their examinations because they were not sick and did not see that they being benefitted." (p. 393).
59. Austin V. Diebert to Raymond Vonderlehr, March 20, 1939, TSS-NLM, Box 1.
60. Murray Smith to Subjects (1938), TSS-NLM, Box 1. See also,

Sidney Olansky to John C. Cutler, November 6, 1951, TSS-NLM, Box 2.
61. The USPHS originally requested that the Julius Rosenwald Fund meet this expense. See Cumming to Davis, October 4, 1934, NA-WNRC. This money was usually divided between the undertaker, pathologist, and hospital. Lloyd Isaacs to Raymond Vonderlehr, April 23, 1940, TSS-NLM, Box 1.
62. Stanley H. Schuman, Sidney Olansky, Eunice Rivers, C. A. Smith, Dorothy S. Rambo, "Untreated Syphilis in the Male negro: Background and Current Status of Patients in the Tuskegee Study," *Journal of Chronic Diseases* 2 (November 1955), 555.
63. R. A. Vonderlehr and Taliaferro Clark, "Untreated Syphilis in the Male Negro," *Venereal Disease Information* 17 (September 1936), 262.
64. J. R. Heller and P. T. Bruyere, "Untreated Syphilis in the Male Negro: II. Mortality During 12 Years of Observation," *Venereal Disease Information* 27 (February 1946), 34-38.
65. Jesse J. Peters, James H. Peers, Sidney Olansky, John C. Cutler, and Geraldine Gleeson, "Untreated Syphilis in the Male Negro: Pathologic Findings in Syphilitic and Non-Syphilitic Patients," *Journal of Chronic Diseases* 1 (February 1955), 127-48.
66. Sidney Olansky, Stanley H. Schuman, Jesse J. Peters, C. A. Smith and Dorothy S. Rambo, "Untreated Syphilis in the Male Negro, X. Twenty Years of Clinical Observation of Untreated Syphilitic and Presumably Nonsyphilitic Groups," *Journal of Chronic Diseases* 4 (August 1956), 184.
67. O. C. Wenger, "Untreated Syphilis in Male Negro," unpublished typescript, 1950, p. 3. Tuskegee Files, Center for Disease Control, Atlanta, Georgia. (Hereafter TF-CDC.)
68. Vernal G. Cave, "Proper Uses and Abuses of the Health Care Delivery System for Minorities with Special Reference to the Tuskegee Syphilis Study," *Journal of the National Medical Association* 67 (January 1975), 83.
69. See for example, Vonderlehr to B. W. Booth, April 18, 1934; Vonderlehr to E. R. Lett, November 20, 1933, NA-WNRC.
70. "Transcript of Proceedings--Tuskegee Syphilis Ad Hoc Advisory Panel," February 23, 1973, unpublished typescript, TSS-NLM, Box 1.
71. Raymond Vonderlehr to Murray Smith, April 30, 1942; and Smith to Vonderlehr, June 8, 1942. TSS-NLM, Box 1.
72. Stanley H. Schuman, Sidney Olansky, Eunice Rivers, C. A. Smith, and Dorothy S. Rambo, "Untreated Syphilis in the Male Negro: Background and Current Status of Patients in the Tuskegee Study," *Journal of Chronic Diseases* 2 (November 1955), 350-53.
73. Raymond Vonderlehr to Stanley H. Schuman, February 5, 1952, TSS-NLM, Box 2.
74. Schuman et al. p. 550.
75. "Minutes, April 5, 1965," unpublished typescript, TSS-NLM, Box 1.
76. "Tuskegee Ad Hoc Committee Meeting--Minutes, February 6, 1969," TF-CDC.
77. James B. Lucas to William J. Brown, September 10, 1970, TF-CDC.
78. Elizabeth M. Kennebrew to Arnold C. Schroeter, February 24, 1971, TSS-NLM, Box 1.
79. See *Medical Tribune* (September 13, 1972), pp. 1, 20; and "Report on HEW's Tuskegee Report," *Medical World News*, (September 14, 1973), pp. 57-58.
80. HEW *Final Report*, p. 7.
81. The notable exception is Jay Katz's eloquent "Reservation About the Panel Report on Charge 1," HEW *Final Report*, pp. 14-15.
82. HEW *Final Report*, pp. 8, 12.
83. HEW *Final Report*, pp. 8, 12.
84. See R. H. Kampmeier, "The Tuskegee Study of Untreated Syphilis," *Southern Medical Journal* 65 (October 1972), 1247-

51; and "Final Report on the 'Tuskegee Syphilis Study,'" *Southern Medical Journal* 67 (November 1974), 1349-53.

85. Leonard J. Goldwater, "The Tuskegee Study in Historical Perspective," unpublished typescript, TSS-NLM; see also, "Treponemes and Tuskegee," *Lancet* (June 3, 1973), p. 1438; and Louis Lasagna, *The VD Epidemic* (Philadelphia: Temple University Press, 1975), pp. 64-66.

86. Quoted in "Debate Revives on the PHS Study," *Medical World News* (April 19, 1974), p. 37.

87. Heller to Vonderlehr, November 28, 1933, NA-WNRC; quoted in *Medical Tribune* (August 23, 1972), p. 14.

88. Although it is now known that syphilis is rarely infectious after its early phase, at the time of the study's inception latent syphilis was thought to be communicable. The fact that members of the control group were placed in the test group when they became syphilitic proves that at least some infectious men were denied treatment.

89. When the subjects are drawn from minority groups, especially those with which the researcher cannot identify, basic human rights may be compromised. Hans Jonas has clearly explicated the problem in his "Philosophical Reflections on Experimentation," *Daedalus* 98 (Spring, 1969), 234-37. As Jonas writes: "If the properties we adduced as the particular qualifications of the members of the scientific fraternity itself are taken as general criteria of selection, then one should look for additional subjects where a maximum of identification, understanding, and spontaneity can be expected--that is, among the most highly motivated, the most highly educated, and the least 'captive' members of the community."

# 4

# AFRICAN AMERICAN CULTURE: HISTORIC ROOTS AND UNIQUENESS

Our Own Song

Beat us a rhythm
O African King
On your African drum,
Tell of how your people were kidnapped
and taken to a land
from which they could not run.

And we in the Diaspora will pause and think quietly . . .

Sing us a spiritual
O African slave
Like "Go Down Moses" or
"Steal Away,"
Tell of how these songs strengthened you
throughout the lashful days.

And we in the Diaspora will pause and think quietly . . .

Blow us a blues tune
O free Black man,
Tell of the lynchings
and of your meagre fare in the land.

And we in the Diaspora will pause and think quietly . . .

And we in the Diaspora will form our own chorus . . .

And we in the Diaspora will sing of Amazing Grace . . .

And we in the Diaspora will tell of how far
    we've come from your place.

*Vernal M. Pope*

Vernal M. Pope is a junior English major at Metropolitan State College - Denver. She has read her poetry at many campus and community events. Reprinted with permission of the author, Vernal M. Pope.

# BURIED TREASURE

*Theresa A. Singleton*

Archaeologists are turning up new treasure these days. Not the fabled Tut jewels, but objects equally precious: slender but telling evidence of what plantation slave life was really like. They are coming up with tangible clues that will help to round out our picture of a people who left little in the way of written records.

A comb here, a pottery fragment three, remnants of mortar, burnt bones. From these tantalizing bits and pieces, specialists are starting to build a better image of the slaves who share life in the New World with their European owners and with the native Americans who preceded them.

The archaeology of slave life is a late entrant on the scene. Investigators were slow to recognize that if they wanted to deepen their understanding of European settlements in the New World, they would have to expand their research to include the places where slaves lived. This need was particularly acute in the case of the plantation societies, where slaves played a large and critical role.

This new component in U.S. archaeology focuses on several questions: How did transplanted Africans adjust to New World settings? How were the three traditions--native American, European and African--fused in the making of household objects and crafts for slaves' own use? Did slaves recreate objects from their homelands? How did the objects associated with slave life change over time?

Nobody has clear-cut answers. The situation resembles, in some ways, the frontiers of biological research, where absolutes are slow to emerge and where, sometimes the most fruitful result of painstaking effort is that one learns to ask better questions. But specialists are far enough along to venture some suggestions.

The Rice Coast has been one of the principal targets for the archaeologist's shovel. The reason is not far to seek. This coastal strip extending some 30 miles inland from Cape Fear, North Carolina to the St. Johns River in Florida and including the outriding barrier islands, had one of the heaviest concentrations of slaves in the country.

Africans first came to the region with Spanish conquistadors, who made unsuccessful attempts to settle there permanently in the 16th century. This early African presence has not been identified from archaeological sources--yet. Who knows what coming generations of searchers may find, to document the exchange we know took place among the three cultures long before English-speaking colonists arrived in 1670?

These "Johnnie-come-latelies" rather quickly developed a colonial plantation economy, based on the introduction of rice to South Carolina in the 1690s. Rice culture required an initial investment of $10,000 to $20,000--a huge outlay at that time--and a large labor force. Ownership was therefore restricted to a few wealthy planters. And black slaved provided the labor. At its peak in 1850, only 550 planters with more than 15,000 slaves had 100,000 acres under cultivation, in an area reaching from the southern tip of North Carolina to the northern tip of Florida. In addition to rice, planters produced indigo (during the colonial period) and cotton, a special variety once grown in coastal areas.

Slaves provided more than labor. They functioned as cultural agents, helping their European owners to adapt to the new environment. They also had two essential assets. Those who came from malarial climates brought with them a genetic trait that produces a partial but heritable immunity to malaria. They also brought with them skilled knowledge of rice growing, cattle raising, woodworking and sailing. Their familiarity with rice growing--a pursuit outside the experience of the English--literally made possible this plantation society.

West African culture was thoroughly woven into the daily lives of South Carolinians in the colonial era. Evidence in support of this little-known fact is emerging from such eighteenth-century archaeological sites in Curriboo and Yaughan in Berkeley County, South Carolina.

At these two sites, an African building technology based on mud walls has been identified in early slave dwellings. Since no standing walls exist, one may well ask how archaeologists are able to make this interpretation. They are relying on their excavations, which revealed wall trenches containing a mortar-like clay--and no evidence of other building materials. (Experts can deduce the use of wood, for example, even when no sliver remains, by the distinct color present in the soil, where a post or foundation has rotted in place.) Evidently, the walls of these structures, in their entirety, were made from this substance--just like the thatched-roof houses to be found in many places in Africa.

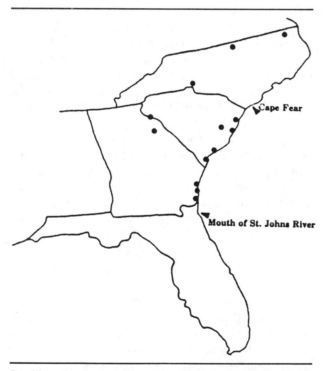

Besides the excavations identified in the map of the Rice Coast above, slave site excavations have been undertaken in the Caribbean, Louisiana, North Carolina, Tennessee and Virginia. The most famous site investigated so far is Monticello, the plantation estate of Thomas Jefferson, third president and author of the Declaration of Independence.

There, a slave quarter that had not been included in Jefferson's records was uncovered. An accumulation of buttons at another Monticello site suggests that slaves converted old clothing to rags to make quilts and other textiles. Additional evidence of slave craftsmanship was found at the weaver's cottage, a nail-making factory, a blacksmith's shop and a joinery.

African influences may also have been incorporated into the clay pots used to prepare and store food. These earthenware, referred to as "colonoware," are common finds at South Carolina plantation sites. Because this ware resembles native American pottery made both before and after the advent of Africans and Europeans, it was assumed until recently that it was produced solely by native Americans.

But now excavations have turned up some colonoware pieces that appear to have been made on site, in slave-occupied areas. And further research has shown that these finds show some similarities to West African and Afro-Caribbean works. The inference--that blacks made at least some of this pottery, out of their own African culture--is strong. To be sure, European influences are also to be found: vessels in such European forms as shallow plates and bowls with ring feet. Accumulating evidence supports the notion that colonoware is a multi-cultural product, fashioned from the collective potting traditions of Africans, native Americans and Europeans.

After the Revolutionary Ware, this African-texture culture dissipated and new objects or forms appeared. Again, the archaeological record documents the change. The items popular in the colonial period show up less frequently, frame houses replace mud wall structures and colonoware use gives way to mass-produced European wares, in slave-site digs associated with later periods.

It is easier to say with certainty that the changes took place than to say why they happened. One theory traces the changes to the abolition of the slave trade in 1807. With this labor supply cut to a smuggled trickle, planters set out to improve the health--and thereby the reproductive capacity--of the slaves they already owned. One approach to this goal was to improve housing--a change they equated with imposing European standards. The crude and makeshift slave housing that prevailed the colonial area began to be replaced with more permanent dwellings. By 1830, the recommended standard for each family was a dwelling measuring 16 x 18 feet, raised on piers, with planked floors and large fireplaces. Granted, these standards were the ideal, not always matched in practice. Even so, most slaves of the 1800s lived in European-styled house.

As for housewares, then, as earlier, their possessions were meager. But what they did have shifted from locally produced objects to inexpensive mass-produced imports.

Post-Revolutionary War slave sites excavated in coastal Georgia document the changes. African-styled or -influenced objects are entirely absent among the excavated debris. While the shift in kinds of housewares can be understood as part of a world-wide trend set in motion by the Industrial Revolution, the changes in housing style appear to be a result of conscious planter policy. They 1940 WPA book, *Drums and Shadows*, relates the story of Okra, a slave on a sea island plantation who built an African mud-walled house that his owner ordered burned down.

The unique contribution that archaeologists can make to our understanding of the past is nicely illustrated by our growing knowledge from these Georgia slave dwelling sites. Historical photographs already documented the fact that Georgia planters favored large two-family dwellings for their slaves. But recent digs have fleshed out precise details about size, construction materials and remodeling over the years.

At Butler Island, a large rice plantation, slave dwellings made from cypress planks measured about 24 x 28 feet, with fireplaces that measured eight feet. The fires in these fireplaces burned very hot at times, a fact attested to by the buckling and separation of the hearths from the outer chimney walls and by findings of food bone burnt to a whitish-blue color. The location of building hardware, such as hinges, locks and shutter pintles, helped these history detectives to work out the placement of doors and windows. And when they found no windowpane fragments, they deduced that the windows were not glassed. Outside the cabins, they spotted the areas where clothes were washed, where gardens were tilled, where trash was burned and where pigs and chickens were penned, using clues uncovered just below the top layer of soil.

Within the cabin outlines, archaeologists have found indications of what residents ate. Analysis of food bone revealed that beef and pork contributed most of the animal protein in their diet. But slaves supplemented these rations, which were supplied by the planter, by hunting and fishing--adding raccoon, opossum, turtle, fish and shellfish to the menu.

Pottery fragments suggest that the typical household had two or three stoneware crocks, manufactured in the piedmont areas of Georgia and South Carolina, for food storage. Inexpensive "Banded" wares from England were most often used for serving food. Fragments of bottles for patent

## What archaeologists do

Archaeologists seek knowledge about the past by finding things—usually buried objects or structures. They reason out the significance of their "finds" by relating the objects to other finds or to information from other disciplines.

For a long time, these experts focused on *prehistory*, the periods before societies developed writing systems. In our own country, inferences from archaeological finds have been the main source of information about native Americans'lives before Columbus—since writing was rare among them before European settlement.

In recent years, some archaeologists have turned their attention to *historical* times. In the United States, sites like Williamsburg, Mount Vernon and Jamestown are testimony to the strength of the historical preservation and restoration movements, which have been picking up speed ever since the 1930s. Projects like these have used the skills of archaeologists to get a more accurate fix on life in colonial times.

When archaeologists excavate at the sites of slave quarters, they are drawing on both streams within the discipline: the slave era in the United States obviously falls within "historical times," but slaves—generally forbidden to learn reading and writing—recorded almost nothing about how they lived.

medicines with a high alcohol content suggest that these potions may have ben imbibed not just for their curative powers but also as an alcoholic drink.

Among personal items found on Butler Island were pocket knives, beads, buttons, clay pipes and occasionally an unusual item such as an umbrella part. One cabin site yielded a harvest of metal parts from chisels, axes and adzes, suggesting that it was the home of a cooper and his family. Why a cooper? Because coopers, who built the wooden barrels and crates used to package rice for market, were essential craftsmen on every rice plantation.

The modest treasures turned up by excavations of slave sites--beads and bones, umbrella ribs and ax heads--are producing a rich harvest. Moreover, slave archaeology is rapidly gaining momentum, as well as attention around the world.

But so far that harvest is stockpiled pretty much away from public view. Specialists share their research with one another but rarely with lay audiences. And black participation in this specialty is scant. Of several hundred professional archaeologists in the country, fewer than ten are black, and only four of these have been involved in investigating Afro-American sites. It is interesting to speculate about what might happen if more young black students were to equip themselves to search for their own past by studying the objects that black people left behind. A treasure trove indeed awaits more seekers.

## Excavations at Butler Island

Butler Island is one of several marsh islands within the Altamaha River drainage in McIntosh County, Georgia. The construction of irrigation systems controlled by the rising and falling of the tide transformed these barren marshlands into rice plantations. Today, these islands function as a refuge area for waterfowl, managed by the Department of Natural Resources.

The archaeological project at Butler Island began as an effort to assist the managers of the waterfowl refuge in developing a plan that would prevent the destruction of any archaeological resources. Certain routine management activities such as seasonal flooding, plowing and dredging, needed to maintain the grounds, could destroy these resources. The study was designed first, to locate and identify areas where people once lived—from pre-Columbian times to the plantation era; second, to establish through testing (excavation) the age, association, and function of each site. In addition to developing a preservation plan for the waterfowl refuge, a significant secondary objective was to undertake a study of slavery at Butler Island using both written records and material resources uncovered from the archaeology.

Before field work began, historical maps, deeds, plantation records and aerial photographs were carefully studied to obtain clues for the location of sites. Sketches drawn by an overseer of the plantation in the 1830s indicated the location of slave villages, structures used to process and store rice, even a pre-Columbian site he identified as "Indian shell."

Informants also offered suggestions of places to search for sites. Present-day workers at the waterfowl refuge pointed out areas where they had unearthed materials, while former tenant farmers at Butler Island remembered places where they had seen ruins of the plantation. The information gathered from these sources provided the basis for the first phase of fieldwork—surface reconnaisance. This involved mapping, recording and taking notes of all "above ground" archaeological resources.

Results from the surface survey determined the excavation strategy. Areas with remains of structures or a high density of artifacts were excavated. At each site, the surface of the whole area was measured into squares forming a grid. The same grid was reproduced on paper to record the position of all major artifacts or features (a pit, posthole, floor or wall that is constructed and cannot be moved without causing alteration or destruction). Digging began in selected squares within the grid, usually around structural remains.

Most of the structures were found to be slave cabins. Slave cabins appeared in the archaeological record as concentrated scatters of brick arranged in rows. These rows once formed a row of slave houses within a slave village and represented the only surviving evidence of abandoned chimneys. Careful removal of soil and other debris revealed hearths of duplex slave cabins.

# FOR MY PEOPLE

*Margaret Walker*

For my people everywhere singing their slave songs repeatedly: their dirges and their ditties and their blues and jubilees, praying their prayers nightly to an unknown god, bending their knees humbly to an unseen power;

For my people lending their strength to the years, to the gone years and the now years and the maybe years, washing ironing cooking scrubbing sewing mending hoeing plowing digging planting pruning patching dragging along never gaining never reaping never knowing and never understanding;

For my playmates in the clay and dust and sand of Alabama backyards playing baptizing and preaching and doctor and jail and soldier and school and mama and cooling and playhouse and concert and store and hair and Miss Choomby and company;

For the cramped bewildered years we went to school to learn to know the reasons why and the answers to and the people who and the places where and the days when, in memory of the bitter hours when we discovered we were black and poor and small and different and nobody cared and nobody wondered and nobody understood;

For the boys and girls who grew in spite of these things to be man and woman, to laugh and dance and sing and play and drink their wine and religion and success, to marry their playmates and bear children and then die of consumption and anemia and lynching;

For my people thronging 47th Street in Chicago and Lenox Avenue in New York and Rampart Street in New Orleans, lost disinherited dispossessed and happy people filling the cabarets and taverns and other people's pockets needing bread and shoes and milk and land and money and something--something all our own;

For my people walking blindly spreading joy, losing time being lazy, sleeping when hungry, shouting when burdened, drinking when hopeless, tied, and shackled and tangled among ourselves by the unseen creatures who tower over us omnisciently and laugh;

For my people blundering and groping and floundering in the dark of churches and schools and clubs and societies, associations and councils and committees and conventions, distressed and disturbed and deceived and devoured by money-hungry glory-craving leeches, preyed on by facile force of state and fad and novelty, by false prophet and holy believer;

For my people standing staring trying to fashion a better way from confusion, from hypocrisy and misunderstanding, trying to fashion a world that will hold all the people, all the faces, all the adams and eves and their countless generations;

Let a new earth rise. Let another world be born. Let a bloody peace be written in the sky. Let a second generation full of courage issue forth; let a people loving freedom come to growth. Let a beauty full of healing and a strength of final clenching be the pulsing in our spirits and our blood. Let the martial songs be written, let the dirges disappear. Let a race of men now rise and take control.

# REDISCOVERING ZORA NEALE HURSTON

*Wali Rashash Kharif*

Zora Neale Hurston (1891-1960) was a leading African American writer of the Harlem Renaissance. Unlike Claude McKay, Countee Cullen, Alain Locke, Langston Hughes and most other African American literary contributors of the period, Hurston was not a writer by training. Rather, she was an anthropologist and was trained to observe. This training is what makes her literary contributions so unique. In addition, Hurston was the only significant female writer of the Renaissance.

Hurston developed skills in careful observation, recording such observations, and presenting them intact to a reading audience. In this sense, she was more than just another writer. She was a folklorist as well. In this is her strength. Since 1973, largely because of the efforts of Alice Walker, there has been a resurgence of interest in Hurston's works. Four of these books, now available in paperback editions, showcase Hurston's talents as a writer and folklorist. Examining them is essential to understanding the mystery of Zora Neale Hurston. Each book contains an afterword, "Zora Neale Hurston: 'A Negro Way of Saying'", by Henry Louis Gates, Jr.

## BOOK REVIEWS

*Jonah's Gourd Vine*, By Zora Neale Hurston. (New York: Harper & Row, Publishers, 1990. xv, 229 pp. Forward, glossary, afterword, selected bibliography, chronology. $8.95 paper.)

*Jonah's Gourd Vine*, Hurston's first novel, was originally published in 1934. It is set in the rural South in the late nineteenth and early twentieth centuries. The novel is based on a combination of Hurston's field notes and family history. The central characters are John Pearson, mulatto son of a white southern judge, and Lucy Potts (i.e., Hurston's mother's maiden name was really Lucy

Reprinted with permission from *The Griot*, Vol. 10, No. 1, Spring 1991.

Potts). John is a strong specimen of a man with a weakness for women. Lucy, though frail of body, is a strong woman with extraordinarily good judgment and foresight. Her marriage to John is the best thing that ever happened to him. He finds success in each of his many ventures thanks to Lucy's inspiration. John is called to preach, (interestingly, Hurston's father--John Hurston--was also a preacher), and with Lucy's help discovers his ability to communicate and to entertain. Yet, in spite of this strength--or gift--he succumbs to his passion for other women.

Hurston cuts across cultural and class lines, captures and portrays the essence of each character within its time. The novel is replete with realism. The reader may find himself identifying with a character and understanding, if not accepting, particular character traits. An annoyance to the male reader may be Hurston's constant depictions of African American men as weak "in the flesh" or otherwise misguided. This is also an important element in the novel *Their Eyes*, and it even creeps into the non-fictional works *Mules and Men* and *Tell My Horse* as well. Certainly, the African American female had been victimized in traditional literature, however, emasculating the black male character is obviously not the appropriate response. If her intention, however, was to point out that as men and women we have weaknesses, and that resolving them comes only after first acknowledging that they exist, then I too must concur.

Finally, the novel also contains historic accounts that are presented in an entertaining manner. Many of these revelations are accurate depictions of events which actually occurred, and are corroborated in the literature. A reader may conclude that fictional characters are placed in the past and through their eyes one may experience that past. Thus, the book also serves as a source of historic interpretation.

The true gift of this book is Hurston's ability to preserve the verbal expressions of rural and migrant African Americans. The expressions are not unique, however. Hurston's decision to incorporate such language usages into almost every page of text is unique. Hurston captures the spirit and oral expressions of a dispossessed, excluded, and overwhelming rural people at a time when leading Renaissance writers often disregarded this transitional phase in the African American trek from slavery to freedom, concentrating on the more cultured "New Negro".

*Mules and Men.* By Zora Neale Hurston. (New York: Harper & Row, Publishers, 1990. xxiii, 309 pp. Contents, preface, foreword, introduction, glossary, appendix, afterword, selected bibliography, chronology. $8.95 paper.)

*Mules and Men*, first published in 1935, is a collection of African American folksayings and tales (or as Hurston dubs them "lies"). The materials were collected in and around Central Florida--an area of the state with an extremely high migrant population during the period leading up to and between the two great world wars. Many of the tales are corroborated by former slaves in the Florida Slave Narratives, collected by the Work Progress Administration. Hurston divides the book into two parts. Part I pertains to "Folk Tales", and Part II deals with "Hoodoo" or voodoo (hereafter referred to as the latter). In addition, there is glossary (which proves quite helpful) and an appendix.

In this non-fictional work, Hurston assesses the overall political, social and economic milieu, and evaluates how the prevailing conditions account for the images in the minds of excluded African Americans. She further relates their impressions on that power structure and reaction to it. This book can be a valuable tool for the social historian of the late nineteenth and early twentieth century American South.

*Their Eyes Were Watching God.* By Zora Neale Hurston. (New York: Harper & Row, Publishers, 1990, iv, 207 pp. Foreword, afterword, selected bibliography, chronology. $8.95 paper.)

*Their Eyes Were Watching God* is considered Hurston's premier work. The novel was published in 1937, and is evidence of the tremendous development of Hurston as a writer. Usually, book cover inscriptions are biased and are intended for hype, however, the following inscription printed on the back cover of *Their Eyes* is accurate:

A classic black literature, it tells with haunting sympathy and piercing immediacy the story of Janie Crawford's evolving selfhood through three marriages. Fairskinned, Janie grows up expecting better treatment than she gets until she meets Tea Cake, a younger man who engages her heart and spirit in equal measure and gives her the chance to enjoy life without being one man's mule or another's adornment.

As with *Jonah's Gourd Vine*, much of *Their Eyes* is based upon actual places, events and most probably characters who lived in the period. The book also utilizes the simple folk language prevalent among the African American rural population. As such, the novel has historic value. The novel depicts life in Eatonville, Florida (which is in fact a small all black town established in the late nineteenth century), and its African American inhabitants relationships with neighboring central Florida localities. While Janie may be a fictious character, through her eyes the reader witnesses actual historic events: life among the migrants workers in the mulk of the Everglades, specifically Clewiston and Belle Glade; racial injustice in the Florida resort city of West Palm Beach; one of the most furious hurricanes to ever touch the United States (judging from the amount of damage and deaths described, it would most probably have been the 1928 rather than 1926 hurricane--though both decimated South and Central Florida).

The novel presents a powerful and moving examination of life and the fact that one person's heaven may well be another's hell. It is meaningful and as timely now (if not moreso) as it was more than fifty years ago.

*Tell My Horse: Voodoo and Life in Haiti and Jamaica.* By Zora Neale Hurston. (New York: Harper & Row, Publishers, 1990, xv, 311 pp. Illustrations, foreword, contents, appendix, afterword, selected bibliography, chronology, $8.95 paper.)

*Tell My Horse*, first published in 1938, is a personal account of voodoo and life in Haiti and Jamaica. The author examines Catholicism as modified among the African slave and their descendants in the Caribbean. She makes a strong case that African ancestral worship practices were preserved in the ritual of the Catholic church. The fact that Catholic Spain and France encouraged their African slaves to worship (while the English in North American discouraged this for some time) provided the African slave in the Caribbean with a medium for preserving traditional practices. For this reason Caribbean Christian practices contained a duality of purpose. On the one hand there was the official church religion as manifested by the Catholic faith. On the other, there was the unofficial church--an embodiment of Catholic ritual and the ancestor worship practices of the African traditional religions--voodoo.

*Tell My Horse*, is the result of Hurston's personal experiences as both an outside observer and as an initiate into the voodoo cult. The book is divided into three parts. Part I is a survey of Jamaica; Part II explores the "Politics and Personalities of Haiti"; and Part III examines "Voodoo in Haiti". The study contains an appendix, comprised of songs of worship to voodoo gods and miscellaneous songs. A working knowledge of French, and ability to read music are required for those wishing to take full advantage of these inclusions.

# SEA CHANGE IN THE SEA ISLANDS

*Charles L. Blockson*

Nowadays Verneda ("Rikki") Lights, M.D., a graduate of Bryn Mawr College and of the University of Pennsylvania School of Medicine, practices in Philadelphia. But in the 1950s, when she was a small girl in Charleston, South Carolina, she was passed over the coffin of her great-grandmother so that she would be free of fear in accepting the mystical powers the old woman had specifically bequeathed to her. Rikki's ancestress, like many other black mainlanders on the Southeast coast, had embraced the traditions and customs deeply embedded in the Sea Islands, just offshore. Rikki's family moved there--to the island of Port Royal--three years after the old woman died.

"My great-grandmother came from a community of Christian mystics," Dr. Light explains. "In the island we all took it for granted that there were spirits, and we had to get rid of the hostile ones."

Dr. Lights, who is descended from West Africans transported to America as slaves, has never doubted that the powers that she inherited are real. Her great-grandmother, a practical nurse and midwife who was expert in the use of medicinal herbs, was famous for her clairvoyance. Dr. Lights herself has a gift for medical diagnosis in internal medicine--a gift, she says, that came from God.

The physician feels that her inheritance has strengthened her natural talent for music and poetry and that the spirit of her island and ancestors is a strong presence in her personal and professional life. "For me there is no separation between medicine and poetry," she told me in the cool tones of a modern scholar as we discussed the treatment of cancer patients with the latest drugs. The miracles of modern medicine, Dr. Lights believes, are every bit as wondrous as the feats of her long-ago neighbor on Port Royal, who would give Rikki's mother "flowers hexed, which would never die."

Reprinted with permission from the author, Charles L. Blockson.

The latter phrase was spoken in Gullah, the headlong Sea Islands Creole that mixes English words and syntax with those from the Caribbean and especially West Africa to create a speech that is all but incomprehensible to outsiders, including blacks who may live only a few miles away on the mainland. This tongue, sometimes called Geechee, is an important reason why Sea Islanders have preserved a way of life that remains African in some of its essentials.

Like many another Sea Islander, Dr. Lights fears that the world of her ancestors, which survived more or less intact into her own childhood, is fading away. Booming development is changing life in the Sea Islands, displacing people who have in many cases lived on family land for generations.

"The situation is horrendous!" says Dr. Lights. "The islands have become a playground for white people. But this will not conquer the spirits of those whom the Lord has spoken to! The land knows who it belongs to."

I heard this emotional, evangelical tone in many voices in this past year as I traveled up and down the Sea Islands, those low-lying, marshy barrier islands that hug the coast of South Carolina and Georgia (map, page 745), In *When Roots Die*, her remarkable book about the life and language of the Sea Islands, the late Dr. Patricia Jones-Jackson explained some of the reasons: "The extended family is the norm in the Sea Islands. Most islands are sectioned off into family communities, where all members of one family, their close relatives, and people remotely related live or have a right to live . . . Land is not normally sold to family members but is passed on through an unwritten contract called 'heir's land.'"

Island tradition also places great importance on burial in home ground, and islanders will pay all their lives on insurance policies designed to provide for funerals that may cost thousands of dollars. Many still living in the islands believe that a person is composed of three parts--body, soul, and spirit. When the body dies, the soul departs, but the spirit remains behind and is capable of doing good or mischief to the living. As in West Africa, graves in the Sea Islands traditionally have been adorned with belongings of the departed, and with charms designed to contain or placate the spirit of the person buried there. Real or imagined threats to graveyards are, therefore, a cause of disquiet.

The island people long lived in isolation, and many of their customs and beliefs closely resemble those of the Ibo, Yoruba, Kongo, Mandinka, and other West African tribes from whom they probably descended.

Signs of development, and reactions to it, are particularly vivid on Daufuskie. Three-quarters of Daufuskie, a particularly lovely island lying off Savannah, has been earmarked for development over the next 20 years, and two large tracts totaling 1,798 acres, or 29 percent of the island's surface, are already being developed to include more than 900 new homes, two inns, two golf courses, two tennis clubs, and two beach clubs, along with buildings for community services.

Local government officials estimate that "buildout," or the completed development of Daufuskie, will result in a population of 10,000 permanent residents in addition to a seasonal and part-time population of 10,000. Daufuskie's population in the 1980 census was 59, of whom 45 were black.

Property values were inflated dramatically by the development plan. A lot that may have been worth almost nothing rose in value to as much as $50,000 depending on its location.

"Yayman!" says Thomas Stafford, who makes his living on Daufuskie as a crab fisherman. "Money talks and you know what walks--some people can't wait to leave!" Thickets of For Sale signs sprang up over the island and are still to be seen.

But the sale of the heir's land is not always entirely voluntary. Under South Carolina law, heir's property (land whose title is often clouded because the original owner died without having made a will) usually cannot be sold until the title is cleared, but heirs living on it must pay taxes in order to continue their residency. As development causes land to become more valuable, taxes rise. Consequently, the occupants of heir's land are sometimes obliged to sell it in order to pay taxes. Because all known heirs must relinquish their interest in the land before title can be cleared, and because there may be hundreds of heirs to any

given piece of land, the process is long, arduous, and fraught with emotion.

Most of the land on Daufuskie has been owned by whites since before the Civil War. In the days of slavery Daufuskie was divided into several large plantations growing long-staple sea island cotton. Profits for the white owners were enormous--the supple, silky sea island cotton sold in European markets for more than twice the price of ordinary cotton. Union forces occupied Daufuskie early in the war. White owners abandoned their plantations, and blacks who had been their chattels were dispersed.

As the Confederacy collapsed, freed slaves moved into the Sea Islands in large numbers. On January 16, 1865, after meeting at Savannah with a delegation of black clergymen who pleaded for land for former slaves, Gen. William Tecumseh Sherman issued Special Field Order 15, ceding most of the Sea Islands In Georgia and South Carolina to them and declaring that no whites apart from military officers and others in helpful capacities were permitted to reside in the islands. After the war, however, President Andrew Johnson allowed plantation owners to return. Many former slaves nevertheless retained small holdings.

During Reconstruction two of the plantations on Daufuskie were subdivided into small tracts and sold to blacks who had moved onto the island, but the others remained under white ownership. A period of prosperity followed, base don sea island cotton, lumbering, and the rich oyster beds that surround Daufuskie. By the early years of the 20th century, a thousand blacks were residing there.

Then disaster struck. By the 1920s the boll weevil had destroyed the cotton industry. In the ensuing economic collapse, many black families sold their land to mainland investors and moved away, and by 1936 fewer than 300 blacks remained on Daufuskie. Many worked at an oyster cannery, but it was closed down in the 1950s after industrial pollution from the Savannah River poisoned Daufuskie's oysters. The population fell steadily as residents departed in search of work and education.

Other islands have experienced similar declines. The exodus has been so marked that some community leaders, such as Bill Jenkins, the heir of a family long established on Johns Island, believe that black ownership of the land will likely be a thing of the past by the turn of the century. Those who remain will be living under conditions that are quite different from the life describe din the Gullah folktales, in which the simple adventures of the islanders almost always involve the soil and the animals--Brer Rabbit, Brer Gator, Brer Deer, the friendly porpoise who leads mullet into the net, the wise buzzard (a favorite creature among black islanders).

"Most people feel, what can we do?" says Tom Stafford. "Sure, I raised some hell at first, but now I don't feel a cuss about the damn pollution and the building that are changing everything."

An elaborate plan of development, approved by the local authorities, seeks to provide adequate protection against overbuilding and the pollution and other problems that can result from it. But golf courses and hotels and villas, pleasing though they may be to the investor and to the city dweller, are not as enchanting to those who grew up on the islands as the salt marsh, the piney woods full of birdsong, the lagoon teeming with ducks.

To the outsider's eye, the Sea Islands remain enchanting. Separated from the mainland and from one another by a system of tidal creeks and salty inlets, wide bays and marshes, they form magnificent beaches and dunes and grow lovely forests of pine and live oak. Their names are pure music: Pawleys, Cedar, Murphy, Bull, Capers, Dewees, and the Isle of Palms off Charleston; then James and Johns, Kiawah, Wadmalaw, Edisto, famous Parris Island, Hilton Head, and Daufuskie, and on down to Tybee, Wassaw, Ossabaw, St. Catherines, Sapelo, St. Simons, Jekyll and Cumberland at the Florida line.

I was charmed by these place-names, in which the languages of two or three continents tumble together. And I was charmed by the vast stretches of brown fields and moss-green marshes, charmed by the sandy beaches pounded by rhythmic surf, and I was charmed above all by the magnetic people of the Sea Islands.

The first people were Indians--Guale and Cusabo--who inhabited the Sea Islands when they were "discovered" by the Spaniards in 1521. The first European colony in what is now the United States, predating St. Augustine in Florida by 39 years, was established by Spain in 1526 on the coast of South Carolina. Among the original settlers were the first black slaves, and they staged the first slave revolt. The colony failed. In time, other Spanish settlements and missions sprouted along the coast. All were eventually uprooted by the English, who founded Charleston in 1670.

James Oglethorpe established Savannah in 1733 and crushed a last-gasp Spanish attack on St. Simons Island nine years later.

The whites who displaced the indigenous Indians were never numerous, but the black population grew apace. In 1835 a South Carolina grand jury complained that during the summer months (when mosquitos made life miserable) there were only 40 white proprietors to oversee a black population of 15,000 on the plantations around Georgetown. By 1860 South Carolina had a white population of 291,300, a slave population of 402,406, and 9,914 freed slaves.

The ratios did not yield to the passage of time. The 1940 census revealed that only 251 of the 1,858 inhabitants of Wadmalaw Island were white. Ratios were similar on other islands, but whites appear in some surprising historical footnotes: Aaron Burr took refuge on St. Simons after killing Alexander Hamilton in a duel, Edgar Allan Poe found the inspiration for "The Gold Bug" on Sullivans Island near Charleston.

Black history was recorded in an oral tradition that is typically African. Every islander, however young, is expected to know his own family history, and older people often subject newcomers, black or white, to a strict interrogation on their lineage. Parentage is the passport to trust and acceptance, and islanders can be cool, even hostile, to outsiders regardless of race. Most black islanders have two names--one for home use and another to be told to strangers. Some older residents are named for months or for days of the week, a system of naming that is common among West African peoples.

Today large tracks of private land are closed to everyone except those with permission to enter. In the opinion of Emory Campbell, the soft-spoken director of the Penn Center on St. Helena Island, the old cohesion of history and everyday life is coming to an end. Development, the latest in a long series of instructions from the outside world, generally gets the blame. "Yayman! Something is slipping away," Mr. Campbell said. "We used to hunt, fish, and play at will. Now we need identification in order to enter certain areas.

Is there no bright side to recent events? Edward A. Chazal, vice president of International Paper Realty Corporation, suggests that the jobs created by development may make it economically possible for Sea Islanders to come back home," he says, pointing out that his firm has created 140 jobs on Daufuskie. Nearly all of these, he concedes, are filled by workers who commute from the mainland.

Certainly development brought employment opportunities to Hilton Head, where development began in the 1950s. But Laura Bush of the Institute for Community Education and Training on Hilton Head maintains that there are few blacks in white-collar positions. "We have set up a system with Beaufort Technical College whereby we prepare students both for high-school equivalency test and post-secondary education, with the hope that they can move ahead into college level classes," says Mrs. Bush. But the 5,000 men and women who arrive daily on Hilton Head at 7 a.m. from five surrounding counties work in construction, service, landscape, cleaning, or maintenance.

Like Mr. Chazal, Donald Martin, former vice president and now a consultant for the Haig Point Realty Corporation, which has been building on Daufuskie since February 1985, sees the resort boom as a long-term source of jobs in the Sea Islands. "Everybody who wants to work can work," Martin says. "Inevitably there will be growth and therefore more jobs."

"We can tolerate what is happening so long as there is progress with pride," says the Reverend Benjamin Williams, pastor of the Mount Calvary Missionary Baptist Church on Hilton Head and member of the board of the Paralleled Land Owners Association. "But surely residents must be given the privilege of traveling about on the islands of their ancestors without showing identification."

Beneath this tense and puzzled surface, old things survive. One elderly woman, who asked that her name not be published, told me, "We have love and understanding here--but I tell you, when the burden becomes too heavy to carry, we go to church."

Churchgoing on the islands is an inspiring experience, and as Dr. Jones-Jackson observed, the sound of singing and praising can be heard from afar on Sunday morning. In her book she quoted this passage from a prayer in an island church:

> As you say the foxes of the forest
> Got hole
> And then the birds of the air has nest
> Master, we are poor son of man
> Nowhere to lay down weary head.

Mrs. Gillian Hinson-White spoke about other traditional activities. "I used to be the best shot on Fuskie," said Mrs. Hinson-White, who told me that she was 86 years old, five feet tall, and had always weighed exactly 98 pounds. "I could shoot alligators between the eyes. I buried two husbands on Fuskie, and now those folks talking about removing the cemetery. If the construction companies bother my husbands' graves, that is the day I'll put *them* in one."

Rikki Lights had told me about a plant known to black island residents as "life everlasting," whose dark leaves and stems can be boiled into an herbal tea to treat many ailments, including asthma. Elsewhere in the islands I heard tales of hexes and other herbal remedies--mullein tea for curing colds, tinctures of wood chips and turpentine for purging the system, secret roots used by midwives, poke leaves for sprains, leaves from the lily bush for sweating out fever.

When I asked Mrs. Hinson-White about these matters, she gave me a searching look and responded with caution: "Yes, there were a few root doctors--years ago. Some people believed in ghosts, hexes, and roots. Sheriff McTeer and Dr. Buzzard were good witch doctors who made a lot of money."

I had heard that blue paint was much in demand in the Sea Islands because it is supposed to protect the home from evil spirits. "That's right," said Mrs. Hinson-White tartly, "but my house isn't painted blue."

Many others are.

Doubtless preparation of herbal medicine and the use of incantation and witchcraft were brought to the islands from Africa. Such practices have been persistent features of Sea Island culture, and they did not always work for the good.

Many believed, and still believe, that malevolent juju men could "put de mout [mouth] on you," as bewitchment is called. In any case the picturesque terminology of Sea Island superstition and folklore is still in everyday use: "When you hear the pig hollering, it's going to rain," the islanders will say. Or "hang a bottle in the tree to keep evil spirits away . . . Pour turpentine, kerosene, or lime around your gate to keep off poisonous snakes . . . Plant a cedar tree near the grave . . . To put a curse on someone, mix up ashes and chicken feathers."

H. L. Mencken, among others, wrote contemptuously of Gullah. Other scholars thought differently, and as long ago as 1949 a linguist reported that he had identified 6,000 names and other words of African origin in the speech of the islanders. Professor William Stewart of the City University of New York has estimated that about 250,000

Gullah speakers live in the United States, including some 10,000 in New York City.

Dr. Jones-Jackson collected many Gullah word sin common use that have survived intact or have been derived form such West African languages as Kongo, Kimbundu, Vai, Twi, and Ga (page 744).

The Reverend Ervin Greene, pastor of Brick Baptist Church on St. Helena and former pastor of First Union African Baptist Church on Daufuskie, has been working with other scholars for nine years to translate the Bible into Gullah.

Mr. Greene believes that Gullah is related to the Creole spoken in the Caribbean. Grady Lights, brother of Dr. Rikki Lights, recalled from his school days that Gullah-speaking students had little problem learning a foreign language, but sometimes had difficulty with standard English. When I asked Grady about the difference between Gullah and Geechee, he smiled. "Folks down the coast speak at a faster clip than we do," he said. "We seldom used the word 'Geechee' in their presence because it had somehow come to mean, well--hick. So if we did, we'd also say, 'Prepare yourself for battle.'"

Sometimes, after talking over old times and new times with the islanders, I would find myself thinking about ancient peoples who lost their history and died. Then the vitality of the islanders would wake me to reality. At the sixth annual Penn School Heritage Celebration on St. Helena Island, pride, love, and smiles reflected the reigning mood of the interracial crowd. It was a feast--fish, oysters, clams, fried chicken, corn on the cob.

There was much talk of the history of the island. Strolling around the shady park, I recalled the contributions of Penn School founders Laura Towne and Ellen Murray, and Charlotte Forten, the first black teacher. These three and others were sent by missionary societies in the North to educate 10,000 newly emancipated slaves who lived on St. Helena Island. Soon schools began springing up on neighboring islands. Abolitionist poet John Greenleaf Whittier sent Charlotte Forten his "St. Helena Hymn" written for the scholars of St. Helena Island, occupied by Union troops. Charlotte taught her students to sing Whittier's verses for the Emancipation Proclamation exercise of January 1, 1863.

In 1858, on Jekyll Island, the slave ship *Wanderer* debarked one of the last major cargoes of slaves ever to land in the United States. Jekyll, lying near the mouth of the Satilla River some 20 miles north of the Florida line, greeted me with a shower of warm rain and a great squawking flock of sea gulls, almost the first I had seen in the Sea Islands. At the turn of the century Jekyll was developed as the exclusive winter retreat for a group of northern industrialists. Some of the great houses that they built and filled with servants brought from Newport, Nantucket, or Southampton still look down stately avenues of live oak.

If present-day luxury is something a person values, then he must not miss St. Simons, for here are exclusive country clubs, opulent private estates, marinas bristling with yachts. Fields where slaves toiled have been converted to emerald golf courses.

In a sense the slaves are still a presence here. It is said that a slave ship landed at high tide on a bank of Dunbar Creek. As the slaves were unloaded, they turned together and marched into the deep waters of the creek, chanting as they drowned: "The water brought us in, the water will take us away." Ghost hunters today say that the chant, and the clanking of chains, can still be heard on dark nights.

On nearby Cumberland Island I sought out more contradictions of history and human nature. There is a dewy freshness about Cumberland--waves of sand, great live oaks, vast stretches of green-brown earth. Here I walked among the ruined chimneys of slave quarters and meditated on tall chimneys on Butler Island in which every brick, I was told, memorialized a soul born into slavery.

But I remembered too the accomplishments of the British actress Fanny Kemble Butler, wife of the master of this famous plantation. Her *Journal of a Residence on a Georgian Plantation in 1838-1839* strengthened antislavery sentiment in the North and, some feel, was a factor in the British decision to refrain from aiding the Confederate cause. God works in mysterious ways.

On one island, at least, God seems to have ordained contentment. On the landing at Sapelo Island I met Tracey Walker, pilot of the ferryboat *Sapelo Queen*. He painted an idyllic picture of his island. "We have 75 or 80 black families all the time," said Tracey. "During the weekend, when my business is at its best, maybe 200 people will come home to the island. Many of them work in Brunswick, St. Simons, or Savannah. People from Sapelo are living all over the world. But they always come home. We have an equal number of men and women, so there is someone for everyone. There are seldom any divorces and never an orphan because every child is welcome. If a person starves on Sapelo, something is definitely wrong. My grandmother Mrs. Annie Walker, who is 95, was born in Sapelo and can still walk around."

"Does Sapelo have *any* problems? I asked. Tracey gave me a jaunty smile. "We have no drugs, crime, or jail," he replied, "and if we did have a drug problem, there is only one way to go, and that is to the boat."

I had been told that they used to have hags on Sapelo--supernatural visitors who terrorize people at night while they sleep--but everyone on the island assured me that the hags have gone away because nobody believes in them any longer.

# 5

---

# THE STRUGGLE FOR THE FREEDOM AND THE LIBERATION OF THE AFRICAN AMERICAN PEOPLE

---

"If there is no struggle, there is no progress."

*Frederick Douglass*

# PART OF A WHOLE: THE INTERDEPENDENCE OF THE CIVIL RIGHTS MOVEMENT AND OTHER SOCIAL MOVEMENTS*

*Judith Rollins*

Thirty years after the Montgomery bus boycott, twenty-five years after the Freedom Rides, twenty years after the scenes of Souther police using dogs and firehoses on demonstrators, and after the March on Washington, the questions remain. Was the civil rights movement a success or a failure? What was the significance of that tumultuous period in American history? What did it all mean? This paper attempts to answer such questions by examining the historical and social place of the American civil rights movement in the world context. It is a preliminary exploration of the linkages between the civil rights movement of the 1960s and other internal and international social movements. In the examination of this interplay between the movement and the events which influenced and were influenced by it, the significance of the movement will become apparent.

My thesis is that the civil rights movement in the United States was a critical part of the world-wide movement since World War II which involves two inextricably interrelated elements: the liberation of peoples of color from the domination of the West and the progressive weakening of capitalism's control over the world distribution of goods and resources. That the American movement was related to the efforts of other peoples of color is immediately apparent: black Americans' efforts to be treated as first-class citizens exhibit clear commonalities with efforts elsewhere to decolonize and achieve national sovereignty. But how can a movement reformist and assimilationist at its essence be linked to the weakening of the capitalist dominance of the world?

The beginning of the answer to that question lies in clarifying the conceptualization of the civil rights movement itself and in identifying those events I consider its salient antecedents. The period of the "classical" civil rights movement extended from the Montgomery bus boycott in 1955

Reprinted with permission from Judith Rollins, *Part of a Whole: The Interdependence of the Civil Rights Movement and Other Social Movements*. Vol. 47, 1986, pp. 61-70.

to the passage of the Voting Rights Act in 1965. But if the interdependence of the American movement with other social movements within and beyond the United States is to be understood, the conceptualization of "the movement" must be broadened to include other aspects of activism of blacks of the 1960s: the Black Power period, the evolution and influence of Malcolm X, the philosophy of the Black Panthers, and the urban rebellions of the late 60s. For the clenched fists and militant rhetoric later observed in movements throughout the world were as much influenced by the undisguised anger of these more revolutionary black activists as by the moderate philosophies of the more mainstream, nonviolent assimilationists.

## THE INTERNATIONAL ANTECEDENTS OF THE CIVIL RIGHTS MOVEMENT

Black America was affected by the news of an independent Ghana in 1957, an independent Nigeria in 1960, and an independent Tanzania in 1961. But the mood of black America was beginning to change even before those events. Black America watched in the late 1940s as dark-skinned people of India successfully challenged and achieved their independence from the British. Afro-Americans were conscious of the anti-Euro-American thrust, if not the details ,of Mao's campaign in 1949 to rid China of the poverty and suffering caused by a hierarchical social structure and an economy controlled externally. And they watched the Mau Mau in their fight against the British in Kenya in the early 1950s. There was a new spirit in the world indeed.

Of course, there had been individuals in black America who had been advocating decolonization for decades. Of course, there were Afro-Americans who recognized the inevitability of the demise of the European empires. The importance of DuBois and the Pan African Conferences to the decolonization efforts of Africa cannot be overstated. Nor can the importance of Marcus Garvey for touching and developing a conscious black pride in the basis of mobilization for self-improvement. But it took the concrete realizations of these ideas, the involvement of hundreds of thousands of people of color in the activities of rebellion to generate the spark in the hearts and minds of a large number of black Americans. These movements of liberation in the Third World made it clear to Afro-Americans that "the world was no longer a white man's world."[1] Then came two events which reverberated throughout the Third World and which are often underestimated in their importance to people of color: the Battle of Dien Bien Phu in 1954 and the Bandung Conference in 1955.

The Battle of Dien Bien Phu, in which the poorly equipped Vietnamese army decisively defeated the well-armed French, demonstrated that the European juggernaut could indeed be stopped. Dien Bien Phu gave heat to all those peoples who shared the common history of having had their land, their minerals, their crops and their bodies used for the economic and psychological benefit of white European and American people. The significance of this event was not lost on black America. Paul Robeson published an article entitled: "Ho Chi Minh is the Toussaint L'Overture of Indo-China," in which he not only compared Ho Chi Minh to the leader of the successful Haitian slave revolt but, with incredible foresight, warned black America about Eisenhower's threats to send Americans to Vietnam "in order that the tin, rubber and tungsten of Southeast Asia be kept by the 'free world'--meaning white Imperialism."[2] Similarly, Mordecai Johnson, president of Howard University, had said:

> For over 100 years the French have been in Indo-China, dominating them politically, strangling them economically, and humiliating them in the land of their fathers . . . And now it looks as though [the Vietnamese] can win, and as they are about to win their liberty, we rush up and say: "What on earth are you all getting ready to do? . . . We are the free people of the world, we are your friends, we will send you leaders . . . [3]

The same perceptive empathy that allowed black Americans to understand what colonized people were fighting for also allowed them to see through the government's propagandistic cliches about "making the world safe for democracy" and to realize that the real issue of these colonial wars was the economic issue, that the real fear behind the "domino theory" was the fear of losing plantations, minerals, markets and cheap labor. Thus, as many black Americans became more pro-decolonization, they became increasingly anti-Western imperialism.

The year after the Battle of Dien Bien Phu, five Asian nations[4] called the first conference ever to bring together representatives of Africa and Asia and to exclude representatives of white countries. Twenty-nine nations were invited to Bandung, Java to discuss "racialism and colonialism." The significance of this event did not escape the white world. *Newsweek* magazine wrote:

> Everybody knows what must come to pass between Asia and the West, the yellow and the white . . . Kaiser Wilhelm II, popularizer of the phrase 'Yellow Peril' . . . was right in foreseeing a crisis that now threatens in a more virulent form than he envisaged--an Afro-Asian combination turned by Communists against the West. The problem, according to those who have to deal with it today and tomorrow, is to prevent is formation.[5]

And the *Christian Science Monitor* stated:

> . . . The West is excluded. Emphasis is on the colored nations of the world . . . Colonialism is out. Hands off is the word . . . This is perhaps the great historic event of our century.[6]

Bandung was, indeed, one of the greatest historic events of this century. Although no American delegation was invited, individual blacks did attend on their own. The two "public figures" were Richard Wright and Adam Clayton Powell. But there were others: Wright described a "Mr. Jones" from Los Angeles, who was so moved when he heard about the conference that he used all of his own and his wife's savings to attend.[7] Richard Wright himself was so excited by what he heard and saw that he produced a book on his experiences there. And, based on Wright's description, we can glimpse the impact of the conference on Powell:

> The astounding aspect of Congressman Powell's appearance at Bandung was that he *felt the call, felt its meaning* . . . At the very moment when the U.S. was trying to iron out the brutal kinks of race problems, there came along a world event which reawakened in the hearts of its '23,000,000 colored citizens' the feeling of race, a feeling which the racial mores of American whites had induced

deep in their hearts. If a man as sophisticated as Congressman Powell felt this, then one can safely assume that in less schooled and more naive hearts it went profoundly deep.[8]

The meaning of Bandung went deep into the psyches of the colored oppressed of the world. Through the Mr. Joneses, Wright and Powell, the importance of the Bandung Conference reached at least some segments of black America. Internationally Bandung shocked and dismayed the West while heartening and inspiring the Third World.

## THE CIVIL RIGHTS MOVEMENT IN THE UNITED STATES

In the midst of these international events, the most significant legal event for black Americans in over fifty years took place: the 1954 Brown vs. the Board of Education Supreme Court decision reversed the separate but equal policy which had received government sanction in the 1896 Plessy vs. Ferguson ruling. While credit must be given to the ongoing efforts of the National Association for the Advancement of Colored People (NAACP) in bringing about the decision, the position taken by the American government was also influenced by the changes going on in the world--specifically, the dissolution of the British, French and Dutch empires and the emergence of new independent nations of color. An official segregationist policy could have caused embarrassment to the U.S. government in its dealings with these nations; therefore, the official government sanctioning of segregation had to be eliminated. This combination of Afro-America's increasing awareness of a worldwide confrontation with colonial oppression and the U.S. government's (at least nominal) commitment to an antisegregationist policy infused black Americans with a new sense of self, with "rising expectations", with an awareness of the vulnerability of "white power," and a readiness for confrontation.

The civil rights movement began that change. But he 1960s movement brought changes to the American society that even the most perceptive of early activists could not have foreseen. While it is not within the purview of this paper to detail the history of the movement, a few analytical remarks are in order.

From the Montgomery bus boycott to the voter registration drives of 1963 and 1964, black Americans initiated confrontations aimed at reforming the American system to force it to implement its own liberal ideology of equality for all under the law. The goal was integration of blacks into the existing system, the destruction of caste barriers, the affording of basic civil rights to all Americans. Civil rights activists were not questioning the structure and goals of the system itself. Because there was no inconsistency between the goals of the movement and the liberal philosophy on which this country was founded and because blacks' achieving these goals did not threaten material losses to whites, this is the period in which the movement enjoyed the strongest support of whites--in terms of money, personnel, the media and the government. As previously stated, this has been called the period of the "classical" civil rights movement.

But my conceptualization of the movement is broader than this limited definition, and the black activism beyond the classical movement was distinct in some important ways. First, in the post-1965 period of the movement--when equal employment, access to trade unions, Affirmative Action and fair housing became the issues (i.e., when the achievement of goals of blacks meant loss to whites, and success to blacks with a real redistribution of wealth and services, changes in the forms and functioning of institutions, and Northern whites too being affected), much of the support of "liberal" whites was withdrawn.

Also noteworthy is the fact that many of the activists outside the classical movement raised more fundamental questions about American society--questions about its values, aesthetics, violent history and hypocritical self-portrait, its role in Vietnam and, most important, it economic structure which by its very nature generates poverty and unemployment in this country and maintains Third World countries in dependent and exploited positions. It was on the margins, then, of the classical movement that one can see the influence of prescient men like Paul Robeson and W.E.B. DuBois more than at its core.

And, finally, it was during the 1960s that many Americans of color began calling themselves "Third World Americans," demonstrating their identification with Third World nations. Clearly, for them the goal of getting a bigger piece of the American pie was not a tenable one.

Thus, although the classical civil rights movement of the late 1950s and early 1960s, as many writers have concluded, was essentially reformist, it both reflected and generated ideologies representing a broader spectrum of political thought and behavior. That the total picture of that movement comprised of chiaroscuro of nonviolence and violence, of love and hate, of assimilationism and separatism does not negate the fact that a single community was moving in various ways toward the single goal of liberating itself from the varied and sometimes contradictory ideas. Other groups, of course, would selected out and adopt what was relevant and useful to them. What was important, however, was the energy itself, an energy about change and liberation and the destruction of domination. Thus the movement of the 1960s, precisely because it encompassed such varied political stances, could offer philosophical inspiration and practical guidance in a variety of kinds of social movements throughout the world, including (but not limited to) reformist movements.

## THE OUTGROWTHS OF THE CIVIL RIGHTS MOVEMENT

What, then, have been some of the effects of the 1960s movement? As stated, the diverse causes and effects can be subsumed under the major heading of the worldwide liberation of oppressed peoples and the weakening of capitalism. But this broad conceptualization does not do justice to its many and uniquely important aspects.

Overseas, the American movement reinforced decolonizing efforts in the Third World, especially Africa and the Caribbean. For example, some leaders of the independence movement of Surinam have articulated their admiration for and inspiration from the militancy of black Americans.[9] (Surinam achieved its independence from the Dutch in 1975.) The Black Power Movement in Trinidad, which was promoted by the National Joint Action Committee and the New Beginning Movement,[10] adopted much of the philosophy, tactics and language of the activism of black Americans of the late 60s. And the influence of black America on the thought and behavior of South Africans cannot be overestimated. A member of the South African Black Consciousness Movement[11] and former classmate of Steve Biko stated:

> Black Americans, particularly those who came as missionaries to South Africa, have had a profound influence on South African thought since the turn of the century. The long-standing nonviolent policy of the ANC [African National Congress] was largely due to the religious influence of these black Americans, the strongest group being the AME [African Methodist Episcopal] church. The Civil Rights Movement had a direct impact but it must be remembered that that was part of a continuing pattern; it was a carryover of earlier influences.
>
> We in the Black Consciousness Movement were certainly influenced by your Civil Rights Movements but you won't find any direct references to it in our speeches or writing--for internal reasons: the writings of all our activists were banned. I clearly remember in 1965 being invited to hear one of King's speeches in secret. It was the one where he talks about "sleeping through the revolution." I was really struck by it. Steve Biko admired King and Malcolm but he could never make a direct reference to them in public. Our listening to or reading of such men had to be kept secret.[12]

The references to the American movement in the writings of Cabral, Mao, Nyerere, Nkrumah and others make clear that Third World people were conscious of developments in the United States. And how could they not be encouraged by these developments? Those very areas of the world which had generated the spirit and energy to cause black America to move against its oppressors, in turn, were energized by the rhetoric, militancy, and anger of the entire movement toward self-empowerment that characterized black America of the 1960s.

In the U.S., the most obvious direct outgrowth of the movement was the awakening of other people of color. Among Mexican Americans (the second largest Third World group in the U.S. which in terms of health, education and employment is "more disadvantaged than any other ethnic group, except American Indians"[13]), there had never been organizations like the NAACP to struggle on behalf of the group as a whole. Though there had been isolated labor strikes of Mexican-American workers dating back as early as 1903, it was not until 1965 that a labor strike took on the additional dimensions created by a new sense of racial-ethnic identity and pride. Under Cesar Chavez' leadership, "La Huelga" (the strike) of the National Farm Workers' Association became " 'La Causa,' a crusade to assert the dignity of the Mexican-American population."[14] Other nationalist organizations soon developed. Reies Tijerina's organization in New Mexico focused on reclamation of lands taken from the original Mexican inhabitants of that state; "Corky" Gonzalez created a militant community organization in Denver; some of the Mexican-American gangs in Los Angeles developed a political consciousness and started calling themselves "Brown Berets"; and nationalist journals, like *Atzlan* and *El Grito,* came into being.[15] As sociologist John Howard has stated, "the black protest movement had . . . generated consciousness of the possibility of reform"[16] and helped Mexican Americans take pride in their racial and cultural distinctiveness.

Even more dramatic forms of activism developed in the late 60s among Native Americans. In fact, the demand for the use of the term *Native American* itself and the rejection of the word *Indian* sprang from the same logic and spirit as some Afro-Americans' rejection of the term *negro.* Both labels were aimed at robbing these groups of their selfhood and culture.

Though most of the "Red Power" movement has remained symbolic, perhaps its most important achievement has been the stopping of the government's "termination" program. This program, instituted in the early 1950s, was designed to solve the problems of the reservations by gradually getting rid of them. As one writer put it: "Those favoring termination of the reservations . . . assumed, implicitly, that three would be no Indian problem if there were no Indians."[17] For Native Americans, more than for any other group in the U.S., the retention of land--some of the land that was once entirely theirs--is a critical element in their effort to retain their distinct ethnic identity. Red Power represents the pride in and value of self and a search for the strategies which can best protect and enhance the quality of life of that racial-ethnic self.

I will not detail here the similar kind of activism among Asian Americans, Puerto Ricans, and other Third World people in the United States. Nor will I detail the renewed pride among white ethnics, especially those from southern and eastern Europe. What is important on the national level is that these movements have forced the American ideology to move even further from that of the melting pot--always a myth, in any case--to one of cultural pluralism.[18] That is, the national ideology, once one which envisioned all Americans eventually becoming culturally homogeneous, now at least in theory recognizes diversity as valuable and seeks to allow ethnic groups to preserve their distinctiveness while being full participants in the American society.

The bilingual education program is one of the practical outgrowths of this continuing change in the national philosophy. And although it may not be important legislation for American-born blacks, it has been a major change for Mexicans, cape Verdeans, Asians, Haitians, Puerto Ricans and other non-English speaking immigrants to this country.[19] This legislation and other manifestations of a significant change in the nation's view of those who are culturally different can be linked directly to ideas generated from the original civil rights movement.

Concomitantly, the shift in the nation's attitude toward those who are "different" in other ways can also be linked to the civil rights movement. Owing an incalculable debt to the 1960s movement are the Gay Liberation movement, the Gray Panther movement, the increased activism of the handicapped and, or course, the women's movement. Because I consider the International women's movement potentially a major force of social and economic change, a few observations are appropriate.

First, the women's movement is made up of far more than middle-class American feminists. But, at the same time, it must be acknowledged that "feminist analyses and the women's movement arose within the ranks of the relatively deprived white, middle-class women in the West, rather than the absolutely deprived majority of poor Third World women."[20] And many of these originators of the modern movement, like their forerunners in the nineteenth century women's suffrage movement, previously had been involve din other progressive causes. That is, as many nineteenth century feminists had been involve din the abolitionist movement, many twentieth century feminists had been involved in the civil rights and other movements.[21] During both periods, the factors that led to the development of a push for women's equality were the same: (1) demographically, the number of highly educated women was rising faster than the labor market cold absorb them in appropriate jobs; (2) their treatment in the abolitionist, civil rights and antiwar movements was in some ways contradictory to the egalitarian philosophies of these movements; and (3) through their involvement in these causes, they learned necessary skills for organizing for political change. "Demographic changes alone . . . were not sufficient to create a movement. They created a mobilizable stratum in the female population, but . . . other conditions [like involvement in the Abolitionist and the Civil Rights Movements'] were required for mobilization to occur."[22]

But the earlier and modern movements differ in other ways. In today's movement, even within the U.S., there is no single unifying issue comparable to women's suffrage. Also, the modern movement has spawned diverse perspectives, including liberal, Marxist, radical and socialist feminism.[23] And, most relevant to Third World people, the modern movement has spread to other classes and races within the U.S. and to women throughout the world. Women in India and Cuba and Tanzania and Vietnam are organizing because of their consciousness of their subordination as women and their country's subordination as a present and/or former dependent and peripheral element to the liberation of their group. Thus, their perspective is different from that of Western middle-class women to whom world capitalist imperialism has afforded not only material comfort but "a higher social status in the world over Third World women"[24] and a position of dominance over all poorer people. For Third World women, as sociologist Asoka Bandarage has written, capitalist development has meant:

> ... the marginalization of women in the least productive and least remunerative sectors of the Third World economies . . . The expansion of private property, wage labor, new technology, and the cash nexus have disadvantaged women categorically.[25]

Therefore, for Third World women to address their oppression is for them to confront the inequities generated by industrial capitalism. Marxist, radical and socialist feminism may be peripheral facets of Western feminism, but a feminism that questions the structure of present economic arrangements as well as the implications of gender is an inevitability in the Third World. Thus the great potential for fundamental socioeconomic change emanating from the international women's movement.

Here, again, can be seen the relatedness of the American civil rights movement of the 1960s to a progressive movement of today. For the international women's movement had its roots in the American women's movement which grew out of women's involvement in the hippie movement, the antiwar movement, and the civil rights movement.

This analysis of the linkages of the civil rights movement to other movements of liberation emphasizes the forward movement of the formerly subordinate toward self-empowerment. There are, of course, complexities and reverses in this movement the detailed discussion of which is beyond the scope of this paper. For example, not every new nation has challenged the Western *Weltanschauung*. And there are examples of progressive changes being successfully reversed by reactionary forces.[26] But these variations do not alter the reality that the trend is toward the decomposition of Western hegemony. And, undoubtedly, a major force behind this decomposition is the struggle of people of color for self-determination and dignity.

This struggles emanates from the desire of Third World people to improve their conditions of living. This desire is what black American has shared with other peoples of color. All of these efforts are a part of the movement of people against those countries, people and systems which have contributed to their impoverishment and degradation. That those countries are mainly Western, that those people are mainly white, that the system is the capitalist system is why DuBois was so incisively accurate when he stated in 1903: "The problem of the twentieth century is the problem of the color-line."[27] The civil rights movement in the United States was a critical part of the ongoing move toward a solution to that problem.

## NOTES

\* This is a revised version of paper read at the "Voices of the Civil Rights Movement" Conference in New Orleans, Louisiana in January, 1964. A note of appreciation goes to Dr. Hussein Abdilahi Bulhan of Boston University and Dr. Elaine Hagopian of Simmons College for their helpful comments on an earlier draft.

1. James W. VanderZanden, "The Non-Violent Resistance Movement Against Segregation," in Studies in *Social Movements,* ed. by Barry McLaughlin (New York, 1969), p. 54.
2. Paul Robeson, *Paul Robeson Speaks,* ed. by Philip Foner (Secaucus, New Jersey, 1978), pp.378-79.
3. Ibid., p. 379.
4. Burma, India, Indonesia, Ceylon and Pakistan.
5. Richard Wright, *The Color Curtain: A Report on the Bandung Conference* (Cleveland, 1956), p. 85.
6. Ibid., p. 86.
7. Ibid., p. 176.
8. Ibid., pp. 178-79.
9. For example, Robin Dobru, Surinamese poet and independence fighter, discussed his awareness of the movement in black America in numerous conversations with the author since 1972.
10. The National Joint Action Committee actually began the Black Power Movement in the late 1960s. The New Beginning Movement was an outgrowth of that Movement.
11. The Black Consciousness Movement was begun in 1968 and became public in 1972.
12. Interview in December, 1963. For political reasons, the interviewee prefers to remain anonymous.
13. Rodolfo Alvarez, "The Psycho-Historical and Socioeco-

nomic Development of the Chicano Community in the United States," in *Majority and Minority,* eds. Norman R. Yetman and C. Hoy Steele (Boston, 1962), p. 169.

14. John R. Howard, *The Cutting Edge* (Philadelphia, 1974), p. 96.
15. Ibid., pp. 100-01.
16. Ibid., p. 97.
17. Ibid., p. 115.
18. For a full discussion of the "melting pot" and "cultural pluralism" ideologies, see Milton Gordon, *Assimilation in American Life* (New York, 1964).
19. To be precise, Puerto Ricans are full citizens of the United States and are, therefore, "migrants" rather than "immigrants."
20. Asoka Bandarage, "Toward an International Feminism,"

in *Brandeis Review 3* (Summer 1963): 6-11.
21. For a full discussion of women's involvement in the abolitionist and suffrage movements of the nineteenth century, see Angela Davis, *Women, Race and Class* (New York , 1963).
22. Howard, op. cit., p. 144.
23. This is the classification system suggested by Alison Jaggar and Paula Rothenberg in *Feminist Frameworks* (New York, 1978).
24. Bandarage, op. cit., p. 7.
25. Ibid., p. 9.
26. The fate of Allende's Chile and Bishop's Grenada would be examples of such reversals.
27. W.E.B. DuBois, *The Souls of Black Folks* (Chicago, 1903), p. 12.

# BLACK RELIGION AND SOCIAL CHANGE: WOMEN IN LEADERSHIP ROLES

*Mary R. Sawyer*

The story of women's leadership in black religion may be viewed as an intertwining of two strands: one strand is composed of women in the church and related religious institutions, the other of women engaged in social change activities having religious underpinnings but whose connections to the church vary in degree and intensity. In a recent issue of the *Journal of Religious Thought*, Delores C. Carpenter addressed the first strand, providing a valuable historical overview of black women in religious institutions.[1] The objective here is to profile in an initial way personalities prominent in the second strand. In some instances, of course, the strands converge, with individual activist women being prominent both in religious institutions and in social movements tangential or external to the formal institutions.

Religiously based social action actually presents a continuum of forms. At one end of the continuum is the "secular" arena, including social protest and reform movements, electoral politics, and service organizations. The secular veneer, however, in no way precludes participation by individuals acting out of religious motivations. At the other end of the continuum are transchurch organizations, that is, interdenominational or ecumenical organizations whose objectives are also social change but whose agendas are overtly anchored in a religious framework. In between are religiously grounded nonchurch organizations (e.g., the YWCA), marginal religious movements (e.g., the Shakers), and quasi-church organizations (e.g., benevolent associations and missionary societies). In all of these, women have played key roles. This is particularly the case in the secular and ecumenical areas, which constitute the primary focus for this inquiry.[2]

Appropriate classification of a given movement or organization on this continuum is not always easy. For example, while some regard the

civil rights movement as a secular movement, others regard it as a church-based, or ecumenical movement.[3] Further, conventional understandings of "leadership" may not adhere. In the present context, no assumptions are made with regard to formal credentials. The women are ordained and lay, formally educated and women they represent--may be regarded as "leaders" to the extent that they were moved by religious tenets, or enabled by religious faith, to take action to address inequities and injustice. For the most part, however, they are the more visible leaders connected to formal organizations. The multitudes of women playing critical leadership roles in an informal capacity to local communities and neighborhood are inevitably more difficult to name, but surely no less to be valued.

My interest in this project comes out of my own journey in seeking to come to terms with the extraordinary complexity of black-white relations. As a white undergraduate enraged by the reality of discrimination on my college campus, but inspired by the courage and commitment of Martin Luther King, Jr., I determined, with all the idealism that the 1960s afforded, that my life's work would be concerned with "doing something" about racism. The passion of that vision carried me through a series of work settings--from human relations to urban management to black electoral politics. In each setting, I was compelled to take note of the persistent presence of the black church. Ultimately, the convergence of the black church, black politics, and social change movements became the focus of my graduate studies.

For many years my attention was given exclusively to racism and the multitude of movements, strategies, and ideologies devised to remedy the insidious consequences of racist policies and practices. Only in recent years have I come to understand at an affective as well as intellectual level the vicious precipitates of sexism, and the complex interrelations of racism, sexism, and classism. As that consciousness developed more fully, it was

Reprinted with permission from *The Journal of Religious Thought* - Howard University School of Divinity, Washington, D.C. 20017.

inevitable that in exploring the intersections of black religion, black politics, and social change, I would begin inquiring about the presence of women.

The actual assembling of this necessarily partial roll call was encouraged not only by my interactions with contemporary black women activists, but with white feminists as well, who, I have come to appreciate, represent a range of values and perspectives. If the more visible component of the white women's movement often seems weighted by upwardly mobile, middle-class individuals seeking preeminently a better place for themselves in the system, it is challenged by small but vocal cadres of women whose goal is transformation of the system, some of whom express preference for the label "womanist." The very appropriation of that label is a measure of their indebtedness to black women in learning how to advance a holistic agenda of liberation: how to address issues of sexism without excluding the distinctive experiences of black women and without ignoring the realities of racism, including their own culpability in participating in an as-yet untransformed, racist system. A repository of role models, both contemporary and historical, is thus an essential resource for all justice-seeking women, whatever their point of origin may be.

## THE "SECULAR" ARENA

A distinguishing feature of black religion is its historic concern with racial liberation. Throughout the nineteenth century, slave revolts, the abolitionist movement, the Negro convention movement, and the nationalist emigration movement all provided testimony to the inextricable relation of black religion and black politics (i.e., organized social change).[4] The relationship has held not only in protest politics but also in electoral politics, as both the Reconstruction ear and the post-civil rights movement ear attest.[5]

Heretofore scholars have tended to examine these arenas of political and religious intersection by focusing on the role of clergy and lay church leaders, who more often than not were men. As is increasingly being acknowledged, women, because of the patriarchal structure of the church, have historically been compelled to take their organizing skills and social consciousness into secular avenues without the benefit of church identify and authority. These extra-church involvements were sometimes in exclusively female organizations, sometimes in male-dominated organizations, and sometimes fiercely independent of any organization.

The antebellum period offers up three powerful examples of women in pursuit of justice: Maria Stewart (1803-1879), Harriet Tubman (c. 1823-1913), and Sojourner Truth (c. 1797-1883). Maria Stewart, upon her religious conversion, took up public speaking on behalf of women and the enslaved, addressing, as well, the severe restrictions imposed on "free" blacks. Without fail, her exhortations were couched in the language of religious morality.[6] The religious symbolism surrounding Tubman is apparent in the popular reference to her as the Moses for her people. That she operated out of a personal religious frame of reference is documented in Sarah Bradford's biography. Tubman's own words attest to her abiding faith:

> I had reasoned dis out in my mind; there was one of two things I had a *right* to, liberty, or death; if I could not have one, I would have de oder, for no man should take me alive; I should fight for my liberty as long as my strength lasted, and when de time came for me to go, de Lord would let dem take me.[7]

That the social activism of Sojourner Truth on behalf of women and slaves was solidly anchored in her mystical experiences is even more amply documented. Indeed, the very name taken by this outspoken Methodist preacher (in replacement of their birth name, Isabelle Baumfree) was a product of her recurring visions and dreams. No less were her public stances rooted in an abiding spirituality.

Few activists were as well known as these three women. But neither were activists so few as conventional histories would lead us to believe. Sara Evans, in her *Born for Liberty: Women in American History*, traces a progression from the evangelical revivals of the Second Great Awakening, to the social reform movements of the eighteenth and nineteenth centuries, to the women's suffrage movement.[8] For free black women before the Civil War, evangelical reform being the Africa-American Female Intelligence Society of Boston. On a more overtly political plane, black women were active in interracial organizations such as the Philadelphia Female Antislavery Society.[9]

From the late 1800s to the 1950s, social activism was carried out largely through women's organizations. Women's auxiliaries and missionary societies of the Baptist and Methodist denominations, respectively, constituted one important avenue for expressing moral concern. In the first two decades of this century, for example, the Women's Convention of the National Baptist Convention, under the leadership of Nannie Helen Burroughs, took political positions on lynching, disenfranchisement, stereotyping of blacks in the media and entertainment industries, and segregation in public transportation, as well as on women's suffrage and the sexism of black men.[10] But more often the opportunities resided in extra-church vehicles. Perhaps most significant of these was the multitude of clubs that began forming after the Civil War and that were brought together in the 1890s as the National Association of Colored Women under the leadership of Mary Church Terrell. Devoted to community service and racial uplift, the clubs provided avenues for leadership and organizing too often denied in the church proper.[11]

In addition to Burroughs and Terrell, prominent names of this period include Francis E. W. Harper, Ida B. Wells-Barnett, and Mary McLeod Bethune. Frances Ellen Watkins Harper is remembered as a strong advocate of the right of women to vote and as one of the most prominent black participants of the women's suffrage movement in the last decades of the nineteenth century. As a nationally respected public lecturer, however, she consistently advanced a holistic civil rights agenda which encompassed the imperative of voting rights for black men. She was equally constant in presenting her ideas in the imagery and rhetoric of the faith, as this brief sample attests:

> Let the hearts of the women of the world respond to the song of the herald angels of peace on earth and good will to men. Let them throb as one heart unified by the grand and holy purpose of uplifting the human race, and humanity will breathe freer, and the world grow brighter. With such a purpose Eden would spring up in our path, and Paradise be around our way.[12]

Ida B. Wells-Barnett, or course, is best known for her unrelenting campaign against lynching, but her journalistic critiques extended over the range of civil rights concerns of the early twentieth century. Although a founder of the NAACP and an early contributor to the women's club movement, she was by and large a solo crusader. The origins of her feminist stance, and of her audacity in challenging the accommodationist ideology of Booker T. Washington, are obscure.

But her appeals to moral conscience and to law as well as pragmatic economic interests as remedies for injustice were no doubt at least a partial result of her formal education at Rust College, a Methodist school in Mississippi.[13]

The entirety of Mary McLeod Bethune's extraordinary career was anchored in her deep religious faith. Intending to serve as missionary in Africa, Bethune attended Moody Bible Institute for two years. When those aspirations were thwarted, she turned to her own country, finding the mission field at home a rich harvest. She served as president of the National Association of Colored Women (NACW), then founded and presided over the National Council of Negro Women (NCNW), the umbrella organization that brought together most of the organizations of black women, including the NACW. The only woman member of the "Black Cabinet" under President Franklin Roosevelt's administration, she played a unique role as both spiritual and political adviser in the crucial New Deal years. She is perhaps best known as the founder of Bethune-Cookman College, a Methodist school, which became her own denominational affiliation.[14]

These individuals, each remarkable in her way, are only suggestive of the contributions made by the multitude of black women in the years of segregation. Nevertheless, they begin to hint of the religiously derived power that infused their collective actions. As B. J. Loewenberg and Ruth Bogin have noted:

> Black American women were persuaded that new attitudes could in fact be nurtured. They wished to awaken new understanding among blacks as well as in the general population. Will they had in overflowing measure, and likewise a limitless faith in their own powers to quicken the feelings of others as they themselves had been stirred. They could hardly feel otherwise. They were Americans. They were democrats. And they were Christians. Christianity and its Bible were their justifications for belief, the warrant for reform.[15]

## TRANSITIONS

By the 1940s the mood and methods of the black community began to turn, and the options for activist women shifted accordingly. While the exemplary women's organizations continued to function, the advent of the civil rights movement provided new forums as well. In contrast to the women's reform movements and clubs, the civil rights movement and the subsequent black power movement dictated women's entrance into a stage of participation in decidedly male-dominated organizations. Nevertheless, women did play important roles, as is increasingly being documented. Before turning to the prominent personalities, in this period, however, it would be appropriate to mention an organization that contributed much to laying a foundation for the civil rights movement, the Young Women's Christian Association (YWCA).

From the time of its formation in the 1860s, the YWCA provided an avenue for Christian women to act on their moral commitments. Sadly, those moral commitments did not extend initially to the problem of race and the conditions of black Americans. In consequence, black participation was for several decades effectively restricted to a parallel YWCA. Only after years of protest by black leaders was the situation remedied. From 1946, however, when an "interracial charter" was adopted, through 1970, when the elimination of racism became its "one imperative," the YWCA was an important training ground for civil rights activists.[16]

One author has noted that the language of the YWCA was evangelical Christian language, and that it was partly for the reason that it became an accessible forum wherein black women could express their concerns to white women.[17] No one was more pivotal in this process of directing the energies of the YWCA toward racial injustice than Dorothy Height, who from 1944 to 1977 served on the national staff of the YWCA as director of the District Action Program on Integration. Height remains an influential personality, of course, as president of the National Council of Negro Women (NCNW).

A second religiously based organization was also a significant predecessor of the civil rights movement. The first black ecumenical organization, the Fraternal Council of Negro Churches, organized by African Methodist Episcopal (AME) Bishop Reverdy Ransom in 1934, had an explicit agenda of social change and racial uplift, framed in religious context. Ransom and other black church leaders had despaired that the predominantly white Federal Council of Churches would ever address black concerns in any substantive way. As they envisioned the new Fraternal Council, it would be the "authoritative voice" of the "united Negro church" to speak on "social, eco-

nomic, industrial and political questions."[18] Organized on a conciliar model, the Fraternal Council had representation from sixteen predominantly black communions as well as a half-dozen predominantly white denominations. Significantly, members of the executive committee were not required to be ministers, which enabled the appointment of women. In fact, two of the original thirty-nine members of the executive committee were women--Belle Hendon from Chicago, representing the National Baptist Convention of American (NBCA), and Ida Mae Myller, of Gary, Indiana from the Community Center Church.[19]

Not until the Fraternal Council entered it second stage, under the leadership of Baptist minister William Jernagin, however, is there again evidence of participation by women in any capacity. Jernagin--for many years as the president of NBC, Inc.'s National Sunday School and Baptists Training Union Congress--served variously as president of the Council, chair of the executive committee, and director of the Council's Washington bureau, which he created. Jernagin maintained a close working relation with Nannie Helen Burroughs, who headed NBC's National Training and Professional School for Women and Girls in Washington, D.C. Burroughs served on at least one committee of the Council,[20] and spoke at the 1949 meeting of the Council in Richmond, Virginia. Significantly, her address was given during the 'women's hour." At that same meeting, the Council voted to "authorize the establishment of women's auxiliaries in various states."[21] Except for a group in St. Louis, no evidence exists that such appendages ever became active. In 1950, however, a women's auxiliary was organized at the national level and was for several years headed by Mrs. Jernagin. In keeping with this typical Baptist model, the participation of women outside the auxiliary was limited, although the same year the auxiliary was formed, a woman, Berta L. Derrick, did serve as associate director of the Council.[22] Several women were involved in the planning of the Prayer Pilgrimage held in Washington, D.C., under the sponsorship of the Fraternal Council following the 1954 Supreme Court decision *Brown v. Topeka Board of Education*. Burma Whitted, Dorothy Ferebee, and Jane Spaulding were all co-chairs of major committees.[23]

Beset by internal decline and overshadowed by the emergent civil rights movement, the Fraternal Council became inactive in the early 1960s. That it supported the objectives of the civil rights movements is certainly evident in the invitation it extended to a young man named Martin Luther King to become its executive director.[24] Had King accepted, the course of the civil rights movement might have been very different. The Southern Christian Leadership Conference (SCLC), for example, might never have come into being, and that loss certainly would have extended to activist women. SCLC, like the Fraternal Council in its later years, was a Baptist-dominated and therefore male-dominated organization, which accounted for the establishment of a "women's auxiliary," known as "SCLC Women." In spite of structural and philosophical obstacles, women still found ways to make substantive contributions.

Septima Clark, who as a staff member of Highlander Folk School was responsible for citizenship education training, ultimately became a member of the board of directors of SCLC. Perhaps more than any other individual, Clark was responsible for blacks in the South challenging the denial of voting rights. When the Highlander citizenship education program was taken over by SCLC, it came under the direction of Dorothy Cotton, a talented musician who trained citizenship instructors to use the singing of spirituals to teach their students to read and write.[25] An equally prominent member of the SCLC staff was Ella Stan Levinson--who conceived of the SCLC following the Montgomery bus boycott and worked with King and his lieutenants to develop the organization. Baker then served as the first staff director of SCLC, although her official title was "associate director," a concession to the preponderance of Baptist ministers on the SCLC board. Throughout her tenure, Baker had serious philosophical disagreements with King over leadership styles, arguing for a more participatory and less Baptist model. She lost, of course. But it was partially this difference that led her to urge student participants to form their own organization, separate from SCLC. The result was the Student Nonviolent Coordinating Committee, or SNCC, which Baker is credited with founding.[26]

Many of the women in the civil rights movement--whether affiliated with SCLC, SNCC, or other organizations--brought with them strong ties to the church. It was Baker's early ambition to become a missionary.[27] In her singing, her teaching, her preaching, her organizing and marching, the religious grounding of Fannie Lou Hamer was ever apparent.[28] Septima Clark, in her autobiog-

raphy, states imply, "I've been working in the church all my life."[29] In this, the known leaders of the movement differed little from the thousands of nameless women who carried the movement. One need only view any film on the civil rights protest rallies held in black churches of the South to be reminded that it was women, as much if not more so than men, who dropped their coins in the collection plate, who spread the word of coming events, who encouraged and prayed for male spokespersons, who planned and marched, and agonized and celebrated.

One of the signal accomplishments of the movement was the passage of the 1965 Voting Rights Act, which opened the door for black voter registration and election of black public officials in numbers that had not been seen since Reconstruction. A key difference, of course, was that during Reconstruction black women could neither vote nor hold public office. Although individuals such as Burroughs and Bethune were active in the Republican party in their day, the contemporary era of black electoral politics afforded women the first opportunity to express their social consciousness in the system of representative government. As of 1989, some eighteen hundred black women held public office, accounting for over a quarter of all black elected officials.[30] It is not surprising to find that religious sentiments and values weight heavily in the public service careers of black elected officials. Certainly this circumstance obtains no less for women than for men, as the words of one woman politician, former Congresswoman Shirley Chisholm, attest:

> There is no room left in the world today for a narrow and individualistic religion. To talk of building a Christ-like character while one is absolutely complacent about an economic and political system that engenders selfishness, greed and power-lust--all of this is sheer vanity.

Chisholm has acknowledged that it was the realization that "faith alone is not enough" that compelled her run for public office in the first place.[31]

If the shift from protest politics to electoral politics was one hallmark of the mid-to-late 1960s, there were other hallmarks as well. One was the transition from civil rights to black power, with its separatist emphasis on black culture and black consciousness, an emphasis that in turn produced other results. Demand grew for black studies in major colleges and universities, and interest was renewed in black religion and its institutional manifestation, the black church. These two developments converged, then, in a new academic field of black religious studies.[32]

Central to the emergence of black religious studies was the systematic formulation of a black liberation theology. Significantly, the early steps toward clarifying such a theology occurred not in an academic context but in the activist context of black ecumenical organizations concerned with social change, a new generation of which was spawned in the late 1960s. These organizations, which constitute an intermediary between black churches and extra-church agencies, joined the discipline of black religious studies in providing new arenas in which religious women could pursue social change.

## BLACK ECUMENISM

The memberships of black ecumenical organizations, with few exceptions, are drawn directly from churches; they tend to represent, however, activists and the more progressive element of the churches. While the organizations are by no means free of the patriarchal presumptions of black churches, collectively they offer an assortment of models that embrace female participation to varying degrees.

The first of these post-civil rights organizations was the National Conference of Black Churchmen (NCBC), organized in 1967 in reaction to confrontations with the white religious establishment, which was offended and threatened by black militancy. NCBC sought not only to explain the militancy to the white churches but also to raise the consciousness of the more conservative ranks of the black clergy. NCBC's most significant contribution, through the leadership of Gayraud Wilmore and James Cone, was the formulation of early statements of a black liberation theology.[33] Like the black power movement itself, however, NCBC was male-dominated, with very minimal participation by women--even though one of the five persons present at the group's initial meeting was a woman. Anna Arnold Hedgeman was the associate to Benjamin Payton, then executive director of the National Council of Churches' Commission of Religion and Race, where the initial meeting was held.[34] Not incidentally, Hedgeman began her influential career in civil rights as a staff member of the YWCA.[35]

Those women who did participate labored to raise their colleagues' consciousness. Among them were United Church of Christ minister Yvonne Delk, Erna Ballentine Bryant, AME minister Mary Ann Bellinger, Jacqueline Grant, and Thelma Adair. As board members in NCBC's latter years, these women were instrumental in bringing about a change in the name of the organization, from National Conference of Black Churchmen to National Conference of Black Christians, so as to include women. Erna Bryant also played an important role as the second executive director of the Black Ecumenical Commission in Massachusetts from 1974 to 1979.

NCBC was only marginally functional from 1973 until the early 1980s, when it became totally inactive. As this group declined, a number of its members turned to the Black Theology Project (BTP) as an avenue for pursuing the theological expressions of black liberation and empowerment. The Black Theology Project was originally organized in 1976 under the auspices of Theology in the Americas, but began meeting on a regular basis only in 1984. Even in its more erratic years, the participation rate of women significantly exceeded that of other organizations. Shawn Copeland, a Catholic sister, became the program director in 1976 and planned the first major consultation, held in 1977. Yvonne Delk served as chairperson in 1981 and 1982, and as cochair from 1987 to 1991. Olivia Pearl Stokes, Baptist minister, was a cochair in 1985 and 1986. As significant a role as anyone's was played by Jualynne Dodson, who served as cochair in 1984, and as the administrative coordinator from 1984 to 1988. The present executive director is Iva Carruthers. Women are well represented on the board of directors, as well as on the programs of BTP's annual convocations.

Women have also played a significant part in a little-known group that predates both the National Conference of Black Christians and the Black Theology Project. The National Black Evangelical Association (NBEA), organized in 1963, is made up largely of members of the evangelical wing of American Protestantism. But in contrast to most evangelicals, members of NBEA place a dual emphasis on spirituality and liberation-oriented social change activity. Of the eight founders of NBEA, one, Dessie Webster, was a woman, and approximately one-third of its members are women.[36] In 1990, five of the twenty-five members of the board of directors were women, as were two of the association's officers.[37] One of NBEA's eight commissions is a women's commission, and among the separate entities spun off from NBEA is one called the Women's Consciousness Raising Seminar. While such a high profile for women may at first glance seem improbable in a group such as this, it is also a reminder that evangelical and pentecostal churches are often more open to leadership by women than are the "progressive" mainstream churches.

Certainly the opposite circumstance is evident in the Congress of National Black Churches (CNBC). One of the younger ecumenical organizations--the Congress was formed in 1978--its agenda differs from those of other groups in that its primary emphases are neither theological formulations nor political activism, but economic development and human services delivery, with particular focus on the black family. The Congress, like the old Fraternal Council of Negro Churches, is organized on a conciliar model, with its membership consisting of five of the seven largest black denominations--two Methodist, two Baptist, and one Pentecostal.[38] According to its constitution, all national officers of the member denominations are members of the Congress. Since most officers are ministers and most ministers are men, this structural arrangement effectively limits the participation of women. All Methodist bishops, for example, by virtue of that office are members of the Congress--but there are no women bishops in any of the black Methodist denominations. In recent years, though, women have assumed significant leadership positions at the staff level. Two of the Congress's three project directors, for example, are women: Vanella A. Crawford and Rev. Alicia D. Byrd.

In contrast to the CNBC is another group also organized in 1978, Partners in Ecumenism (PIE). Although PIE has been only marginally active in recent years, it is still extant as a unit of the National Council of Churches (NCC). Its mission was to challenge the white churches, as did NCBC, to be more sensitive to black concerns, and additionally to bring black and white churches into a partnership to address the needs of urban residents in concrete ways. The first national coordinator of PIE was Joan Campbell, A Disciples of Christ minister who held that title from 1978 to 1980. For several years thereafter, Campbell played an important role in PIE as the assistant general secretary of NCC responsible for the Commission on Regional and Local Ecumenism (CORLE). The steering committee of PIE Has had strong representation by women, including, at one point, the vice president at-large for the national program, two of six regional vice presidents, one of six regional representatives, and four of twenty-two at-large members. An estimated 20 percent of PIE's members are women, a circumstance due in part to PIE's emphasis on lay participation. In addition, one-half of PIE's membership is made up of the historic black denominations and the other half of blacks in predominantly white denominations, which enlarges the pool of ordained women.

Recently, a number of individuals previously active in PIE have turned their energies to the newest adventure in black ecumenism, the Black Ecumenical Advocacy Ministry (BEAM), whose purpose is to function as a legislative lobby on behalf of the black community nationally.

Chronicling the presence of women in black religious organizations is an inexact undertaking at best, especially with older organizations for which historical records are scarce and incomplete. What becomes apparent, however, even in this brief review, is that a change is taking place: Women have been conspicuously more prominent in the Black Theology Project and Partners in Ecumenism than in the Fraternal Council of Negro Churches or the hierarchy of the Southern Christian Leadership Conference. It is no longer so easy to exclude women; nor, as many men have come to appreciate, is such exclusion desirable. That change in itself is among the most important contributions women have made, and it portends greater change to come.

A parallel observation may be made with regard to the field of black religious studies. An early critique of black liberation theology was its omission of the experience of women. The black womanist movement, aided by the emergent field of women's studies, inevitably had its impact not only on black theology but on black religious studies as a whole. Today, women are not only theologians, but sociologists of religion, biblical scholars, and ethicists. These individuals are themselves agents of change, for just as male scholars of black religion have south to raise the consciousness of black church leaders regarding empowerment around the issues of class and race, so womanist scholars are pointing to alternative paths where gender is at issue. In this, they have been joined by activist women in church structures, prominent among whom, in addition to Yvonne Delk, are such personages as Leontyne Kelley, retired United Methodist bishop; Theresa Hoover, for many years associate general secretary of the United Methodist Women's Division; the late Pauli Murray, Episcopal priest and longtime civil and women's rights advocate; and, more recently, Episcopal bishop Barbara C. Harris, and Presbyterian moderator Joan Salmon Campbell.

A development of particular moment within the church institution is the formation of a separate convention of Baptist women ministers. The National Baptist Women Ministers Convention, founded in 1981, presently claims some 250 participants. In 1990, the convention also admitted to its membership a delegation of recently ordained women in the Church of God in Christ. The unmistakable statement of these women is that if they cannot be preachers, pastors, and activists in the patriarchal communions, they will create alternative structures and develop alternative models of ministry.

And so it has been, from the time of Tubman and Truth, to the dawn of the twenty-first century.

## NOTES

1. Delores C. Carpenter, "Black Women in Religious Institutions: A Historical Summary from Slavery to the 1960s," *Journal of Religious Thought* 46, no. 2 (1989): 7-27.
2. Particularly where the secular arena is concerned, this essay relies on pioneering efforts during the last fifteen years to document the contributions of women. The new Carlson Publishing Company series, *Black Women in United States History*, edited by Darlene Clark Hine, is the most comprehensive collection of resources to date. An older and still useful compendium on black women's activism is Gerda Lerner's *Black Women in White America: A Documentary History* (New York: Vintage Books, 1973).
3. See Aldon Morris, *The Origins of the Civil Rights Movement* (New York: Free Press, 1984). It is my considered opinion that the civil rights movement is appropriately regarded as an ecumenical movement led albeit by a dissenting "remnant" of the church.
4. Gayraud S. Wilmore, *Black Religion and Black Radicalism*, 2d ed. (Maryknoll, N.Y.: Orbis Books, 1983).
5. Mary R. Sawyer, "Black Politics, Black Faith," master's thesis, Howard University Divinity School, 1982.
6. B. J. Loewenberg and Ruth Bogin, eds., *Black Women in Nineteenth-Century American Life* (University Park: Pennsylvania State University Press, 1976), pp. 183-85.
7. Sarah Bradford, *Harriet Tubman: The Moses of Her People* (Secaucus, N.J.: Citadel Press, 1961).
8. Sara M. Evans, *Born For Liberty: A History of Women in America* (New York: The Free Press, 1989).
9. Lerner, *Black Women in White America*, pp. 435, 437-40.
10. Evelyn Brooks, "Religion, Politics, and Gender: The Leadership of Nannie Helen Burroughs," *Journal of Religious Thought* 44, no. 2 (1988): 14-21.
11. See Charles H. Wesley, *The History of the National Association of Colored Women's Clubs: A Legacy of Service* (Washington, D.C.: National Association of Colored Women's Clubs, Inc., 1984). Also, see Lerner, *Black Women in White America* pp. 435-37, and Cynthia Neverdon-Morton, *Afro-American Women of the South and the Advancement of the Race, 1895-1925* (Knoxville: University of Tennessee Press, 1989),

chap. 10. Significantly, Burroughs was also active in the NACW as the head of the Young Women's Department. See Carpenter, "Black Women in Religious Institutions," p. 14.
12. Loewenberg and Bogin, eds., *Black Women in Nineteenth Century American Life*, pp. 243-44 and 247.
13. See Thomas C. Holt, "The Lonely Warrior: Ida B. Wells-Barnett and the Struggle for Black Leadership," in John Hope Franklin and August Meier, eds., *Black Leaders of the Twentieth Century* (Urbana: University of Illinois Press, 1982).
14. See Clarence G. Newsome, "Mary McLeod Bethune As Religionist," in Hilah F. Thomas and Rosemary Skinner Keller, eds., *Women in New Worlds* (Nashville, Tenn.: Abingdon, 1981).
15. Loewenberg and Bogin, *Black Women in Nineteenth-Century American Life*, p. 28.
16. For an extended treatment of the special role played by the student division of the YWCA in applying social Christianity to racial matters prior to the mid-1940s, see Frances Sanders Taylor, "On the Edge of Tomorrow: Southern Women, the Student YWCA, and Race, 1920-1944" (Ph.D. diss., Stanford University, 1984). For a brief history of blacks in the YWCA up to 1920, see Neverdon-Morton, *Afro-American Women of the South*, pp. 207-22.
17. Sara Evans, "Redefining Public and Private: The History of Women in American," lecture delivered at Iowa State University, Ames, Iowa, March 22, 1990.
18. Reverdy C. Ransom, ed., "The Fraternal Council of Negro Churches in America, *The Year Book of Negro Churches* (Philadelphia, AME Book Concern, 1939-1940), p. 123.
19. *1972 Heritage Brochure: Brochure of Examples of Work Done by the Fraternal Council of Churches* (Washington, D.C.: Fraternal Council of Churches, 1964), pp. 4-5.
20. Burroughs served on the National Coordinating Committee of the Fraternal Council in Civilian Defense. Jernagin to Burroughs, April 15, 1942, Nannie H. Burroughs Papers, Library of Congress, Washington, D.C.
21. Press release to the Associated Negro Press, June 8, 1949, Claude A. Barnett Papers, Chicago Historical Society, Chicago, Ill.
22. *1972 Heritage Brochure*, p. 9.
23. "Program," Lincoln Thanksgiving Pilgrimage, September 22, 1954, Claude A. Barnett Papers, Chicago Historical Society.
24. Interview with Rev. George W. Lucas, executive secretary of the Fraternal Council, cited in Spurgeon E. Crayton, "The History and Theology of the National Fraternal Council of Negro Churches" (Master's thesis, Union Theological Seminary, 1979), p. 52.
25. Donna Langston, "The Women of Highlander," lecture delivered at the Conference on Women and the Civil Rights Movement, Atlanta, Ga., October 1988.
26. See Morris, *The Origins of the Civil Rights Movement.*
27. Nydia D. Thomas, "Remembrances: Masters of Coalition Building--Ella Baker, 1905-1987," *Point of View* (Winter 1988): p. 21.
28. See "Fannie Lou Hamer: Prophet of Freedom," *Sojourners* (December 1982).
29. Cynthia Stokes Brown, ed., *Ready from Within: Septima Clark and the Civil Rights Movement* (Navarro, Calif: Wild Trees Press, 1986), p. 97.
30. *Black Elected Officials: A National Roster, 1989* (Washington, D.C.: Joint Center for Political Studies, 1990).
31. Shirley Chisholm, "The Relationship Between Religion and Today's Social Issues," *Religious Education* 69 (March-April 1974): 120, 122; cited in Sawyer, "Black Politics, Black Faith," p. 104.
32. See Mary R. Sawyer, "C. Eric Lincoln, Scholar and Prophet of Black Religious Studies," *Quarterly Review* 10, No. 3, Fall 1990.

33. For early statements on black theology issued by NCBC, see Gayraud S. Wilmore and James H. Cone, eds., *Black Theology: A Documentary History, 1966-1979* (Maryknoll, N.Y.: Orbis Books, 1979).

34. Others present at the July 1986 meeting were Gayraud Wilmore, J. Oscar Lee, and H. R. Hughes.

35. Carpenter, "Black Women in Religious Institutions," p. 19.

36. Dessie Webster is a Baptist. The diversity of NBEA is evident in the denominations represented by other founders: Open Bible Pentecostal Churches, Evangelical Friends, Presbyterian, Christian and Missionary Alliance, Church of Christ Holiness, United Holy Church of American, and United Brethren.

37. NBEA differs from other black religious organizations in that approximately one-third of its five hundred members are white; in 1990, one member of its board of directors was white.

38. Presently, the five member bodies are the AME Church, CME Church, National Baptist Convention of America, Inc., National Missionary Baptist Convention of America, and the Church of God in Christ.

# ELLA JO BAKER: A CIVIL RIGHTS WARRIOR

*Joan C. Elliot*

Born in Norfolk, Virginia, in 1903, Ella Jo Baker grew up in a small town in North Carolina, the granddaughter of former slaves. Her grandfather was a rebellious slave minister. Her grandmother, equally rebellious, refused to marry a light-skinned slave whom her master had selected for her. As a result, she was banished from working as a house servant to toiling as a field hand. In spite of this punishment, she married the grandfather, the person she loved. With this kind of background, Ella Baker had no choice but to grow up militant.

Baker received her education in the state of North Carolina, where she attended Shaw University in Raleigh and graduated as valedictorian of her class. As a young woman, she yearned to be a missionary. However, due to finances, she studied sociology and became involved with domestic radicalism. Her energy and resonant voice stood in contrast to her weak constitution, for she was a petite woman who suffered from acute asthma during her entire lifetime.

Ella Baker was married at tone time, but she seldom mentioned the marriage. Although she had no children, she did rear a niece. However, she used her maternal instincts in nurturing the civil rights movement during protests from the early thirties to the late sixties.

She came into contact with radical politics for the first time in her life after arriving in New York City in 1927. Harlem provided new social and political ideas and drew her into the political and social climate of the city. New York's Washington Square Park became the scene for debates over such ideas as communism, socialism, and capitalism. From here on, she would only join organizations which yearned for social change and political action.

In 1932, Ella Baker became an ally of a black writer with the *Pittsburgh Courier*, George Schuyler. Together, they organized the Young Negro Coop-

erative League whose goal was to promote consumer cooperatives. In her role as a group organizer, she learned how to understand group dynamics and how groups worked. Throughout the thirties, she identified with movements in the areas of workers' education, consumer protection and community organizing. By now, she identified with the problems of the unemployed and became aware of the suffering and poverty which the depression produced.

In the early 1940s she began her affiliation with the NAACP as an assistant field secretary. Eventually, she became National Field Secretary and traveled throughout the South to organize NAACP branches and develop membership drives. In two years, she attended 362 meetings and traveled 16,244 miles. Eventually, she was promoted to the National Director of Branches of the NAACP. Under Baker's leadership, the New York branch became the best organized and most active branch.

She became disillusioned with the NAACP because it was directed from the top rather than by the branches. She wanted the branches to be more active and in complete control. In spite of the fact that she resigned her national position, she remained active with the New York branch. When the United States Supreme Court handed down its decision in 1954 in the case *Brown vs. Topeka, Kansas*, Ella Baker was serving as chairperson of the Educational Committee of the New York branch. The committee analyzed the evidence presented in the case which revealed that de facto segregation caused the achievement levels of black children to decline after they entered elementary school. She served on the mayor's committee on school integration including the subcommittee on zoning. In 1957, she organized a group called parents in Action for Quality Education. As president of the group, she assisted in the implementation of community action against de facto segregation in the New York public schools.

I went to the upper West side, and the people very

Reprinted with permission from *The Griot*, Vol. 11, No. 1, Spring 1992.

eagerly said they wanted school integration. But when you raised the question of whether they would permit or would welcome blacks to live in the same houses with them, which was the only practical way at that stage to achieve integration, they squirmed. Integration certainly had to be pushed concurrently with changing the equality of education that the black children were getting, and changing the attitudes of the educational establishment toward the black community. (Lerner p. 348)

From her NAACP experiences, she had first hand knowledge of the South, southern blacks, southern communities, and southern organizations and leadership. In addition, she had personal contacts with numerous persons across the South whose commitments to civil and human rights were deepened because they knew Baker at a crucial time in their development. Among these was Mrs. Rosa Parks, who started the Montgomery bus protest in 1955, but who long before that worked with Baker in Alabama through the local NAACP branch (lerner p. 346). Rosa Parks, a seamstress in Montgomery, Alabama, refused to give up her seat to a white man on the city bus. This singular act of defiance caused the blacks to begin to protest and to resist the indignities of segregation.

The treatment of blacks on the buses, especially of women who utilized them to go to work, was a natural starting point. (Giddings p. 264).

At this point the bus boycott erupted into full bloom in Montgomery. Blacks organized the Montgomery Improvement Association to give structure to the protest which eventually attracted national attention. Civil groups and organizations, black churches and organized labor provided financial support and other kinds of assistance for the protestors.

One of the MIA's staunchest supporters was an organization called In Friendship. Organized in 1956 in New York, In Friendship provided financial assistance to southern blacks who were suffering reprisals for their political activity. (Giddings, p. 267)

Three prominent members of In Friendship (Bayard Rustin, Stanley Levinson and Ella Baker) were the first civil rights activists to offer voluntary assistance to Martin Luther King in the early weeks of the Montgomery boycott.

On June 4, 1956, the federal court rules in favor of the Montgomery Improvement Association to end segregation in public accommodations, which included segregation of the buses. On November 13, the United States Supreme Court confirmed, in a court order that reached Montgomery by December 20, 1956, the lower court's ruling. After the success of the boycott, according to Ella Baker, the movement literally came to a halt, for no plans existed for a continuance of activities.

It was Ella Baker who exhorted the leadership of the Montgomery Improvement Association to continue its fight against racial injustice. At age 52, she was a key figure in the formation of the Southern Christian Leadership Conference (SCLC) in 1957 to fight against all types of racial injustice. As associate director, Baker's organizational expertise and unique leadership style were crucial to its success. She felt that the leadership of the civil rights movement should be in the South and that the movement needed a counterbalance to the NAACP whose leadership was mainly in the North. (Giddings p. 268). Besides, she felt that the leadership in Montgomery had not realized how important it was to keep the momentum going. Martin Luther King became the leader of SCLC, but it was Ella Baker who ran and developed its office and coordinated the program. SCLC, whose headquarters were moved to Atlanta, became an organization with sixty-five affiliates in various souther cities with blacks providing leadership locally. By now, she had become disillusioned with the NAACP and put her energies into SCLC. Baker intended to work for six weeks. However, due to the lack of funds to replace her skills and expertise, she remained as SCLC's coordinator for two-and-a-half years. (Lerner p. 349).

Several research articles on the Southern Christian Leadership Conference identified Ella Baker as the first executive director of the organization. In actuality, she was the first associate director; Rev. John Tilley from Baltimore was the first executive director, elected in May, 1958. The Executive Council of the Southern Christian Leadership Conference chose Rev. Tilley because he had recently directed a successful voter registration drive in Baltimore and felt that he would be ideal to direct the crusade for the citizenship movement. Tilley was also elected as director because he was a minister. Although Martin Luther King stated that the director did no have to be a minister, the other members on the executive board insisted that a minister be a part of the qualifications. The Executive Council thought that another minister who had had experience with the voting rights movement would fit well with the church-based leadership in the Southern Christian Leadership Conference (Branch p. 247).

Before Tilley's arrival, Ella Baker established a central office for the Southern Christian Leadership Conference and had performed all of the duties and tiresome work of an administrator. The ministers resisted her as the chief executive officer of SCLC because of her age, sex, a nd genius to organize and inspire people. They were accustomed to women doing all of the work in the church in the background and not questioning decisions or seeking changes. Because of these forces, the ministers differed from Ella Baker. (Branch p. 258)

At the time (November, 1957) she was 25 years older than most of the leadership in the Southern Christian Leadership Conference and possessed skills for organizing and inspiring people. Entering the organization controlled by black ministers, she collided with them, for they still had condescending attitude which did not envision women as full-fledged leaders. Since Ella Baker, a self assured woman, did not necessarily defer to men, she was bound to have friction with the leadership of the Southern Christian Leadership Conference. Because he had to shuttle back and forth between Baltimore and Atlanta, and serve as the minister of a church in Baltimore, Tilley proved to be negligent. In the meantime, Baker continued to run the office and provide leadership and ideas. Although she was eventually named director of the Southern Christian Leadership Conference, the friction still remained. (Giddings p. 268).

In fact, the feminist issue in the civil right movement was not different that in any other patriarchal society. Black women were placed in the back to do daily administrative tasks, to perform the leg work, to organize the fund-raising and to provide shelter for Freedom Fighters, while the men made the speeches and took the credit. Baker did not want credit for her work although she provided ideas, energy, money and hard work. Yet, she was instrumental in awakening the nation to women's struggle for equality and justice and fought against the tendency to relegate women to subordinate positions in the movement.

The movement of the '50's and '60's was carried largely by women, since it came out of the church groups. It was sort of second nature to women to play a supportive role. How many made a con-

scious decision on the basis of the larger goals, how many on the basis of habit pattern, I don't know. But it's true that the number of women who carried the movement is much larger than that of men. Black women have had to carry this role, and I think the younger women are insisting on equal footing. (Lerner p. 351).

Sexism did not become a major issue in the United States until after the 1964 civil rights legislation. Black women and black men protested so vigorously against the racism of the white establishment that black women of the '50's did not speak against sexism of the black males.

Ella Baker, who was not as well known as some of the other black civil rights leaders, knew that she would not play a major role in the circle of leaders among a group of ministers. However, the movement and its results were more important to her than her visibility on a television screen. She acknowledged that women had always played a supportive role in church groups, and the civil rights movement was not different. She has served black people without fame, publicity, and recognition. Secure in herself, she served her people continuously. (Lerner p. 350).

At this point the Southern California Christian Leadership Conference had affiliates in many southern states, but the main body of the Southern Christian Leadership Conference was stationed in Atlanta under the leadership of Martin Luther King. By now, he had developed into a charismatic leader by way of the media. Baker had a different concept of leadership and organization for the SCLC. She thought that an organization should not be centered around one or a few leaders, and maintained that a people's movement is most effective, if participants are encouraged to develop local leadership among the masses.

Instead of "the leader"--a person who was supposed to be a magic man--you would develop individuals who were bound together by a concept that benefitted larger numbers of individuals and provided an opportunity for them to grow into being responsible for carrying on the program. (Giddings, p. 268).

She especially felt that the civil rights movement centered around and depended too heavily on Dr. King. The complete idolization of King prevented the development of potential leadership from women, young people and other members of the community. According to Ella Baker, mass movements and their organizations should be structured around "group centered leadership." With this approach a mass movement can be more democratic and responsive to the people. (Lerner p. 351).

In spite of her perspective and warnings, the elected officials of the Southern Christian Leadership Conference acknowledged Martin Luther King as the leader of SCLC. The ministers felt that the country would listen to a charismatic leader and would respond financially to him. (Branch p. 247).

While the crusade was contributing to the slow process of building local movements between 1958 and 1960, it did not accomplish its goal of doubling the number of black voters in local communities. External and internal factors contributed to the failure. The chief external factor was white resistance when confronted by blacks seeking votes. Southern whites used every repressive measure in their power to block voter registration. These measures included economic reprisals and delaying tactics by white registrars. These measures did have an impact on the crusade. For example, in Louisiana, blacks were cut off of welfare if they tried to register. In Tuskegee, Alabama the city council gerrymanded all blacks out of voting districts in town except four persons. (Giddings p. 269).

The internal factors which caused friction among blacks were jealousy, envy, the lack of resources and the emphasis on one leader. The ministers on one hand idolized Martin Luther King; but on the other hand, they experienced envy and jealousy. Many claimed behind his back that they did all the work, while he received all of the credit. Reverend Ralph Abernathy was Dr. King's best friend and at the same time his jealous competitor. (Branch p. 247).

By 1959, the sit-ins began to sweep across the country. Baker was a key in the network of sit-ins in the summer of 1960. Since the sit-ins were mainly led by students in historically black colleges, she saw the need for the students to form one cohesive umbrella organization. Through her producing she persuaded SCLC to organize a conference in Raleigh, North Carolina. Anticipating about one hundred young student leaders, she found two hundred dynamic students in attendance. (Lerner p. 351).

To fight against all types of racial injustice, she helped organize student leaders into SNCC (Student Nonviolent Coordinating Committee) on April 15, 1960 at Shaw University in Raleigh,

North Carolina. This group sponsored sit-ins, wade-ins, knell-ins and boycotts of retail establishments. Baker, executive secretary of SCLC, asked that SCLC give support in the amount of eight hundred dollars for the sit-in campaign, but allow SNCC to remain independent of SCLC. The Southern Christian Leadership Conference wanted the Student Non-Violent Coordinating Committee to become an arm of the SCLC. Again, disharmony arose between Ella Baker and the executive council of the SCLC when she did not encourage the students to join them.

In spite of her difficulties with SCLC, she continued her work with the young students. She had no problems relating to them and their goals.

> I had no difficulty relating to the young people. I spoke their language in terms of the meaning of what they had to say. I didn't change my speech pattern and they didn't have to change their speech pattern. But we were able to communicate. (Lerner p. 350).

Civil rights activist James Foreman, credited Ella Baker among all black leaders with understanding the significance of the student sit-in movement and helping to organize these campus groups into SNCC. The established civil rights groups (SCLC, NAACP, and CORE) wanted SNCC to ally with them as the youth wing of the parent group. Since Ella Baker at the time identified with SCLC, the latter group thought it automatically had an inroad to SNCC. However, Baker supported an independent student-oriented group rather than a leader-centered group. In an interview Baker stated:

> I have always felt it was handicap for oppressed peoples to depend so largely upon a leader, because unfortunately in our culture, the charismatic leader usually becomes a leader because he has found a spot in the public limelight. It usually means he has been touted through the public media, which means that the media made him, and the media may undo him (Gerda Lerner, interview with Ella Baker, December 1970, Lerner p. 351).

This idea further exacerbated the friction between her and SCLC.

Besides the sit-ins, she assisted the students in the organization of voter registration drives. SNCC became the most significant student-activist movement in United States history. Her touch was felt as the students pricked the conscience of the nation over the Vietnam War, the free speech movement, and the women's movement.

Ella Baker in the sixties looked like the average black mother, but when she talked, she gave an additional facet to her personal appearance, that is, a committed dedicated leader. Her personal appearance did not indicate that she was the major political advisor to the Student Nonviolent Coordinating Committee. Although she looked like a southern school teacher or church goer, she was defined as a radical activist. Her voice patterns let the listener know that he or she was listening to a true leader with convictions. She especially made the students feel that the struggle for justice was possible. An organizer, she could persuade people to do their best for the cause of freedom. Shunning the limelight, she was a social activist and tough negotiator behind the scenes. While Martin Luther King made the public speeches, she managed the office, conceived ideas, developed strategies and nurtured the movement. Adamant in her convictions, she supported the right of the students to set up their own independent organization. As a result of her stand, she broke with SCLC.

Baker was recognized for her organizational skills. Barbara Omolade recalls that Baker was known for her fearlessness when organizing community groups to protest and to vote. She went to the people, went to the streets, knocked on doors. Others preferred meeting in a downtown office building or a hotel. As an activist, she went where the people were. And she went whether the group was large or small or whether the problem was big or little. (Omolade p. 53).

> Ms. Baker was a subversive who mobilized people to organize for decent wages for Black teachers, for paved streets in the Black community, against police brutality and for the right to vote. (Omolade p. 54).

She helped people to understand there was strength in unity when she served as a NAACP field worker. In spite of danger, she organized in the rural South during the 1940's when lynching and shotgun justice was the norm and membership in the NAACP could mean death. Yet she believed that one must be a soldier in the army for black people. In addition, she believed very firmly in the right of people to be the ones to decide what actions they were going to take to get from under their oppression. (Omolade p. 30).

In 1964, Ella Baker helped to found the Missis-

sippi Freedom Democratic Party (MFDP), gave the keynote address at its founding convention, and helped to prepare its challenge to the National Democratic Party in Atlantic City. She moved to Washington, DC, until the convention was over, closed up the office, and moved back to New York from Atlanta. (Lerner p. 346).

As a community organizer, civil rights advocate, and voice of many activists, Ella Baker both made history and observed it during a career of leadership which started in 1929 and lasted over five decades. Like Martin Luther King, Ella Baker was an effective leader and bold strategist pioneering the direct-action tactics which were so successful in the 1960's. She is considered one of the most foremost organizers of the freedom movement. Known as a woman of determination and conviction, she quietly planned strategies to overcome prejudice and discrimination in the United States.

In 1983, the Public Television Broadcast System presented a documentary on her amazing life, called "Fundi: The Story of Ella Baker." *Fundi* a Swahili word means "one who hands down a craft from one generation to another."

In her own words she states:

> In my organizational work, I have never thought in terms of my "making a contribution." I thought of myself as functioning where there was a need. And if I have made a contribution I think it may be that I had some influence on a large number of people. (Lerner p. 346).

In December, 1986 she died on her eighty-third birthday.

## REFERENCES

"About Ella Baker," *Jet* Vol (19 January 1987): 71:18

Bergman, Peter M. *The Chronological History of the Negro in American*, New York: Harper, 1969.

Branch, Taylor, *Parting the Waters: America in the King Years 1954-63*, New York: Simon and Schuster, 1988, p. 231-33, p. 330-31, p. 292-93.

Canterow, Ellen, Gushee O'Malley Gushee and Sharon Hartman Strom. *Moving the Mountain*. Old Westburg, NY: Feminist Press, 1979.

Forman, James. *Making of Black Revolutionaries*. New York: Macmillan, 1972.

Giddings, Paula. *When and Where I Enter: The Impact of Black Women on Race and Sex in America*. New York: Bantam Books, 1984, p. 268-69, p. 274-75.

Hentoff, Nat. "A New Year's Toast to Those Who Reject Fate." *Village Voice* 1 January 1979. 30.

Lerner, Gerda. *Black Women in White America: A Documentary History*. New York: Vintage Books, 1973. p. 345-352.

Morris, Aldon D. *The Origins of the Civil Rights Movement*. New York: Free Press, 1984.

Omolade, Barbara. "Black Womanhood Images of Dignity: Ella Baker and Miriam Makeba." *Black Collegian Vol.* (April/May 1981): 52-60, Contains a photograph of Ella Baker.

Payne, Charles. "Ella Baker and Models of Social Change." *Signs* 14 (Summer 1989): 885.

Seitz, Michael H. Review of "Fundi: The Story of Ella Baker." *The Progressive* 47 (January 1983).

Wiley, Jean. "On the Front Lines; Four Women Activists Whose Work Touched Millions of Lives." *Essence* 20 (February 1990): 45. Contains a photograph of Ella Baker.

# BLACK GROUPS NEED 'NEW TACTICS, LEADERS'

*Marty Baumann*

**PROFESSOR ALDON MORRIS SAYS GROUPS ARE SO TIED TO TRADITIONAL WAYS THEY ARE NOT MEETING BLACK PROBLEMS HEAD ON.**

*Aldon Morris is chairman and professor of sociology at Northwestern University in Chicago. As the Southern Christian Leadership Conference holds it annual convention this week in Dayton, Ohio, the civil rights expert explains in an interview with USA TODAY's Sharon Shahid the changing black community and the need for new leadership at the top of black organizations to keep up with those changes. His comments:*

"At this juncture, black organizations need the kind of leadership that can deal with the contemporary problems confronted by the African-American community. They have to give some very serious thought to how to develop a young, dynamic leadership within the African-American community. The older leaders have to know that what they did was important, but each generation is given challenges, experiences and insights that can go beyond the leadership of their elders. They need to try to come to grips with generating bold new strategies and tactics to brings about change. Until the Urban League, the NAACP, the SCLC and other groups are creative enough to get their financial support from the black community, they are limited in their vision and in what they actually do."

*On why he thinks many groups are out of touch with mainstream blacks:* "I would certainly have to say that when you look at what is happening in the black community, especially in the inner cities, and given the levels of poverty and neglect, if the civil rights organizations aren't addressing those kinds of issues head on, then they are going to really miss the gravity of what is happening within those oppressed communities. Part of the problem stems from the fact that the mainline civil rights organizations are so tied into their traditional ways of doing things, that's the reason why they aren't addressing these things head on."

*On issues important to blacks:* "Black people are very much concerned with the economy and not just when it's in a recession. Crime and violence are another high priority. This whole notion that somehow crime is something intrinsic to black people is nonsense. Any group of people who are caught in the kinds of circumstances that you have in the inner city, where they are crowded on top of each other, where there are not jobs, where there's anger and hostility, you are going to have this kind of violence and crime. The whole problem of police brutality is another major issue that has not been solved. Also, African-Americans are so aware that racism hasn't gone anywhere, that it remains an important issue they have to deal with daily. Another thing is that many members of the black community are well aware of the international picture and, in many ways, they share a similar fate with non-whites in other parts of the world. They're very concerned about foreign policy as it relates to places like South Africa and Haiti. Another problem is education. You could go on forever."

*On the presidential election:* "The African-American community is caught in the traditional dilemma it often finds itself, in, and that is they must choose between candidates who are not focused directly on solving the problems of the African-American community. Bill Clinton pushes the whole idea of racial harmony, but he has not yet come up with anything concrete that would bring about the sort of change where you can have racial harmony. He has not outlined anything that would change the fact that black people make only about half of what whites make in this country. He has not solved the problem of coming up with any solutions that would increase the decision-making power of African-Americans in this society. And, certainly, the Bush administration is simply more of the same. We already know from the

Reagan era through Bush that there are no creative solutions or even political will to bring about any fundamental change on the racial front."

*On the L.A. riots:* "There's a message in the L.A. riots that is often overlooked. It's easy in this country, given the racial history, to simply view these things as black-white confrontations. But if we really look at the faces of the L.A. situation, what we saw were many other groups--Hispanics, whites, along with African-Americans--who were participating in that rebellion. And we need to ask, 'What does that mean?' rather than simply saying that it was a confrontation between blacks and whites. What that uprising suggested is that poverty and inequality cut across racial and ethnic lines and, even though the black community is disproportionately affected by these problems, they're certainly not limited to the black community."

*On preparing for the 21st century:* "That's the million-dollar questions. I don't think that black or white leadership has come up with any viable solutions to deal with the questions of poverty, corporate irresponsibility or how we restructure the school system so everyone can be educated so they can function as productive citizens in the 21st century. These are the kinds of issues that are confronting us as an entire nation."

---

### Black Status

---

The median household income for blacks in 1990 was $19,758, up 1.4% from 1980, but significantly lower than the $31,435 for whites. Other trends:

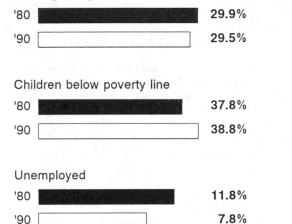

Below poverty line

| '80 | 29.9% |
| '90 | 29.5% |

Children below poverty line

| '80 | 37.8% |
| '90 | 38.8% |

Unemployed

| '80 | 11.8% |
| '90 | 7.8% |

# APPENDICES

# A

# SOME SIGNIFICANT DATES IN BLACK AMERICAN HISTORY

*Mary Francis Berry*
*John W. Blassingame*

| | |
|---|---|
| **1502** | First Africans arrive in New World. |
| **1619** | Twenty Africans arrive on Dutch man-of-war at Jamestown, Va. |
| **1619-1803** | Legal slave trade: 400,000 to 1 million of the 10 to 50 million Africans forcibly transported to America arrive. Other smuggled in illegally until 1860. |
| **1662** | Virginia enacts a statute making slavery hereditary, following the status of the mother. |
| **1770** | Crispus Attucks, first of five men killed in the Boston Massacre. |
| **1787** | Richard Allen and Absalom Jones found the Free African Society, precursor of the Bethel AME Church, founded in 1794. |
| **1800** | Gabriel Prosser, a Virginia slave, hanged together with a number of his followers, for plotting to lead a slave attack on Richmond, Va. |
| **1815** | Free Negro battalion fights in the Battle of New Orleans against the British. |
| **1815** | Paul Cuffee carries thirty-eight Negro immigrants to Africa at his own expense. |
| **1817-1842** | Blacks and Indians fight against federal troops in the First and Second Seminole wars. |
| **1816-1817** | American Colonization Society organized by Bushrod Washington, Henry Clay, and other whites to take blacks to Africa. |
| **1820** | Missouri Compromise enacted prohibiting slavery north of Missouri. |
| **1822** | Denmark Vesey's slave conspiracy takes place in Charleston, S.C. |
| **1827** | Samuel E. Cornish and John Russwurm found *Freedom's Journal* in New York. |
| **1829** | David Walker publishes *Walker's Appeal*, a militant antislavery pamphlet. |
| **1831** | William Lloyd Garrison founds the *Liberator*. |
| **1831** | Nat Turner's slave rebellion takes place in Southhampton County, Va. |
| **1833** | Free Negroes and whites found the American Anti-Slavery Society, which meets in Philadelphia. |
| **1834** | Prudence Crandall's School for Negroes attacked by citizens and closed by local authorities in Canterbury, Conn. |
| **1838** | *Mirror of Liberty*, the first black magazine, begins publication in New York City. |
| **1849** | Benjamin Roberts loses court challenge to segregation in Boston schools. |
| **1852** | Publication of Harriet Beecher Stowe's *Uncle Tom's Cabin*. |
| **1853** | Publication of *Clotel*, the first novel by a black American, William Wells Brown. |
| **1857** | The Supreme Court decides *Dred Scott v. Sanford*. |
| **1858** | William Wells Brown publishes the first American black-authorized play, *The Escape*. |
| **1859** | Martin R. Delany and Robert Campbell lead the Niger Valley exploring party to explore possible settlements of American blacks in Africa. |
| **Oct. 1859** | John Brown's raid on Harpers Ferry. |

| | |
|---|---|
| **Jan. 1863** | Lincoln issues the Emancipation Proclamation. |
| **Mar. 1863** | First National Draft Act passed; does not exclude blacks. |
| **Mar. 1865** | Freedman's Bureau Act, including provision for land for the freedmen, passed. |
| **Apr. 1865** | Opening of the government-chartered Freedmen's Bank; goes bankrupt after being milked by directors in June, 1874. |
| **Dec. 1865** | Ratification of the Thirteenth Amendment abolishing slavery. |
| **Apr. 1866** | Civil Rights Act passed by Congress, giving black citizens civil rights equal to those of whites. |
| **Mar. 1867** | Reconstruction Act, including voting rights for blacks, passed by Congress. |
| **July 1868** | Ratification of the Fourteenth Amendment protecting civil rights from the state interference. |
| **1869** | First of twenty blacks to serve in the House of Representatives during Reconstruction seated. |
| **1870** | Hiram Revels elected to the Senate from Mississippi. |
| **Mar. 1870** | Ratification of the Fifteenth Amendment prohibiting denial of the right to vote on the grounds of race or previous condition of servitude. |
| **1873-1879** | Exodus of blacks from the South to Kansas. |
| **1874** | Blanche K. Bruce elected to the Senate from Mississippi, the only black elected to a full term until 1966. |
| **1875** | Civil Rights Act providing equal public accommodations passed by Congress. |
| **1877** | Reconstruction ends with withdrawal of the last federal troops from the South. |
| **1881** | Booker T. Washington founds Tuskegee Institute. |
| **1883** | Civil Rights Act of 1875 declared unconstitutional by the Supreme Court. |
| **1895** | Booker T. Washington's Atlanta University speech. |
| **1895** | Frederick Douglass dies February 20. |
| **1896** | *Plessy v. Ferguson* decided by the Supreme Court, approving separate by equal facilities. |
| **June 1898** | Ninth and Tenth Cavalry, two of four black regiments in the Regular Army, and Theodore Roosevelt's Rough Riders at San Juan Hill during the Spanish-American War. |
| **1900** | Booker T. Washington founds the National Negro Business League. |
| **1903** | W. E. B. Du Bois publishes *The Souls of Black Folk.* |
| **1905** | W. E. B. Du Bois, Monroe Trotter, and others found the Niagara Movement to fight for civil rights. |
| **1906** | Brownsville, Texas, shooting incident involving black troops. |
| **1909** | Springfield, Ill., lynching and subsequent white attacks in black neighborhoods leads to founding of the National Association for the Advancement of Colored People. |
| **1910** | W. E. B. Du Bois starts *Crisis* as the official NAACP publication. |
| **1915** | NAACP wins *Guinn v. U.S.*, finding use of the grandfather clause of qualify voters unconstitutional. |
| **1915** | Booker T. Washington dies in Tuskegee, Ala. |
| **1915** | Ghanaian Alfred Sam leads black emigration movement to Africa from black towns organized earlier in Oklahoma. |
| **1916** | Marcus Garvey arrives in New York from Jamaica and founds the Universal Negro Improvement Association. |
| **1917** | Houston, Texas, shooting incident involving black troops. |
| **1919-1945** | Five Pan-African Congresses organized by W. E. B. Du Bois. |
| **1928** | Oscar DePriest elected to Congress, the first black since the term of George White of North Carolina ended in 1901. |
| **1930** | Black Muslims founded by W. D. Fard, succeeded by Elijah Muhammad in 1934. |
| **1935** | National Council of Negro Women founded with Mary McLeod Bethune as president. |
| **1941** | A. Philip Randolph's threat of a march on Washington leads Roosevelt to issue |

|          | Executive Order 8802. |
|----------|-----------------------|
| **1946** | *Ebony* magazine started by John Johnson. |
| **1949** | Secretary of Defense Lewis Johnson issues orders to desegregate opportunities in the miliary service. |
| **1950** | Ralph Bunche becomes the first black man to receive Nobel Peace Prize. |
| **1954** | *Brown v. Board of Education* decided by Supreme Court. |
| **1955** | Court order requiring desegregation with all deliberate speed issued in the Brown case by the Supreme Court. |
| **1956** | Montgomery, Ala., bus boycott led by Martin Luther King, Jr. |
| **1956** | Autherine Lucy expelled from the University of Alabama. |
| **1957** | Eisenhower orders use of troops in enforcing Little Rock, Ark., school desegregation. |
| **1957** | Congress passes the Civil Rights Act creating the U.S. Commission on Civil Rights and a Civil Rights Division in the Justice Department. |
| **1960** | Sit-ins at lunch counters in Greensboro, N.C. |
| **1961** | W. E. B. Du Bois joins the Communist party, renounces his U.S. citizenship, and moves to Ghana. |
| **1961** | CORE Freedom Rides in interstate transportation. |
| **1962** | Mississippi officials attempt to keep James Meredith out of the University of Mississippi; leads to violence. |
| **1963** | Assassination of Medgar Evers, leader of the NAACP in Mississippi. |
| **Aug. 1963** | March on Washington for jobs and freedom. |
| **Sept. 1963** | Four black children killed in bombing of a black church in Birmingham, Ala. |
| **1964** | Civil Rights Act creating the Equal Employment Opportunity Commission and ending discrimination in public accommodations, passed by Congress. |
| **July 1964** | Lemuel Penn shot by the Ku Klux Klan while driving along a road in Georgia. |
| **Aug. 1964** | Three civil rights workers--James Chaney, Michael Schwerner and Andrew Goodman--murdered in Mississippi; bodies found. |
| **Oct. 1964** | Martin Luther King, Jr. receives the Nobel Peace Prize. |
| **Feb. 1965** | Malcolm X murdered. |
| **Mar. 1965** | Civil rights march from Selma to Montgomery, Ala., leads to passage of the Voting Rights Act. |
| **Aug. 1965** | Riot set off by police arrest in Watts, Los Angeles, Calif. |
| **1965** | Robert C. Weaver appointed Secretary of Housing and Urban Development, the first black cabinet officer. |
| **June 1966** | On the march for freedom from fear led by James Meredith in Mississippi, "Black Power" slogan attributed to Stokely Carmichael, head of the Student Non-Violent Coordinating Committee. |
| **1966** | Edward Brooke of Massachusetts elected to the Senate, the first black elected since Reconstruction. |
| **1966** | Founding of the Black Panther party by Huey Newton and Bobby Seale in Oakland, Calif. |
| **June 1967** | Muhammad Ali convicted for draft evasion and his heavyweight boxing title taken away. After he wins on appeal, he has to fight George Foreman three years later to win back the title. |
| **1967** | In *Loving v. Virginia* Supreme Court declares illegal the ban on interracial marriage. |
| **1967** | Thurgood Marshall appointed first black Supreme Court Justice. |
| **Apr. 4, 1968** | Martin Luther King, Jr., assassinated. |
| **1971** | Jesse Jackson founds Operation PUSH. |
| **1972** | Gary National Black Political Convention. |
| **1974** | Sixth Pan-African Congress convened in Tanzania. |
| **1978** | *Bakke v. University of California* decided by Supreme Court. Racial quotas cannot be used in university admissions decisions, but race may be taken into account. |
| **1979** | *Weber v. Kaiser Aluminum* decided by Supreme Court. Voluntary agreements to give |

preferential training opportunities to blacks in an industry are legal.

**1980** *Fullilove et al. v. Klutznick, Secretary of Commerce et al.* decided by Supreme Court approves minority fund set-aside in public works act included in an amendment proposed by Congressman Parren Mitchell.

**May 17, 1980** March for Jobs, Peace, and Justice in Washington, D.C. led by Rev. Jesse Jackson.

*Editor's Note:* During the past 12 years, the Black struggle for justice and equality has continued and African Americans have made contributions to the American society at all levels. Students are required to update this listing of significant dates in Black American history - 1980-1992 (see question #8 of study guide for Part V.

# B

## THE CONTINENT OF AFRICA

*Editor's Note:* Africa is the second largest landmass on earth, after Eurasia. The continent is more than three times the size of the continental U.S.A. The roots of the African American culture and heritage are found in Africa. Today, there are fifty-one independent countries in Africa. Africa has witnessed tremendous political, cultural, and economic changes during the last several years.

# C

# THE AFRICAN DIASPORA

*Editor's Note*: The concept African Diaspora is used in reference to those geographical areas with a large number of people of African descent. Africans were imported into these geographical areas during the period of the slave trade. Haiti, Barbados, Jamaica, Bahamas, Grenada, Dominica, Saint Lucia and Belize are examples of countries of the African Diaspora (countries located in Caribbean, South and Central America) with over 85% of the population being of African descent. Brazil (located in South America) is second to the United States in the number of people of African descent, excluding nations on the continent of Africa. The population of people of African descent in these countries is a rough estimate due to the following factors: definition of racial and ethnic groups, the frequency and the method of enumerating the population.

# D

---

# THE AFRICAN AMERICAN POPULATION

---

I.  Total African American Population - 29,986,060
    Percentage of the United States' Population of 248.7 million - 12.1

II.  Concentration of African American Population According to Regions
    Midwest     -     24%
    Northeast   -     19%
    West        -     9%
    South       -     53%

III.  U.S. Cities With African American Population of 150,000 or Greater, 1990.

| African American Rank | Overall Rank | City | Percent African American |
|:---:|:---:|:---|:---:|
| 1 | 1 | New York, NY | 29% |
| 2 | 3 | Chicago, IL | 39% |
| 3 | 7 | Detroit, MI | 76% |
| 4 | 5 | Philadelphia, PA | 40% |
| 5 | 2 | Los Angeles, CA | 14% |
| 6 | 4 | Houston, TX | 28% |
| 7 | 13 | Baltimore, MD | 59% |
| 8 | 19 | Washington, DC | 66% |
| 9 | 18 | Memphis, TN | 55% |
| 10 | 25 | New Orleans, LA | 62% |
| 11 | 8 | Dallas, TX | 30% |
| 12 | 36 | Atlanta, GA | 67% |
| 13 | 24 | Cleveland, OH | 47% |
| 14 | 17 | Milwaukee, WI | 31% |
| 15 | 34 | St. Louis, MO | 48% |
| 16 | 60 | Birmingham, AL | 63% |
| 17 | 12 | Indianapolis, IN | 22% |
| 18 | 15 | Jacksonville, FL | 24% |
| 19 | 39 | Oakland, CA | 44% |
| 20 | 56 | Newark, NJ | 59% |

---

*Editor's Note*: The data relative to "The African American Population" are based upon the 1990 Census count. While census-taking has become more sophisticated, it is the belief of many that the 1990 African American percentage (as with the counts of the past) is an undercount. African Americans are among the population groups most difficult to count in a census. Several factors are responsible for this fact. Several civil rights groups, municipal officials called for the Census Bureau to adjust the 1990 census figures.

IV.     Percentage of African American Population in State's Total Population

| | State | % of African American Population | | State | % of African American Population |
|---|---|---|---|---|---|
| 1. | Alabama | 25.3 | 27. | Nebraska | 3.6 |
| 2. | Alaska | 4.1 | 28. | Nevada | 6.6 |
| 3. | Arizona | 3.0 | 29. | New Hampshire | 0.6 |
| 4. | Arkansas | 15.0 | 30. | New Jersey | 13.4 |
| 5. | California | 7.4 | 31. | New Mexico | 2.0 |
| 6. | Colorado | 4.0 | 32. | New York | 15.9 |
| 7. | Connecticut | 8.3 | 33. | North Carolina | 2.2 |
| 8. | Delaware | 16.9 | 34. | North Dakota | 0.6 |
| 9. | Florida | 13.6 | 35. | Ohio | 10.6 |
| 10. | Georgia | 27.0 | 36. | Oklahoma | 7.4 |
| 11. | Hawaii | 2.5 | 37. | Oregon | 1.6 |
| 12. | Idaho | 0.3 | 38. | Pennsylvania | 9.2 |
| 13. | Illinois | 14.4 | 39. | Rhode Island | 3.9 |
| 14. | Indiana | 7.8 | 40. | South Carolina | 29.8 |
| 15. | Iowa | 1.7 | 41. | South Dakota | 0.5 |
| 16. | Kansas | 5.8 | 42. | Tennessee | 16.0 |
| 17. | Kentucky | 7.1 | 43. | Texas | 11.9 |
| 18. | Louisiana | 30.8 | 44. | Utah | 0.7 |
| 19. | Maine | 0.4 | 45. | Vermont | 0.3 |
| 20. | Maryland | 24.9 | 46. | Virginia | 18.8 |
| 21. | Massachusetts | 5.0 | 47. | Washington | 3.1 |
| 22. | Michigan | 13.9 | 48. | West Virginia | 3.1 |
| 23. | Minnesota | 2.2 | 49. | Wisconsin | 5.0 |
| 24. | Mississippi | 35.6 | 50. | Wyoming | 0.8 |
| 25. | Missouri | 10.7 | 51. | Dist. of Columbia | 65.8 |
| 26. | Montana | 0.3 | | | |

*Source*:  William P. O'Hare, Kelvin M. Pollard, Taynia L. Mann, and Mary M. Kent, "African Americans in the 1990's, "Population Bulletin, Vol. 46, No. 1 (Washington, D.C.: Population Reference Bureau, Inc., July 1991).

# E

## BLACK MEMBERS OF THE 103 CONGRESS

(Alphabetically by State)

**ALABAMA**
1.  Rep. Earl Hillard - Democrat

**CALIFORNIA**
2.  Rep. Ronald Dellums - Democrat
3.  Rep. Julian Dixon - Democrat
4.  Rep. Walter Tucker - Democrat
5.  Rep. Maxine Waters - Democrat

**CONNECTICUT**
6.  Rep. Gary Franks - Republican

**DISTRICT OF COLUMBIA**
7.  Rep. Eleanor Holmes-Norton - Democrat

**FLORIDA**
8.  Rep. Corrine Brown - Democrat
9.  Rep. Alcee Hastings - Democrat
10. Rep. Carrie Meek - Democrat

**GEORGIA**
11. Rep. Sanford Bishop - Democrat
12. Rep. John Lewis - Democrat
13. Rep. Cynthia McKinney - Democrat

**ILLINOIS**
14. Sen. Carol Moseley Braun - Democrat
15. Rep. Cordiss Collins - Democrat
16. Rep. Mel Reynolds - Democrat
17. Rep. Bobby Rush - Democrat

**LOUISIANA**
18. Rep. Cleo Fields - Democrat
19. Rep. William J. Jefferson - Democrat

**MARYLAND**
20. Rep. Kweis Mfume - Democrat
21. Rep. Albert Wynn - Democrat

**MICHIGAN**
22. Rep. Barbara Rose-Collins - Democrat
23. Rep. John Conyers - Democrat

**MISSISSIPPI**
24. Rep. Mike Espy - Democrat

**MISSOURI**
25. Rep. William Clay - Democrat
26. Rep. Alan Wheat - Democrat

**NEW JERSEY**
27. Rep. Donald Payne - Democrat

**NEW YORK**
28. Rep. Floyd Flake - Democrat
29. Rep. Major Owens - Democrat
30. Rep. Eugene Rangel - Democrat
31. Rep. Ed Towns - Democrat

**NORTH CAROLINA**
32. Rep. Eva Clayton - Democrat
33. Rep. Mel Walt - Democrat

**OHIO**
34. Rep. Louis Stokes - Democrat

**PENNSYLVANIA**
35. Rep. Lucien Blackwell - Democrat

**SOUTH CAROLINA**
36. Rep. Jim Clyburn - Democrat

**TENNESSEE**
37. Rep. Harold Ford - Democrat

**TEXAS**
38. Eddie Bernice Johnson - Democrat
39. Craig Washington - Democrat

**VIRGINIA**
40. Bobby Scott - Democrat

# F

# SELECTED SCHOLARLY JOURNALS FOR RESEARCH IN AFRICAN AMERICAN STUDIES

*Africa Report,* published by African American Institute - New York City.

*Black Music Research Journal,* published by Columbia College - Chicago, IL.

*Callaloo: A Journal of Afro-American and African Arts and Letters,* published by Johns Hopkins University - Baltimore, MD.

*Obsidian II. Black Literature in Review,* published by North Carolina State University, Department of English - Raleigh, NC.

*Phylon - Review of Race and Culture,* published by Clark - Atlanta University, Atlanta, Georgia.

*Review of Black Political Economy,* published by Transation Publishers - Rutgers State University, New Brunswick, NJ.

*SAGE: A Scholarly Journal on Black Women,* published by Sage's Women's Education Press, Atlanta, GA.

*The Afrocentric Scholar,* published by the National Council of Black Studies - West Virginia University, Morgantown, WV.

*The Black Scholar, Journal of Black Studies and Research* - California.

*The Griot,* published by the Southern Conference on Afro American Studies, Inc. - Berea College, KY.

*The Journal of Black Psychology,* published by the Association of Black Psychologists.

*The Journal of Black Studies,* published by Sage Publication - Newbury Park, CA.

*The Journal of Negro Education,* published by the Bureau of Educational Research, under the auspices of Howard University Press - Washington, DC.

*The Journal of Negro History,* published by the Association for the Study of Negro Life and History, Inc. - Washington, DC.

*The Journal of Religious Thought,* published by Howard University School of Divinity - Washington, DC.

*The Journal of Social and Behavioral Sciences,* published by The Association of Social and Behavioral Sciences.

*The Negro Educational Review,* published by The Negro Educational Reviews, Inc. - Jacksonville, FL.

*The Western Journal of Black Studies,* published by Washington State University Press - Pullman, WA.

# G

---

# BIBLIOGRAPHICAL AND REFERENCE SOURCES FOR RESEARCH IN AFRICAN AMERICAN STUDIES

---

Asante, Molef: K. and Mattson, Mark, editors. *Historical and Cultural Atlas of African Americans.* New York City: MacMillan Publishing Company, 1991.

Brelin, Christa, editor. *Who's Who Among Black Americans.* Detroit, MI: Gale Research Inc., 1992-93.

Cantor, George, *Historical Landmarks of Black America.* Detroit: Gale Research, Inc., 1991.

Davis, Lenwood and Sims, Janet. *Marcus Garvey: An Annotated Bibliography.* Westport, CT: Greenwood Publishing Company, 1980.

Davis, Lenwood O. and Hill, George. *A Bibliographical Guide to Black Studies Programs in the USA: An Annotated Bibliography.* Westport, CT: Greenwood Press, 1986.

Harlon, Louis and Smock, Raymond, editors. *The Booker T. Washington Papers*, Urbana: University of Illinois Press.

Herod, Augustina and Herod, Charles C. Afro-American Nationalism: *An Annotated Bibliography*, New York City: Garland Publishing Company, 1986.

Hill, Robert A., editor. *The Marcus Garvey and Universal Negro Improvement Association Papers.* Berkelcy: University of California Press, 1986.

Hine, Darlene Clark, editor. *Black Women in United States History.* Brooklyn: Carlson Publishing Inc.

Hornsby, Alton, Jr. *A Chronology of African American History.* Detroit: Gale Research Inc., 1991.

Howard, Sharon M. *African American Women Fiction Writers 1859-1986.* Camden, CT: Garland Publishing Company, 1992.

Johnson, Timothy. *Malcolm X - A Comprehensive Annotated Bibliography.* New York City: Garland Publishing Company, 1986.

Logan, Rayford and Winston, Michael L. *Dictionary of American Negro Biography.* New York City: W.W. Norton and Company, 1982.

Lowery, Charles D. and Marszalek, John F., editors. *Encyclopedia of African American Civil Rights.* New York City: Greenwood Press, 1992.

Martin Luther King, Jr., *Papers Project - A Guide to Research on Martin Luther King, Jr. and the Modern Black Freedom Struggle.* Stanford: Stanford University Libraries, 1989.

Payne, Wardell J. *Directory of African American Religious Bodies.* Washington, DC: Howard University Press, 1991.

Ploski, Harry A., editor. *The Negro Almanac, 5th edition.* Detroit: Gale Research Inc., 1989.

Smith, Jessie Carney. *Notable Black American Women.* Detroit: Gale Research Inc., Detroit, 1992.

Smith, Randall M. *Dictionary of Afro-American Slavery.* New York City: Greenwood Press, 1988.

Thernstrom, Stephan, editor. *Harvard Encyclopedia of American Ethnic Groups.* Cambridge: The Belknap Press of Harvard University.

# H

# THE TEACHINGS OF MALCOLM X: A STUDENT'S PERSPECTIVE WITH RECOMMENDED READINGS *Dennis Green*

Malcolm X probably better understood more so than any other leader in his time that the only real revolution needed by African American people was indeed a revolution of the mind. With that in mind, he attempted to teach African American people about the true nature of not only their country, but the world they were living in. Analyzing the racism in this country, Malcolm demonstrated time and time again through keen knowledge and usage of history, politics, culture, economics, sociology and psychology that the condition of millions of African American people was not an accident. The gut wrenching essence of Malcolm's teachings has to be what he taught African American people about themselves, and the way he induced them to think for themselves. He attacked and exposed self hate, and almost singlehandedly changed the way African American people think about themselves, bringing racial pride and self-esteem to unimaginable heights as he, in the image of a master teacher, taught daily about the achievements that African American civilizations on the African continent accomplished long before the intrusion of the White race and made millions for the first time proud to be connected to the continent of Africa.

The teachings and background of Malcolm X provide indepth insight into the psychological trauma of ghetto life and how one man learned to survive. Malcolm constantly emphasized the special significance that comes with feeling like a "somebody" and made many aware that in order for one to succeed, individuals must be made to feel a positive sense of self-worth. Malcolm stressed the importance of education and presented a perfect example of intellectual development being spawned in the bleakest of moments, all by an individual who was practically given up for lost. Beginning social science students are introduced to a slogan that reads "I am what I think you think I am." Malcolm understood perfectly the psychology behind the statement, realizing that everyone needs a platform of support to operate from in order for the recognizing of self respect from within to blossom. With the teaching of his philosophy of Black Nationalism, Malcolm not only put forth pride in an historical and emotional sense, but explained thoroughly how his concepts made sense in an economic realm.

It is impossible to discuss the legacy of Malcolm X without some reflections on Dr. King. Malcolm X and Martin Luther King, Jr. both had fathers who were strict, rigid and domineering Baptist ministers. However, Martin grew up in the world of the African American middle class and Malcolm grew up poor. Martin Luther King, Jr. tried to get things changed by appealing to the conscience of White America in hopes of getting laws passed to insure equal treatment for all and his home base was primarily the South. Malcolm X tried to get things changed by uplifting the conscience of Black America first, and then adding the spice of cooperation from others and his home base was primarily the North.

The most distressing element within the romanticizing of both Malcolm and Martin has to be the tendency of the followers and others to deal with the two men as adversaries. Both were men of high moral character, deeply committed to helping the African American race, and their backgrounds and life experiences demanded that each one take a different turn at the fork in the road. However, the philosophy and methods employed by each one were not only valuable, but needed to complement and further the cause of the other. There was a difference in the structure of the problems within the

Reprinted with permission from the author, Dennis Green.

geographical areas that Malcolm and Martin operated, and each man was quite adept at developing and implementing methods to battle forces in their area of operation. It is nothing short of counterproductive to pit the two against each other and to do so only reflects upon a lack of indepth study into the lives of the two men. The numerous legislative actions passed and the uplifting of many African American minds were accomplished only because of the dedication of Malcolm X and Martin Luther Kings, Jr.

Malcolm's main contribution to the Black Revolution lies in his efforts to stir the consciousness and bring a sense of identity among African Americans, enabling many, for the first time, to see themselves as a worthy people. He refused to allow African Americans to lie to themselves about why the African American race was constantly exploited, and stood up to the White race in an uncompromising and non-begging manner, saying all the things publicly and out loud that so many African Americans secretly wished to have the courage to say. He had freed himself from the psychological chains that bind so many African American people, and he made other African Americans aware of the intricate weaving of inequality in the American system. In addition, one area in which Malcolm was equally relentless was his insistence that African Americans take more responsibility for their daily lives and what goes on in the African American community.

The resurgence of the popularity of Malcolm X should be viewed within the context of the world which the African American population finds itself at odds with. The hostile racial climate in America has contributed to African Americans, especially African American youth, being systematically eliminated from the labor force, and misused and abused in a manner unlike any other group. Thus, the rage felt and expressed by the group is linked to Malcolm's undying insistence upon the positive worth of the African American race.

Those who wish to link the resurgence to *only* the rage felt by many African American youth, put forth the same disservice to the youth as rendered to Malcolm X by those who wish to focus on just one segment of Malcolm's evolving ideas. Other examples of linkage would be the many individuals who look to Malcolm as a tremendous source of inspiration, strength, and hope while attempting to accomplish goals when the future looks dismal and hopeless. Also of importance are the individuals involved in various types of civil/human rights organizations who have worked tirelessly over the years only to look behind themselves and see that the masses of African Americans are still at the bottom of the heap and catching more hell than 30 years ago. Many of these individuals are now realizing the truth of Malcolm's statements regarding the importance of Black Nationalism and the controlling of the economics of the African American community by African American people rather than by everyone else. Also to take under consideration is the fact that overall the so-called national African American leadership is fragmented at best, weak, in disarray, and the look toward Malcolm is a cry out for strong African American leadership with direction and African American unity.

A glimpse into the historical aspects reveals that the resurgence really started to gather the most steam in the early 1980's after Ronald Reagan became President of the United States. Reagan's treacherous assault on the African American community by way of merciless policies that he enacted was so severe and potentially long-term devastating, that Reagan soon came to symbolize for many the evil in the American nightmare that Malcolm so often talked about African Americans receiving. African American rap groups also helped to spread the word about Malcolm through messages in their songs.

African countries and observed international unity of African American people throughout the world and the concepts of Pan Africanism are all examples of the survival of Malcolm's philosophy. In the summer of 1964, Malcolm's every move was being monitored by the State Department, CIA, and Muslims from the Nation of Islam. Death threats followed and on February 13, 1965, his home as bombed, but Malcolm and his family escaped unharmed. On February 21, 1965, Malcolm was assassinated while at the Audubon Ballroom in Harlem.

The commercialism of Malcolm X cannot be overlooked or denied; however, he must not be reduced to being just a slogan or caricature on a shirt or poster. Malcolm stood for truth and self determination for African American people by way of re-education. Extolling the virtue of Black Nationalism to the end, he was more real than most of us even dare dream to be.

Few other figures in United States History have captured the imagination of the African American community, or the press, as Malcolm X did during and after his lifetime. The following are examples of books that will be of interest to those wanting to know more about Malcolm X's significance and legacy.

## BIBLIOGRAPHY

Breitman, George (ed). *Assassination of Malcolm X*. New York: Pathfinder Press, 1976.

Breitman, George. *Last Year of Malcolm X: The Evolution of a Revolutionary*. New York: Merit Press, 1967.

Clarke, John. *Malcolm X: The Man and His Times*. New York: MacMillan, 1969.

Cone, James H. *Martin and Malcolm and America - A Dream of a Nightmare*. New York: Orbis, 1991.

Davis, Lenwood. *Malcolm X: A Selected Bibliography*. Westport, CT: Greenwood Press, 1984.

Haley, Alex and Malcolm X. 1992. *The Autobiography of Malcolm X*. New York: Ballantine Books.

Lee, Spike and Wiley, Ralph. *By Any Means Necessary: The Trials and Tribulations of the Making of "Malcolm X"*. New York: Hyperion, 1992.

Lomax, Lewis, *To Kill A Black Man*. Los Angeles: Holloway House, 1968.

Paris, Peter. *Black Leaders in Conflict; Joseph H. Jackson, Martin Luther Kings, Jr., Malcolm X, and Adam Clayton Powell, Jr*. New York: Pilgrim Press, 1978.

Perry, Bruce. *Malcolm X: The Last Speeches*. New York: Pathfinder, 1989.

T'Shaka, Oba. *Political Legacy of Malcolm X*. Chicago: Third World Press, 1983.

Wood, Joe (editor). *Malcolm X in Our Image*. New York: St. Martin's Press, 1992.

*Editor's Note:*   Dennis Green received a B.A. degree in Sociology, May 1992, from Metropolitan State College of Denver. Presently, he is completing the requirements for a B.A. Degree in African American Studies at Metropolitan State College of Denver, and is a teaching assistant in the African American Studies program at the same institution.

# I

# THE LEGACY OF MARCUS GARVEY: A STUDENT'S PERSPECTIVE WITH RECOMMENDED READINGS   *Charles White*

Integration and nationalism represent the broad streams of Black though in response to slavery and segregation in society (Cone, 1991:4). There have been many articulate voices and important movements of Black Nationalism throughout the history of the Black presence in the United States. Among them were David Walker and Martin Delaney during the antebellum period and Henry McNeal Turner, Marcus Garvey, Noble Drew Ali, and Elijah Muhammad during the nineteenth and early twentieth century (Cone, 1991:1).

Since Garvey's centenary year in 1987 there have been an increase in discussion about the teaching of his life works. The revolutionary tradition of the Caribbean and the history of freedom movements in the United States produced a Marcus Garvey. The stories of the Maroons, Toussaint L'Overture and Nat Turner were passed down from generation to generation to a young Garvey through the oral tradition while growing up in St. Ann's Bay, Jamaica.

Too often Marcus Garvey is viewed as an irrational bombastic, rabble rouser that wanted all Blacks to return to Africa. Molefi Kente Asante, a leading proponent of Afrocentricity, in his discussion of Garvey stated (1990:10):

> He proposed the most perfect, consistent, and brilliant ideology of liberation in the first half of the twentieth century. In no nation in the world was there a more philosophical treatment of oppressed people in any more creative way than Garveyism. It was used as a vehicle for a people's up lift as well as a weapon against those Whites and Blacks who had vested interest in the status quo. Garvey was an idea fulfilling its time. It took the common man of Africa descent, uprooted from his culture and fortified him.

The accomplishment of the Garvey Movement can best be understood through an awareness of the Afrocentric approach to the experiences of African peoples. Asante (1990:23) discussed the elements of Afrocentricity in his book - *Afrocentricity, Kenet and Knowledge*:

> History is the coherent record of the achievement of a people. Religion or mythology is the ritualized manner in which a people present themselves to humanity. Motif represents the icons and symbols through which a people announce themselves. Ethos is how you are projected to the world. Economics, political and social organizations give legitimacy and power.

The goals of the Garvey Movement were carried out through the Universal Negro Improvement Association (UNIA). The UNIA became the largest mass movement among Black people in this century, with 996 branches in 43 countries and five million members (Martin, 1983:96). Who were the people who supported the UNIA? They were born in the nineteenth century many were migrants, some had experienced slavery especially those born in Cuba and Brazil. They were drawn from a variety of social and class backgrounds but shared the common fate of racial discrimination. A careful examination of the UNIA reveals consistent application of elements of Afrocentricity through the teaching and the activities of the organization.

Marcus Garvey being a student of history realized the importance of history to a people. He understood that if Black people were to fight the negative idea that oppressed them they would have to know their history. He realized that knowledge of self was the first step to instill self confidence and "racial"

Reprinted with permission from the author, Charles White.

emancipation. The UNIA taught the glorious history of Egypt and Ethiopia. The members were exposed to the contributions of Black heroes such as Frederick Douglas, Toussaint L'Overture and Prince Hall. Lectures were given by great historians such as Carter G. Woodson and J. A. Rodgers. Garvey realized that with a strong sense of history people knew what they had done. Pride and spirit was fostered through such teachings.

The manner in which a people foster and nurture pride is through religion. The religion espoused by Garvey expressed oneness and racial imagery. In Afrocentricity religion encompasses all areas of life - political, economic and social. Garvey's African Orthodox church penetrated all of these areas. The church founded in 1921 paid no attention to special religious denomination. The ground work for Black liberation theology was laid by the religion advanced by Garvey through its emphases on racial imagery. In his discussion of Garvey's points of view on religion, Martin (1976: 69) stated:

> Black men should depict a God in their own image likeness which would inevitably be Black. Garvey pointed out that the practice of western hemisphere Africans to worship a God of another race had few parallels anywhere else. It is quite normal for people to visualize and depict their Gods in their own color....Jesus Christ was canonized as a "Black man of sorrows" and the Virgin Mary as a Black Madonna.

The concept of racial imagery in religion expanded to the concept of Black beauty was meaningful for a people who had previously bleached their skin and "pressed" their hair to look "white". Black beauty manifested itself in all areas of life including art and magazines depicting Black men and women with Black features. So that people would also learn to accept and appreciate their physical characteristics.

Garvey understood that Black people had to be shown and not just told. Garvey was a printer and journalist by trade, so he knew how to spread information. In this newspaper the *Negro World*, he published articles that fostered Black pride and kept the Black population informed. Many writers that would later achieve popularity in the Harlem Renaissance wrote for the *Negro World*. The publication penetrated every area where Black people lived and had regular readers as far away as Australia (Martin, 1976:93).

The newspaper gave accounts of the huge parades sponsored by the UNIA's many auxiliaries: The Universal African Legion, the Universal Black Cross Nurses, the Universal African Motor Coups, the Juvenile and the Black Flying Eagles all equipped with uniforms and symbols. Dr. Francis Cress Wesling, a leading Afrocentric psychiatrist, explains the meaning of symbols (1991:56):

> The major forms of symbolism is a power system/culture that constitute powerful and subtle messages about how and why the culture came into being, and what the people must do to survive and manifest itself. Symbolism is thus the glue that holds the individual and the collective psyche of the people and its culture together.

Garvey had a strong sense of nationhood. He set up a provisional government, and he was elected provisional President of Africa and President General and administer of the UNIA.

In making his dream of connecting with the continent of Africa a reality, Garvey purchased four ships. The ships were to be used in transporting goods and people to Africa. This venture was Garvey's largest enterprise and was responsible for his downfall. Garvey lacked business skills for an operation of the magnitude of his Black Star Ship line. He advertised the company in his newspaper and encouraged his followers to buy stock in his company. The ships, purchased by one of Garvey's assistants were in dire need of repair and almost worthless. Garvey was arrested, indicted and changed with "knowingly using" fraudulent and deceptive articles in the sale of stocks through the mail and for advertising and selling space on a mythical ship. After a lengthy trial he was sentenced to five years in prison. Many felt that Garvey's conviction was political. However, in 1927, President Coolidge commuted the sentence and in December of that year, Garvey was deported from the United States as an undesirable alien. He returned to Jamaica where he continued to work for Black emancipation. He later went to London where he established the headquarters of the UNIA, but died there on June 10, 1940.

In conclusion, Marcus Garvey achieved in a few years what perhaps no other Black leader achieved and that's eternal life. Every Black Nationalistic Organization in the United States and abroad can trace its roots back to Garvey. The "Black is Beautiful" and Black Power Movement of the 60's owe its roots to Garvey. As African Americans start to look for hope and inspiration thanks must go to the Honorable Marcus Garvey. He gave us a plan for liberation based upon the principles of Afrocentricity.

## LITERATURE CITED

Asante, Molefi Kete. 1990. *Afrocentricity, Kenet and Knowledge*. Trenton: African World Press.

Cone, James. 1991. *Martin and Malcolm and America - A Dream or a Nightmare*. Maryknoll, N.Y.: Orbis Books.

Martin, Tony. 1976. *Race First: The Ideological and Organizational Struggles of Marcus Garvey and the UNIA*. Dover: The Majority Press.

1983. *Marcus Garvey Hero: A First Biography*. Dover. The Majority Press.

Wesling, Francis Cress. *The Isis Papers*. Chicago: Third World Press.

## RECOMMENDED READINGS

Clark, John Henry. 1974. *Marcus Garvey and the Vision of Africa*. Trenton: African World Press.

Cronon, E. David. 1969. *The Story of Marcus Garvey and the UNIA*. Madison: The University of Wisconsin Press.

Garvey, Amy Jacques. 1986. *The Philosophy and Opinions of Marcus Garvey*. Dover: The Majority Press.

Harris, Robert (editor). 1992. *Corlos Cooks; Black Nationalism from Garvey to Malcolm*. Dover: The Majority Press.

Hill, Robert. 1987. *Marcus Garvey: Life and Lesson*. Los Angeles: University of California Press.

Hill, Robert (editor). 1986. *The Marcus Garvey and Universal Negro Improvement Association Papers*. Berkeley: University of California Press.

Martin, Tony. 1976. *Race First: The Ideological and Organizational Struggles of Marcus Garvey and the UNIA*. Dover: The Majority Press.

Martin, Tony. 1984. *The Pan African connection: From Slavery to Garvey and Beyond*. Dover: The Majority Press.

*Editor's Note:* Charles White received his B.A. degree in History, May 1992, from Metropolitan State College-Denver. During his senior year, he was a teaching assistant in the African American Studies Program. He is presently enrolled at Louisiana State University pursuing an M.A. in History.

# J

## OUR TIMES IN '92

*Vernal M. Pope*

Our hands are folded now
the last ship has arrived
from Africa.
The tribes have gathered to
count their loss,
and drum rhythms still
resound with the wind . . .

Our times are in Thy Hand.

Our hands are folded now
the last slave has been sold.
The severe red welts have healed.
And thorns and thistles
surround and consume
    the big house . . .

Our times are in Thy Hand.

Our hands are folded now
the last lynched body hanging
in southern Mississippi has been loosed for burial,
the "colored only" signs have been repainted
And the identities behind the masks
    are disclosed . . .

Our times are in Thy Hand.

Our hands are folded now
The last dog has been chained
the fire hydrants have been shut down
The sirens have ceased
and all the votes are in.

Our times are in Thy Hand.

Our hands are folded now
The qualified man for the job is too black
It's affirmative the white is
too white.
And the suburban jury in '92
peered past obvious perils
performed on a brother of color
to pry the guilty free.

Our times are still in Thy Hand, but
Our hands are unfolded now.

Vernal M. Pope is a junior English major at Metropolitan State College - Denver. She has read her poetry at many campus and
    community events. Reprinted with permission from the author, Vernal M. Pope

# STUDY GUIDE AND
# DISCUSSION QUESTIONS

# I

## STUDY GUIDE

1.  African American Studies can be defined as *scientific, interdisciplinary, holistic* and *intercontinental*. Explain.

2.  According to Professor Harris, there have been four stages in the intellectual and institutional development of Africana Studies as an area of scholarly inquiry. List and characterize each one of these four stages.

3.  How did the early social scientists of European background advance the untrue belief of the innate inferiority of people of African background?

4. Cite examples of White/European social scientists who challenged the proponents of White superiority and Black inferiority.

5. Race relations became the focus of study for the early Black social scientists (late 1800's - early 1900's). Explain the factors/conditions responsible for this emphasis.

6. Professor Young's bibliography of recent social science literature relative to the African American experience included the time frame of 1960 to 1976. Update this list with some of the major social science publications dating from 1976 to 1992.

7. Professor Quarles presented a fourfold typology to illustrate the major contemporary uses of Black History. Describe the aims, general content and style of each.

8. Discuss the contributions of "the newer Black History," as termed by Quarles, to the Black and White publics.

9. Discuss the reasons why historically, the American Anthropologists overwhelmingly chose Native Americans and neglected African Americans as the subjects of their studies.

10. The study of American Blacks is in keeping with the scope of the "new" anthropology. Explain.

11. The study of the Black experience in the United States cannot be reduced to the Ethnic Studies construct. Explain.

12. Apply Professor Long's concept of "oppugancy" to a study of the African American experience.

13. According to Professor Jones, the Euro-American orientation to society is *organization* and the African American orientation is *individual*. Explain.

14.   Discuss the contribution of the following to the study of the African American experience:

Joyce Ladner
Nathan Hare
W. E. DuBois
St. Clair Drake
Horace Cayton
Mary Berry
Arthur Schomburg
Charles S. Johnson
Melville Herskovits
Kenneth Clark
Chancellor Williams
Maulana Karenga
Alex Haley

George W. Williams
Teresa Singleton
Carter G. Woodson
Alain Locke
E. Franklin Frazier
John Hope Franklin
Charles H. Thompson
John Henrik Clarke
Langston Hughes
Darlene Clark Hine
John Blassingame
Margaret Walker Alexander
Angela Davis

2. molifi Asante

# II

---

## STUDY GUIDE

---

1. Based upon the arguments presented in the essay **Afrocentrism in a Multicultural Democracy**, respond to the following:
   (a) The points of agreement concerning Afrocentricity;


   (b) relationship of Afrocentricity to multiculturalism;


   (c) some of the limitations of the concept in developing a comprehensive understanding of the African American experience.


2. Some of the critics of Afrocentricity have terms such theories as "cultural separatism" or "radical chauvinism". Summarize Professor Asante's response to these critics.


3. According to Professor Asante some of the problems that plague many African American students relate to the fact that they are not culturally centered and empowered in their class-rooms. From his essay, **Afrocentric Curriculum**, cite the requirements for "centering" and "empowering" African American students in the classroom.

Afrocentricity should be based upon an understanding of African life, culture and history. In view of this fact discuss the following:
(a)   classic myths concerning Africa and Africans; debunk such myths with facts;

(b)   the ancient West African Kingdoms;

(c)   West African life and culture prior to European control;

(d)   the impact of colonialism on the African continent;

(e)   contributions of Africa/Africans to human civilization

NOTE: The following references are recommended for answering #4.
      Franklin, John Hope. *From Slavery to Freedom: A History of Negro Americans.*
      Quarles, Benjamin. *The Negro in the Making of America.*

How would the following publications add to an understanding of Afrocentricity:
Diop, Cheith A. *The African Origin of Civilization.*

Davidson, Basil. *The Lost Cities of Africa.*

Van Sertima, Ivan. *They Came Before Columbus.*

# III

## STUDY GUIDE

1.  Many social scientists attempt to explain variation in I.Q. and academic achievement between groups (dominant-White and Ethnic Minorities-African Americans) through an application of the *genetic theory* or the *cultural deficit theory*. According to Persell, in the article *Genetic and Cultural Deficit Theories-Two Sides of the Same Racist Coin*, both of these theories embrace racist concepts. Explain.

2.  Discuss the following based upon Ladner and Stafford's article *Defusing Race: Developments Since the Kerner Report*:
    (a)  the purpose and the findings of the Kerner Commission

    (b)  striking characteristics of the Kerner Commission

    (c)  reason(s) why the government did not establish a Commission after the riots of the 80's

    (d)  forces responsible for the emergence of the "new minorities" during the late 60's and 70's. How did these forces serve as a disadvantage to Black Americans?

3. What argument did the author present to explain racism in the White community in the article *Socialization and Racism: The White Experience?* In this article, the author cited autobiographical accounts of experiences that occurred during the sixties in the South. During the past five years the media has reported many examples of racism experienced by African American students enrolled at predominately White colleges and universities outside of the deep South. Explain.

4. Discuss the following based upon Professor Marable's article *Blacks Should Emphasize their Ethnicity*
   (a) differentiate between race and ethnicity

   (b) what assumptions about intelligence have proven false

   (c) requirements for racial peace

5. In retrospect, the Tuskegee Study revealed more about pathology of racism than the pathology of syphilis; more about the nature of scientific inquiry than the nature of the disease process. Explain.

6. Discuss the following based upon the article *Ethnicity the New Ideal*.
   (a) the meaning of multiculturalism

   (b) the assumptions of the melting pot/assimilation theory

   (c) implications of the present demographic profile in the United States

7. Define/identify the following:

> ideology of racism
> race
> theory of natural selection
> amalgamation
> Loving vs. Commonwealth of VA. 1967
> miscegenation
> intra-racial prejudice
> inter-racial prejudice
> prejudice
> stereotypes
> discrimination
> scapegoat
> projection
> ethnocentrism
> overt racism
> covert racism
> individual racism
> institutional racism

# IV

## STUDY GUIDE

1. The research of Dr. Theresa A. Singleton (one of the few African American archaeologists in the United States) has added to our understanding of the "roots" of African American culture. Discuss the following based upon her article *Buried Treasure*:

   (a) reason(s) why the "Rice Coast" has been one of the principal geographical areas for African American archaeology

   (b) evidence in support of the fact that West African culture was thoroughly woven into the daily lives of South Carolinians during the colonial era

   (c) the relationship between the excavations at Butler Island and an understanding of the African American cultural past

2. Discuss the contributions of Margaret Walker to our understanding of Black history and culture.

3.  The Harlem Renaissance was a period when Black writers and other creative Black artists began to look to their historical and cultural roots for revitalization. Discuss the following concerning this important historical period:
    (a)  the historical and socio-cultural climate that ushered in the Harlem Renaissance.

    (b)  the racist notions that the Harlem Renaissance defeated

    (c)  the important contributions of Alain Locke and Marcus Garvey to the Harlem Renaissance

    (d)  the major writers, artists and musicians of the period and their contributions

    Note:    In answering #3 the following is suggest as a reference:
             Franklin, John Hope. *From Slavery to Freedom: A History of the Negro American.*

4.  Zora Neal Hurston was a leading African American Writer of the Harlem Renaissance. Based upon the article *Rediscovering Zora Neale Hurston*, discuss the following:
    (a)  her training made her more than just another writer. Explain

    (b)  examples of the publications indicating their uniqueness when compared with others during the period

    (c)  her politics differed from the politics of many African Americans during the period. Explain

    (d)  factors responsible for the resurgence of interest in Hurston's work

5.  A study of the Sea Islands of South Carolina and Georgia provides an understanding of the following:
    (a)  the retention of the African culture in the United States

    (b)  the dismantling of elements of the African American culture

    (c)  the collective efforts on behalf of the Sea Islanders to resist and to counteract the efforts of cultural dismantlement

    Using Blockston's article *Nowhere to Lay Down Weary Head* discuss the three aforementioned points relative to the Sea Islands of South Carolina and Georgia.

# V

## STUDY GUIDE

1. Discuss the following based upon Rollins' article *Part of a Whole: The Interdependence of the Civil Rights Movement and Other Social Movements*:

   (a) the national and international events that generated the "spark" that resulted into the Civil Rights movement of the 50's and 60's

   (b) the impact of the Civil Rights movement in the U.S.A. on "Third-World" political and socio-economic developments

   (c) the impact of the Civil Rights Movement on other liberation movements in the United States - cite organizations, goals and the relationship of goals to the Civil Rights Movement

2. It has been assumed by some that Black women were passive supporters of the Black liberation movement. Refute this assumption using the research presented by Sawyer, in their article *Black Religion and Social Change: Women in Leadership Rules*.

   Your discussion should focus upon the historic involvement of Black women in the Black liberation struggle as well as their involvement during the 50's and 60's.

3.    According to Sawyer, some regarded the Civil Rights movement as a secular movement, other regarded it as a church-based or ecumenical movement. Select a position and explain the reason(s) for your choice.

4.    Ella Baker is considered one of the foremost organizers of the freedom movement of the 50's and 60's. Answer the following based upon Elliot's article *Ella Baker: A Civil Rights Warrior*.
      (a)   the reasons why she disagreed with the structure of the NAACP and SCLC

      (b)   she corrected what she considered to be major problem for the NAACP and SCLC through the structure and the activities of SNCC. Explain

5.    According to Professor Morris, author of *The Origins* of the Civil Rights, until the Urban League, the SCLC and other groups are creative enough to get their financial support from the Black community, they are limited in their vision and in what they actually can do. Explain the main point being conveyed.

6.    Cite the major problem facing the Black community today and the reason(s) why some of these problems are not being addressed by the mainstream civil rights organization.

7. In his book, *Martin and Malcolm and American: A Dream or a Nightmare*, Dr. James H. Cone, stated "they complemented and corrected one another, King moved closer to Malcolm's critique of America, and Malcolm moved closer to some aspect of King's solution to the problem. Explain with concrete examples.

8. Supplement Berry and Blassingame's list of *Some Significant Dates in Black American History* by adding the significant dates and events that have occurred since 1980.